Gender and Sex in Counseling and Psychotherapy

Lucia Albino Gilbert

University of Texas at Austin

Murray Scher

Wipf & Stock
PUBLISHERS
Eugene, Oregon

Resource Publications
A division of Wipf and Stock Publishers
199 W 8th Ave, Suite 3
Eugene, OR 97401

Gender and Sex in Counseling and Psychotherapy
By Gilbert, Lucia Albino and Scher, Murray
Copyright©1999 by Gilbert, Lucia Albino
ISBN 13: 978-1-60608-890-6
Publication date 6/15/2009
Previously published by Allyn and Bacon, 1999

Photos: Chepstow Place Garden, 1997 (p. xiii); Kiki and Ben—Timmendorforstrand, 1997 (p. 2); Lotte, Nancy, and Ingie—Chepstow Place, 1997 (p. 24); Dr. Werner and Frau Nickel, 1993 (p. 46); Lotte balancing, 1997 (p. 58); Lilly and Banji Adu, 1992 (p. 72); The Jackson Twins, Powis Terrace, 1997 (p. 88); Ben and Lilo, 1997 (p. 104); Two Boys, 1989 (p. 124); Self portrait—London, 1996 (p. 142); Lisa and Ken Vandy—Hayling Island, 1987 (p. 156); Louise—Kensington Gardens, 1997 (p. 176)

To our spouses, Jack and Rita,
and our daughters, Melissa and Elena

Brief Contents

Contents

Part JJ   Fundamentals   45

3 Jdentifying Gender Bias in Practice   46

4 Gender-Jnformed Theories of Counseling and Psychotherapy   58

9 Gender and the Dynamics of Counseling   142

10 Strategies for Disrupting Gender Processes   156

11   Ethical Practice   176

References   187

Author Index   199

Subject Index   203

 Preface

We believe this is an exciting, vital, and accessible book. We have been concerned about the effects of gender on therapeutic interactions for several decades and have researched and written about our concerns for most of that time. Our concern has not abated in recent times. Gender is still largely ignored as an "active" variable in counseling and is typically, and erroneously, viewed as pertaining to women's issues or problems. The field has leapfrogged over gender, perhaps because it is too complex, perhaps because we resist change, or perhaps because our gender socialization is sufficiently effective to keep us from seeing the power of gendered elements and dynamics in our personalities, our perceptions, our interactions, and our society.

This book makes clear *why* gender *must* be considered in understanding the client's concerns, the process of therapy, and the counselor's role in the therapeutic interaction: "Therapy that does not acknowledge gender issues and sexism cannot be fully therapeutic" (Marecek & Hare-Mustin, 1987, p. 36).

Key goals for the book are to help the reader:

- Understand gender theory and the complexity of gender processes;
- Grasp the centrality of gender in clients' lives and in the psychotherapeutic/counseling process; and
- Obtain sufficient knowledge to work therapeutically to enhance, and not further limit or diminish, the lives of individuals who seek help.

In the book, the terms *counselor* and *therapist* as well as *counseling* and *psychotherapy* are used interchangeably.

Themes of the Book

The book has three interconnected themes woven throughout: First, gender and issues of gender apply to all people. To view gender as about women is to miss the point entirely.

Second, gender is an active process that emerges between clients and counselors or therapists. In the complex process of development across the life cycle, each of us internalizes societal-based constructions of women and men and each of us, to varying degrees, is encouraged and rewarded for playing them out in our interpersonal interactions.

Third, gender is best understood within interpersonal and societal-cultural contexts. Throughout the book we provide examples of clients from diverse backgrounds and describe a number of client-therapist interactions to illuminate gender processes.

Organization of the Book

The book's three main parts are: Theory, Fundamentals, and Applications. *Part I: Theory* introduces key theory and research about gender and *Part II: Fundamentals* builds on this material in presenting research and theory pertaining to counseling and therapy practice. *Part III: Applications* then applies the material from the first two Parts to different aspects of therapy and to different kinds of clients. All the chapters in Parts I and II begin with relatively brief cases that illustrate key points and issues. The chapters in Part III use longer cases and provide more detailed gender analysis of therapeutic work.

Part I: Theory

Part I, on gender theory, contains two quite lengthy chapters. These chapters are crucial in laying the foundation for the remainder of the book. Gender is complex, so we ask that readers take the time to consider these chapters in some depth. Chapter 1, Gender and Its Many Faces, explains how and why gender relates to the making or constructing of women and men across cultures. Using everyday examples, we detail helpful ways to understand the power of gender in shaping who women and men actually become or think they should become. We label these various ways gender operates in cultures as "the four faces of gender."

In Chapter 2 we expand on the material in the first chapter. We discuss the process of gender socialization and summarize several important bodies of research that inform the theoretical ideas described in the first chapter. Here again, we ask readers to take the time needed to understand the key points, which are crucial to using the concepts in later chapters on counseling and therapy. Presented here, for example, are summaries of empirical studies on sex-related differences in such areas as personality characteristics and cognitive abilities as well as ways to determine for oneself the meaning of statistical differences in the context of gender socialization and culture. Some connections to counseling are made in the chapter, although more detail about application to therapeutic settings is left to later sections and chapters.

Part II: Fundamentals

Part II, Fundamentals, concerns the application of gender theory to various aspects of practice. Chapter 3 starts with a relatively brief discussion of understanding and developing an ability to detect gender bias in therapeutic practice. Then in Chapter 4 we describe gender-informed theories of therapy including several forms of feminist therapy as well as gender-aware therapy.

Earlier chapters looked at different ways in which theories guide counseling and therapy. In Chapter 5 we look at a somewhat different aspect of theory. We consider the language used in theories and in describing client concerns and everyday behavior. We also look at language in the form of dominant discourses. Dominant discourses can guide and shape our thinking about client concerns and what we say and do in counseling. Chapter 6 continues this discussion, but in the area of sexuality. We discuss the place of sexuality in the life and psyche of clients and how gender socialization shapes women's and men's sexual experiences and their beliefs about those experiences. Also considered in the chapter is how views of sexuality relate to the many faces of gender and to gendered processes in counseling.

Finally Chapter 7 describes in some detail a number of gender issues male and female clients commonly bring to therapeutic settings. Included are discussions of male gender role strain, sexual harassment and rape, and issues facing dual-earner families.

Part III: Applications

In Part III, Applications, we describe in greater detail the connection between gender and the practice of counseling and psychotherapy. Chapter 8 focuses on what makes up a person who comes for counseling with special reference to gender, and Chapter 9 demonstrates how gender can influence various aspects of the counseling process, including what is seen and heard and what is less visible. The cases of Jonathan and Allison (Chapter 8), and Donald and Eloise (Chapter 9) not only further elaborate on material presented in the chapters but also illustrate gender case analyses using the four faces of gender described in Chapters 1 and 2.

Then in Chapter 10 we examine in greater detail crucial aspects of the counseling process associated with the doing and undoing of gender in therapy. In this chapter we also describe problematic areas in counseling, including the particularly troublesome area of sexual relations with clients, which violates the ethics of all the helping professions. An illustrative gender analysis of the case of Anthony and Rose appears as an appendix to the chapter. Finally, in Chapter 11 we consider what is needed for ethical practice.

Throughout the book we provide opportunities for the reader to consider ways to "undo gender" and illustrate this process with examples from the counseling setting. We also provide questions for class discussion and suggestions for further reading. Our intent is to be as inclusive and broad as possible in considering sex, gender, and counseling and psychotherapy. Thus, as best as possible, given the very real constraints of a single book, we have attempted to present clients in a context that reflects the very real and rich diversity of their lives.

Acknowledgments

Our appreciation goes to the many students, clients, friends, and colleagues who shared their thoughts and experiences with us, and by so doing, helped in our understanding of the importance of gender in everyday life as well as in psychotherapy and counseling. Special appreciation goes to the students who commented on earlier versions of the book: Tamatha Dake-Walden, Judy Glaister, Don Jones, Diana Laura, Hsin-Tine Liu, Alicia Meuret, Laymoi Ng, and especially Jessica McFaddin, who provided extensive comments. We also wish to thank past and present doctoral students at the University of Texas at Austin whose studies helped inform our book: Karen Rossman, Sarah Walker, Sherry

Goss, Betty Gregory, Elette Estrada, Laura Rencher, Natalie Eldridge, James Werrbach, Beverly Davis, Jim Etzkorn, Jeanne Schillaci, Cynthia De Las Fuentes, Marybeth Hallett, Brian Thorn, Stella Kerl, Eric Benjamin, and Tanya Shan. Our thanks to Ray Short, series editor, for his vision and to Karin Huang for her unfailing assistance and to Kathleen Copeland for obtaining permissions.

Enormous gratitude is expressed to Melissa Carlotta Gilbert who not only prepared the book's references and index but also devoted many hours to providing insightful comments and thoughtful editing.

Very special appreciation goes also to Emily Anderson for her marvelous and sensitive photographs. Emily received an MA from the Royal College of Art in London. She works as a freelance photographer in London. Having published extensively in books and magazines her work is shown frequently and she is represented by a gallery. She has work in the collection of the National Portrait Gallery. She received the John Kobel Prize for Outstanding Contribution to Portraiture, 1997.

Our spouses Jack and Rita have only to read the dedication to know how important their contributions have been. Finally, we want to acknowledge our parents who first introduced us to gender some time ago: Carmelina and William Albino, inspiring in their willingness to challenge traditional gender roles and Lea Rubenstein, whose struggles as a single parent informed her son of the plight of women in our culture. Their visions for their children were instrumental to our life paths.

Lucia Albino Gilbert and Murray Scher

About the Authors

Lucia Albino Gilbert, Ph.D. is Professor of Educational Psychology and Director of Women's Studies at the University of Texas at Austin. She teaches in the department's program in counseling psychology. She is a fellow of the American Psychological Association and the American Psychological Society, Associate Editor of *Psychology of Women Quarterly,* and current editorial board member of *Journal of Family Issues, Journal of Family Psychology,* and *Applied and Preventive Psychology.* Her research and publications focus on understanding gender processes in families and society and in psychotherapeutic treatment. In addition to *Gender and Sex in Counseling and Psychotherapy,* her recent books include *Two Careers, One Family: The Promise of Gender Equality* and *Men in Dual-Career Families.*

Dr. Gilbert has conducted many continuing education workshops and has published widely in the areas of counseling and psychotherapy, work and family, and career development. She has received two teaching excellence awards during her 15 years at the University of Texas at Austin and is also the recipient of the John Holland Award for Excellence in Research and the Caroline Wood Sherif Award for excellence as a scholar and teacher in the psychology of women.

Dr. Gilbert is very committed to the educational process and often speaks to media representatives (radio, television, and magazines) as well as to professional and lay audiences on topics associated with her major areas of research and teaching. This past year, for example, Dr. Gilbert was interviewed by writers from *Newsweek, New Women, Men's Health,* and *McCall's* magazines; the *Chicago Tribune, Wall St. Journal,* and *New York Times,* among others. She has also been a guest on a number of national programs including the *Oprah Winfrey Show* and *ABC News Washington.*

Murray Scher, Ph.D. has been involved in the study of gender and its effect on counseling and psychotherapy for the last twenty years. He is the lead editor of *The Handbook of Counseling and Psychotherapy with Men,* published by Sage. He has also been guest editor of *The Personnel and Guidance Journal's Special Issue on Counseling Males* as well as guest editor of *VOICES'* issue Reflections on Therapist Gender. He was co-editor of the special section Gender Issues in Counseling of the *Journal of Counseling and Development.* He was also co-editor of *Changing Men in Higher Education,* published by Jossey-Bass. He has published and presented extensively on male gender roles and their impact on psychotherapy. Dr. Scher has given two invited presentations to the American Psychological Association on gender role issues for men. Dr. Scher is a Fellow of Division 51, The Society for the Psychological Study of Men and Masculinity, of the American Psychological Association. He was chair of the Standing Committee on Men of the American College Personnel Association. He is one of the original members of the National Organization of Men Against Sexism. He is currently President-elect of the American Academy of Psychotherapists.

Theory

Part

The two chapters in the first part of the book provide an in-depth understanding of the concept of gender. These are particularly crucial chapters because they lay the foundation for the remainder of the book. Gender is complex, so we ask that you take time to consider these chapters in some depth. Indeed some readers may find the theoretical ideas we present startlingly new, quite intriguing, and very useful in making sense of things they have long found puzzling.

Chapter 1 explains how and why gender relates to the making or constructing of women and men across cultures. We begin with working definitions of sex and gender and explain the theoretical importance attached to the proper use of the term *gender*. Using everyday examples, we then detail helpful ways to understand the power of gender in shaping who women and men actually become or think they should become. We label these various ways gender operates in cultures as the four faces of gender.

In Chapter 2 we discuss the process of gender socialization and summarize several important bodies of research that inform the theoretical ideas described in the first chapter. This may be a difficult chapter for some readers, as it presents a wealth of research-based material. Here again, we ask that you take the time you need to understand the key points, which are crucial to making sense of the later chapters on counseling and therapy. Presented here, for example, are summaries of empirical studies on sex-related differences in such areas as personality characteristics and cognitive abilities, as well as ways to determine for yourself the meaning of statistical differences in the context of gender socialization and culture. Some connections to counseling are made in the chapter, although more detail about application to therapeutic settings is left to later chapters.

1

Gender and Its Many Faces

Pat enters therapy with a presenting problem of "feeling down, fatigued, and unmoti-vated." The client has been in the same position for the last ten years, and is disappointed by the absence of any significant promotions. The therapist begins by asking the client the reasons for the lack of promotions. Pat attributes it to only working 40 hours a week and not going into the office on weekends; Pat avoids working overtime in order to make time for family recreation and chores. In addition, Pat admits to being less assertive and less well-organized than co-workers. (Rencher, Schillaci, & Goss, 1995, p. 1).

Does it matter in counseling Pat whether Pat is a woman or a man? Is Pat's sex, resulting gender socialization, and life context important in understanding the presenting concern about work? Is Pat's sex relevant to your theories about what the client is experiencing and what you might say or do to be helpful? Would therapy with Pat be limited or even harmful should a therapist lack an under-standing of the many faces of gender?

This first chapter provides an overview of current thinking about gender and presents a framework for conceptualizing gender in counseling. We start with a discussion of current views of gender and how they differ from the past, and describe what these changes mean for counseling and therapy. We then ex-plore the many faces of gender in some detail. We end the chapter with a con-sideration of the faces of gender with regard to race and ethnicity.

What Is Gender?

Simone de Beauvoir (1970) noted some time ago that, "One is not born, but rather becomes a woman (or a man)." Biological sex has long served as a looking glass or lens through which we view decisions about how to think about and interact with girls and boys, women and men (Bem, 1993). To a large degree we are molded into what our culture views as desirable, proper, and appropriate for our biologi-cal sex. We all have deeply held views of what it means to be a woman and a man in our culture, and often these views are developed and shaped in subtle and nonconscious ways. It is this view of gender that guides and informs this book.

Use of the term gender, rather than the term sex, represents a *fundamental* change in how we think about women and men. We cannot overemphasize how fundamental and important a change this is for counseling. Sex and gender are dif-ferent concepts (although, as we see later, they are frequently treated as if they were identical). The definitions of sex and gender we use in this book are as follows:

Sex: Refers to whether one is born biologically female or male

Gender: Refers to the psychological, social, and cultural features and char-acteristics that have become strongly associated with the biological cate-gories of female and male

Sex—being a woman or a man biologically—distinguishes human individuals. Women and men differ in a number of ways biologically. The most obvious biological differences have to do with each sex's role in reproduction. Apart from traits directly involved with procreation, however, women and men are not very different physically. For example, the sexes are similar biologically in "normal" pulse rates, basal temperature, and blood pressure, and in the needs for food, water, and rest. The physical traits of height, weight, and strength show enormous overlaps between women and men, with some women being heavier, taller, and stronger than some men, and some men being lighter, shorter, and weaker than some women.

Gender, in contrast, pertains to what we *assume* is true or will be true of someone who is born biologically female or male. Gender concerns societal beliefs, stereotypes, and ingrained views about the fundamental nature of girls and boys, women and men. Thus, gender refers not only to biological sex but also to the psychological, social, and cultural features and characteristics associated with the biological categories of female and male (Deaux, 1985; Sherif, 1982; Unger, 1979, 1990). As de Beauvoir observed, unlike biological sex, a person is not born with gender. One is not born a man or a woman, but learns to become what is considered to be a man or a woman in the eyes of a particular society at a particular time. Films such as *Hoop Dreams, Sense and Sensibility, Love Has Nothing to Do with It, Lonesome Dove, The Joy Luck Club,* and *Gentleman Prefer Blondes,* portray very differing views of the female and male gender, reflecting changing cultural views of what it means to be a woman or man. The four examples presented in Box 1.1 illustrate the link between sex, gender, and societal norms and practices.

BOX 1.1 Views of Sex and Gender Are Linked to Societal Norms and Practices

The term gender makes more explicit the broader meaning typically associated with being born biologically female or male. These examples help illustrate how views of gender are constructed within a society.

- Example 1: *Who wears the pants?* In most Western cultures, women wear skirts and men wear trousers. The kind of clothing people wear is not caused by their biological sex, but is associated with their biological sex. Men could wear skirts and women trousers, and indeed in some non-Western societies they do. The kind of clothing worn by women and men is dictated not by their biology but by the cultural norms of their society.
- Example 2: *Who wears pink?* Consider the powerful symbolic meaning associated with the colors pink and blue in our culture. At birth, an infant's sex is identified by a pink or a blue bow. Try as you might, it is impossible to find a pink congratulatory card for the new parents of a boy and it is nearly as difficult to locate a blue card for the parents of a girl. Infant clothing presents a similar problem. Few parents would be so thoughtless as to dress their son in

pink; parents of girls have more leeway, although pink predominates. (Have you ever asked yourself why pink is a "girl" color?)

- Example 3: *Who cares for children?* Women and men in our society are equally likely to become parents (i.e., biologically, conception requires a female and a male), but disproportionately more women than men involve themselves in the day-to-day care of children (i.e., culturally, women rear children). From a gender perspective, women typically rear children, not because men lack innate nurturing tendencies, but because societal expectations associated with sex prescribe that women, more than men, engage in nurturing activities.
- Example 4: *Who brings home more money?* Even today women earn significantly less than men on average. This "gender" gap in salary is not brought about by women and men having different intellectual capacities and abilities, but by differential and complex reward systems associated with views of women and men and what they are "worth."

Views of gender, then, are constructed within a society; they are not located in a person's biological sex. They are created and maintained through complex processes within a cultural environment that considers them just and appropriate (see Deaux & LaFrance, 1998). Before 1920, for example, the law denied women the right to vote. At that time it was considered as just and appropriate for men to speak for women and to make decisions that would be in women's best interests. This assumption relates to views of traditional heterosexual marriage in which a couple legally became "man and wife," a view also reflected in conventional wedding vows.

Traditional "Opposite Sex" versus Current Thinking about Gender and Identity

In the past, if we knew someone's biological sex, it was implicitly assumed that we knew a great deal about that person. If Pat, introduced at the start of the chapter, were a white female, we would have assumed she would be in a relationship with a man; would describe herself as emotionally expressive and nurturing, and as submissive in her relationships with men; would put care-taking roles first in her life; and would have few ambitions for herself other than caring for her husband and family. In the case of Pat, a white male, we would have assumed he would be "opposite" to Pat, a white female. Thus, his romantic relationships would be with women and he would describe himself as self-reliant and instrumental, and as dominant in relationships with women. We would have assumed he would marry, that marriage would be incidental to what gave his life meaning, and that female significant others would support his personal ambitions and life goals.

Box 1.2 depicts the relative simplicity of the "opposite sex" traditional model, which directly linked biological sex to life roles, personality characteristics, and choice of sexual partners. According to traditional thinking, all females engaged exclusively in care-taking roles and were members of the sex who possessed expressive personality characteristics and desired men as sexual partners. Similarly, all males engaged in a totally different (opposite) set of roles—those of provider, and were members of the sex who possessed instrumental personality characteristics. They, too, were heterosexual by virtue of being biologically male.

The "women and men as opposites model" may appear somewhat simplistic and out of date today, but we ask that you not dismiss the power it has on how you think about women and men. A few examples help illustrate how deeply embedded these ideas are in our thinking. Suppose one is a woman and also a successful athlete, business leader, or scientist, a possibility that does not fit the traditional model depicted in Box 1.2. How do we describe this individual, make sense of who she is? Generally speaking, such individuals are viewed as exceptions to the rule, as acting like men, as taking on male characteristics and roles, or as lacking in warmth and other feminine characteristics (Crawford & Marecek, 1989). The underlying assumption that such behaviors and characteristics could not be normative for women is, of course, derived from the traditional model depicted in Box 1.2. Consider a man who identifies himself as gay.

BOX 1.2   The Traditional Model of "Opposite" Sex (Gender) Identity

The traditional model of sex and identity assumed that biological sex made women and men "opposite" and thus destined them for "opposite" roles in life, "opposite" personality characteristics, and "opposite" desired sexual partners.

Sexual (Gender) Identity

Biological Sex	Female	Male
⇓⇑	⇓⇑	⇓⇑
Life Roles	Care taking	Provider
⇓⇑	⇓⇑	⇓⇑
Personality	Expressive	Instrumental
⇓⇑	⇓⇑	⇓⇑
Sexual Partner	Man	Woman

Note: ⇓⇑ symbolizes the bidirectionality of these implicit views. For example, because a man was assumed to be instrumental by nature it was also assumed that he could provide; the fact that he could provide meant that he must be an instrumental person by nature.

To make this situation fit the model, the man who is attracted to another man is often perceived as acting like a woman, and thus stereotypically defined by expressive characteristics and female roles and behavior (Eldridge, 1987). Similarly, the man who wants to parent full-time is stereotypically viewed as acting like a woman, and therefore lacking in such essential male characteristics as ambition, instrumental and independent strivings, and wanting power in the world (Gilbert, 1993).

Such traditional views continue to hold great power in how we think about women and men. Perhaps most important, they shape women's and men's lives and the nature of heterosexual romantic relationships in most cultures (Ker Conway, 1994). The accepted female life plan and story line conceals that women are instrumental and capable of a sense of self separate from the needs of others. Further, a woman's life ends with the "marriage plot," when she is subsumed within the man's history and becomes his wife (Heilbrun, 1988). The standard male life plan, in contrast, is fused with a personal instrumentality that is tied to proving that he can control his fate and make his own way in the world (Ker Conway, 1995). Story lines reflecting female acquiescence and male self-determination form the basis of the traditional happy marriage.

In contrast, current thinking about gender uses societal context rather than biology as a lens. This broader lens allows our thinking to move away from views of individuals as solely determined by their biology to views of individuals who are developing in social and cultural contexts. Rather than considering biological makeup and reproductive organs as the only valid explanation for women's and men's personality characteristics and behavior, gender perspectives allow us to view individuals' behavior as emerging from a web of interactions between their biological being and their social and cultural environment.

Karen Horney was one of the early theorists to recognize the power that culture exerted on human development. Her paper, "The Overvaluation of Love" (Horney, 1934) described how being loved by a man was one of the few ways women of her culture and era could attain financial security and status. Women's dependence on men for love was not innate, she argued, it was learned. Women were expected to marry, and when they married, the law required that they give up their name, their property, and their personhood.

When one changes the frame of inquiry away from the traditional opposite-sex model, in which sex determines our partner, our personality, and our life roles, to a broader contextual gender perspective, new possibilities emerge. In the case of Pat, a man, his unhappiness may stem from the lack of support he feels for making a close relationship with his family a priority in his life. If a counselor focused on Pat's sense that he is not as assertive as his colleagues, conceptualizing the problem as Pat's needing to be more assertive and manly, the counselor may miss the importance of exploring possible dynamics associated with Pat's going against the norm in his work situation. For example, Pat's self-perceived lack of assertiveness may be a way for him to survive in a nonsupportive environment or a way to blame himself for the lack of promotions rather than challenge the attitudes and policies of his workplace, which he may view as unchangeable. Moreover, should Pat be a partner in a same-sex relationship, a counselor or therapist who conceptualizes the problem as Pat's needing to be more assertive and manly may be perceived as holding homophobic attitudes. Finally, returning to Box 1.2, a counselor who views the problem as Pat's not possessing the right personality characteristics or not engaging in appropriately instrumental behaviors may "make sense" of Pat's giving priority to home roles by erroneously assuming that Pat possesses expressive characteristics and therefore lacks instrumental ones.

By broadening explanatory models, counselors and therapists working with individuals such as Pat, woman or man, are better able to identify the importance of contextual variables shaping personal experiences and are less likely to mistakenly attribute client difficulties entirely to intrapsychic causes. In the case example of Pat, male or female, it is crucial to explore with the client his or her own and partner's attitudes about life roles, partner participation in family work, child-care availability and quality, employers' work and family policies, and workplace attitudes.

It is typical in our culture for individuals to blame themselves for feeling overwhelmed and upset in their lives or, as in the case of Pat, for feeling stalled in their work. Using broader contextual models can help clients to see other aspects of their current distress which, in turn, allows them to use different strategies for changing the situation. For example, if Pat's fear of appearing too family oriented, or his fear of being open about his gay relationship, makes him hesitant to use his employer's work-family policies such as telecommuting or restructuring work hours to maximize family time, options commonly used by colleagues, his life context would call for different interventions and strategies than if Pat says he hates his work and wants to retrain for another field, but is hesitant to ask his partner to carry the financial responsibility for the family in the interim. In these instances, counseling and therapy must focus on the context of these individuals' lives in association with the unique aspects of who they are as human beings. Later chapters consider contextual variables in greater detail.

The Many Faces of Gender

Gender has become a ubiquitous term in our society. The old-fashioned term sex is out and the more sophisticated term gender is in. Unfortunately many people today, including researchers and mental health professionals, are simply replacing the term sex, referring to one's biological sex, with the term gender. The forms we fill out in offices and the surveys we complete for various studies ask us to identify our gender. Headlines in newspapers, lead-ins in magazines, and titles of books use the term gender. This practice is regrettable because it obfuscates the crucial distinction social scientists have worked so hard to make clear. Gender was introduced by feminist theorists as a term connoting context— events and processes located outside of individuals which get tied to their biological sex, such as wearing lipstick for women but not for men, or expecting men to appear more muscular than women. Using the term gender to denote biological sex unwittingly locates gender right back within the person. It moves us back to the old sex difference models and theories (as described in the next section) but with a new term, gender.

The "dangers of a sexist nonconscious ideology" are real—it is all too easy as a counselor or therapist to use the new word gender but to assume the same old sex differences (Gilbert, 1994). Social meanings and societal institutions are deeply rooted in sexual difference and in the notions that women give care and men take care (Pogrebin, 1983) and that men are superior to women (Wollstonecraft, 1792/1989). Not too long ago the syndicated magazine section of a local newspaper included a section on "Fresh Voices." The topic was sexism. Reproduced here is the entire article (Minton, 1995, p. 20).

They Think They're Joking

Sexism is so accepted in my school that people just don't realize it. I know many guys who make comments. They think they're joking. There's a group of boys in one class, and they love to say stuff like, "Yeah, my woman's gonna be barefoot and pregnant"—all the stereotypes. One guy said, "If I take a girl out to a prom, and I spend a bunch of money on her, I better be getting something in return." I just kind of shrug it off, because I don't want to deal with these guys. But it really bugs me.

In class, we discuss all these issues—but sexism is ignored. Sexism is acceptable. Teachers who wouldn't dream of saying anything racist make comments about women. Like, one said, "Men are better drivers, and it's a proven fact." I was like, "Where did this come from?"

—Amanda Zeiger, 16, Glendale, AZ

In one of my classes, the teacher jokingly said stuff to guys like, "Uh-oh, she's a girl, and she's catching up to you. She's better than you." Like, "Watch out!" We don't really talk too much about sexism. It's like it doesn't exist. But it does exist. It exists a lot.

—Mara Posada, 17, San Antonio, TX
(Reprinted with permission from Parade, *copyright © 1995)*

Imbedded in this brief article about a sexist nonconscious ideology are the many faces of gender. The next sections describe these faces and show how these two student comments are illustrative. (Box 1.4 on page 14 uses examples from this article in summarizing current views on the many faces of gender.)

Gender as Difference

Gender as difference is the assumption that one set of characteristics, abilities, and interests belongs to one sex, and that another set belongs to the other or "opposite sex." Amanda (in the quote above) is irritated by the expressed certainty of male superiority in areas such as driving. (Interestingly, women have far fewer accidents and pay less for their insurance as a result). Mara refers to the idea that teachers motivate boys to perform by shaming them (and girls) if girls outperform boys or do as well as boys. The assumption here is that boys are superior, or should be.

Historically when researchers studied the behavior of women and men, it was often done with the assumption that the sexes were opposite by nature and thus possessed nonoverlapping attributes and abilities, assumptions tied to the model depicted in Box 1.2. Researchers' interpretations of their findings both reflected and preserved traditional views of women's and men's opposite natures. Men were assumed to be superior to women, and stronger and more active. Thus, the different shape and size of women's skulls were interpreted as evidence of women's weaker brain power, and the normal processes of menstruation as rendering women weak and diseased (Russett, 1989). These assumptions extended to views of sexuality; in this activity men were assumed to be the pursuers and aggressors, and women were passive recipients. In conception the ovum was seen as passive and static, and the sperm energetic and mobile. (Although many children's books still present the egg as a passive object waiting for the sperm to fertilize it, in reality, the two cells fuse, a process in which both the egg and the sperm participate actively.)

The assumption that women and men basically differ often results in interpreting observed differences between women and men on various tests or measures as "differences in kind" rather than as "differences in degree."

- *Differences in kind* means that Groups A and B do not have the same characteristic in common—Group A possesses one set of attributes or behaves in one way, and Group B possesses a different set of attributes or behaves in another way (e.g., women are one way, men are another way).
- *Differences in degree,* in contrast, means that Groups A and B have a particular characteristic in common but they differ in the degree to which that characteristic is present or observable in each group.

As an example, take the two scales of the well-known and widely used Personal Attributes Questionnaire (PAQ; Spence, Helmreich, & Stapp, 1974). The *Instrumental (I) Scale* provides an assessment of self-assertive, instrumental traits that had been judged to be more characteristic of men than women, but socially desirable to some degree for both sexes. Similarly, the *Expressive (E) Scale* provides an assessment of expressive characteristics judged to be more characteristic of women than men, but also socially desirable for both sexes. Each trait is presented in a 5-point bipolar format and respondents are asked to place themselves on the continuum (e.g., not at all competitive to very competitive; not at all warm to very warm). Items from these scales are shown in Box 1.3. (Readers are encouraged to respond to these items and to calculate their scores on the I and E scales.)

BOX 1.3 Items from the Expressive (E) and Instrumental (I) Scales of the PAQ

Most counselors and therapists describe themselves as high on both the E and I scales. Effective counseling typically demands that the therapist be able to engage in both instrumental and expressive behaviors. This questionnaire concerns how you see yourself. Each item consists of a pair of personal characteristics, with the letters A to E in between. For example:

Not at all outgoing   A   B   C   D   E   Very outgoing

The letters form a scale between the two extremes. You are to choose the letter that describes where *you* fall on the scale. For example, if you think you are not at all outgoing, you would choose A. If you think you are pretty outgoing, you might choose D. If you are somewhat outgoing, you might choose C, and so forth.

1.	Not at all independent	A B C D E	Very independent
2.	Not at all emotional	A B C D E	Very emotional
3.	Very passive	A B C D E	Very active
4.	Not at all able to devote self completely to others	A B C D E	Able to devote self completely to others
5.	Very rough	A B C D E	Very gentle
6.	Not at all helpful to others	A B C D E	Very helpful to others
7.	Not at all competitive	A B C D E	Very competitive
8.	Not at all kind	A B C D E	Very kind
9.	Not at all aware of feelings of others	A B C D E	Very aware of feelings
10.	Have difficulty making decisions	A B C D E	Can make decisions easily
11.	Give up very easily	A B C D E	Never give up easily
12.	Not at all self-confident	A B C D E	Very self-confident
13.	Feel very inferior	A B C D E	Feel very superior
14.	Not at all understanding of others	A B C D E	Very understanding of others
15.	Very cold in relations with others	A B C D E	Very warm in relations with others
16.	Go to pieces under pressure	A B C D E	Stand up well under pressure

Scoring Instructions for the PAQ

Items on the I scale are 1, 3, 7, 10, 11, 12, 13, and 16. Items 2, 4, 5, 6, 8, 9, 14, and 15 are on the E scale. Assign a score of 1 to option A, 2 to B, 3 to C, 4 to D, and 5 to E. Add the item scores for each scale to obtain scores for that scale.

Source: Spence, J. T., Helmreich, R., & Stapp, J. (1974). The Personal Attributes Questionnaire: A measure of sex-role stereotypes and masculinity-femininity. *JSAS Catalog of Selected Documents in Psychology, 4,* 43–44, MS 617.

Typically women score a little higher than men on the E scale and men a little higher than women on the I scale, findings consistent with gender socialization. For example, in a study conducted with juniors and seniors at the University of Texas (Gilbert, Walker, Goss, & Snell, 1997), the mean scores for female students who participated were 32.80 for the E scale and 29.84 for the I scale; the mean scores for male students who participated were 30.96 for the E scale and 32.0 for the I scale. These mean scores, accurately interpreted, reflect *differences in degree* or magnitude. That is, both the female and male students described themselves as possessing these personal characteristics, although females did so to a somewhat greater degree on the E scale (32.80 versus 30.96) and males did so to a somewhat greater degree on the I scale (32.0 versus 29.84).

However, researchers tied to a nonconscious ideology of female-male differences are likely to interpret these findings as *differences in kind* (Unger, 1992), particularly if a *t*-test or an *F* test indicates a statistically significant difference. That is, the finding that one group scored higher or lower than the other on a particular measure is interpreted to mean that one group possesses the characteristics assessed by the measure and the other group does not. In this example, should the study's results be filtered through an unconscious "gender as difference" lens, the finding that women scored higher than men on the E scale, and men scored higher than woman on the I scale, would be viewed as women, not men, are expressive and men, not women, are instrumental. The "gender as difference" lens perpetuates the stereotypic view of women and men as possessing "opposite" and nonoverlapping attributes.

You likely have determined by this point that views of "gender as difference" are still alive and well. At a ceremony marking one girl's graduation from kindergarten, the girl's parents were astonished to see the chart of awards presented on the board for parents to see (Deveny, 1994). Boys' awards included Very Best Thinker, Most Eager Learner, Most Imaginative, Most Enthusiastic, Most Scientific, Best Friend, and Hardest Worker. Girls' awards were much different: All-Around Sweetheart, Sweetest Personality, Cutest Personality, Best Sharer, Best Artist, Biggest Heart, Best Manners, and Best Helper. The boys were awarded for their intellectual skills and the girls for their pleasing personalities. The girl's parents brought this example of gender stereotyping to the attention of the teachers and also purchased readers that included female characters in nontraditional roles for every student in their daughter's first-grade class.

The persistence of a nonconscious ideology of female-male differences helps underscore the fact that behavior occurs in a social context, which takes us to descriptions of other faces of gender.

Gender as Organizer or Structurer

Amanda and Mara, in the earlier quotes, both alluded to persistent, highly visible dynamics in their high school culture which they say are never discussed. Amanda noted that, "In class, we discuss all these issues—but sexism is ignored.

Sexism is acceptable. Teachers who wouldn't dream of saying anything racist make comments about women." Another face of gender is as a pervasive organizer in society that extends beyond individual women and men and their socialization to the social structures and principles of organizations (Sherif, 1982).

Persistent, highly visible dynamics in the culture reflect the power of gender as organizer and structurer. Researchers of educational environments have documented the implicit and explicit policies from kindergarten through college that serve to structure the opportunities and behaviors of girls and boys. Thorne's (1993) book, *Gender Play: Girls and Boys in School,* presents many examples of social arrangements that organize or structure female and male students' activities. "Space, an especially valuable resource in the crowded environment of schools, is the locus of one basic asymmetry between girls and boys" (p. 83). In Thorne's studies, boys controlled as much as ten times the space on school playgrounds as girls. Also, boys more often interrupted, invaded, or disrupted all-female games and play much more often than girls interrupted all-male games and play. Adults in these environments encouraged and rewarded these behaviors, viewing them as normal and healthy.

Laws and implicit policies also become ways to structure women's and men's lives along traditional lines. Historical examples include barring women from an advanced education or from entering certain professional fields, not allowing women to vote, and requiring women to leave their places of employment when they became pregnant. These laws and policies were consistent with the view that men were the providers and women the caregivers. Women who were employed were often paid less and viewed as support staff for their male bosses. Behaviors that we now know constituted sexual harassment were for many, many years so much a part of the social order, so customary and so synchronized with traditional views of how women and men interact in environments in which men have more power, they were invisible. (Recall Amanda's comment that, "Sexism is so accepted in my school that people just don't realize it.")

Another example is what is referred to as the "glass ceiling," which frequently underlies issues that women bring to therapy, and a possible variable to consider in the case of Pat, a woman. These transparent but powerful artificial barriers are based on attitudinal or organizational biases that keep women and minorities from advancing upward in their organization into management level positions (Morrison, White, Velsor, & The Center for Creative Leadership, 1987). A study conducted by the U.S. Department of Labor (1995) found that the glass ceiling occurs far below middle management and appears early on in "pipelines to the top." The same stereotypes and misperceptions documented by researchers were found in companies' decisions and records. Women were simply assumed not to possess leadership qualities. Contrary to these stereotypes, comprehensive meta-analytic studies on gender and leadership find no overall sex differences in leader effectiveness (Eagly & Johnson, 1990). These examples concern women because the underlying issue is allowing women into areas long considered by society to be male turf. Similar barriers occur when men want to enter areas considered by society as female turf—namely home and family.

BOX 1.4   Current Views on the Many Faces of Gender with Examples from "Fresh Voices"

- Gender in the form of *difference* based on belief systems about women and men as the "opposite" sex.

   Men are better drivers, and it's a proven fact.

- Gender in the form of societal *structures*, laws, and policies that reflect assumptions about women's and men's rights and roles

   Sexism is so accepted in my school that people just don't realize it.

- Gender in the form of *language and discourse*

   One guy said, "If I take a girl out to a prom, and I spend a bunch of money on her, I better be getting something in return."

- Gender in the form of *interactive process*

   I just kind of shrug it off, because I don't want to deal with these guys. But it really bugs me.

Relatively few men today grow up with the assumption that they will be full-time caregivers to their children. Even fewer, if any, feel pressured by society to do so. Men's involvement in parenting and household work is still greatly influenced by traditional views of men's roles, which in turn are tied to whether men decide to use work-family policies offered by employers and thus perhaps alter traditional paths to career success. Our earlier discussions about possible issues in the counseling of Pat, a male client, brought up some of these dilemmas. Even today, men are less expected to use employer benefits and policies for combining work and family responsibilities (e.g., taking paternity leave or requesting flexible schedules) and some men fear that they will be labeled as insufficiently committed to their work if they use these benefits.

In summary, factors relevant to gender as organizer or structurer revolve around societal views of women's and men's roles and characteristics, but manifest themselves as structural barriers to women's and men's personal wishes, goals, and desires (see Box 1.4). Such factors would be important to explore in counseling Pat, woman or man.

Gender as Language and Discourse

Amanda and Mara both commented on how language was used to depict certain views of girls and boys. The boy who says, "If I take a girl out to a prom, and I spend a bunch of money on her, I better be getting something in return," is of course referring to women owing men their bodies in exchange for men's economic power. This language reflects a powerful discourse in the culture about what entitles men to sex with women. Conventional dating assumes that a man's duty to ask and pay for the date as well as determine its activity has implications for expected sexual intimacy for the couple. A survey of male and female college students indicated that a sizable percentage, around 40 percent, thought women owe male dating partners sex when the men had spent a lot of money on a date, and that under these conditions it was "OK" for guys to force themselves sexually on their female dates (Gandara, 1995).

When the teacher described by Mara says to the boys in the class, "Uh-oh, she's a girl and she is catching up to you," the teacher is conveying the view that boys outperform girls if they really try and that boys *should* outperform girls. These examples are not unusual. In *Secrets of Life,* Keller (1992) describes the subtleties of language and the ways in which linguistic conventions assert traditional assumptions about gender and thus play a powerful role in maintaining nonconscious views about women and men. The first example, "If I take a girl out to a prom, and I spend a bunch of money on her, I better be getting something in return," asserted the traditional assumption that under certain conditions men are entitled to women's bodies; and the second example, "Uh-oh, she's a girl and she is catching up to you," fostered the traditional assumption that men are supposed to be superior to women.

The language used by counselors to describe women's and men's changing roles can also reflect underlying stereotypic views. Pat, a woman employed outside the home, may be thought about and referred to as a working mother, but Pat, a man, also employed outside the home, may *not* be thought of or described as a working father. This difference in language is likely tied to a traditional gender ideology in which women are assumed to be the primary parent, and men the primary provider, regardless of their actual involvement in these roles.

Views about women's and men's differing psychological natures often are embedded in the language we use in therapy, and in the theories that guide our work. A case in point is a phrase used by a student in describing a client in a supervisory session. The therapist-in-training referred to a female client as "having lost her virginity." Struck by this phrase, the supervisor wondered what the student thought it conveyed. As was mentioned earlier in the chapter, we often use passive language when describing women's experiences, a convention that portrays women as separate and removed from their sexual experiences. Rather than using phrases such as a woman having her first experience of intercourse, the common expression is a woman losing her virginity or losing some aspect of herself. This language of course also reflects a long-standing cultural view of women's sexuality and what makes women more or less valued by men and by the culture. (Also relevant here is the earlier example of the egg and sperm; the stereotypic but inaccurate notion of the passive egg and active sperm reflects the ideology of gender relations in which men pursue and women yield.)

Later chapters describe in more detail how language can be used in therapy to maintain conventional views about women and men. Both language and normative discourses, and gender as interactive process, the last face of gender we describe, are particularly crucial to what happens in counseling and psychotherapy.

Gender as Interactive Process

This last face of gender speaks to its active, alive quality. Gender processes such as socialization are not something that happened to people growing up—it happens every day. As Deaux and LaFrance (1998) noted, it is in social encounters that "gender gets materialized." This active quality or process engaged in by women and men is referred to as the *doing or making of gender* (Deaux & Major, 1987; Sherif, 1982; Unger, 1990; West & Zimmerman, 1987) or gender as performative, that is, unfolding as a series of "performed" acts (Butler, 1990).

The doing of gender refers to the process in which women and men not only internalize societal constructions of women and men, but also are encouraged and rewarded for playing them out in their interpersonal interactions, particularly in those kinds of interactions in which gender is salient. Here again the experiences described by Amanda and Mara provide a good illustration. The boys act in offensive ways and Amanda tries to ignore it, although it clearly affects her: "I just kind of shrug it off, because I don't want to deal with these guys. But it really bugs me." The teacher in Mara's class assumes boys will outperform girls and interacts with them accordingly. The interactions that both girls described serve to preserve stereotypic views of women's and men's basic nature—girls passively endure and boys are smarter—and more than that, a social order in which men dominate women.

A common example of doing gender concerns physical height. Overall, many women are taller than or as tall as many men. Yet if we conducted a study of the heights of women and men in heterosexual couples we would conclude that male partners are almost always taller than female partners (Biernat, 1993). It is important in the culture to project an image that the man is taller than the woman; both women and men engage in interpersonal behaviors to preserve this view either by whom they select as partners or by the size heel they wear when they are with their partners. The motivations for doing this are likely tied to views held by both women and men, namely, that men should be bigger and stronger than women.

Another illustrative example comes from a leadership study conducted by Davis and Gilbert (1989). In these studies, when high dominant men were paired with low dominant women or men, the high dominant man became the designated leader, as predicted by theories of personality. However, when high dominant women were paired with low dominant men, contrary to expectations, the man again became the designated leader. Observing the process of the decision making indicated that a high dominant woman suggested that her low dominant male partner become the task leader, a behavior that was in accordance with both her personality disposition and societal views of gender. By deferring to the man, partners in these dyads "did gender" in that they both acted in ways to preserve societal views of how women and men should behave in a leadership situation.

The case of Pat helps illustrate some of the ways therapists can do gender. Pat mentioned avoiding working overtime in order to make time for family recreation and chores. In counseling Pat, the heterosexual woman, we may assume that she has made the right choices and see the counseling as helping Pat to deal with the inevitable stresses for working women. We run the risk of doing gender in this situation because we are interacting with the female client in ways that preserve societal views of women's roles and responsibilities. That is, we assume women want to give priority to their family regardless of possible tradeoffs at work. In so doing, we do gender by disallowing other kinds of conversations from emerging that would be contrary to, and perhaps challenge or change, this conventional societal view of women. Pat may need assistance in recognizing and effectively confronting sexist attitudes at work or in reframing what represents a fair division of responsibilities in the home, interventions that would challenge conventional practices and arrangements.

In counseling Pat, the heterosexual man, we may question whether he has made the right choices and see the therapy as helping Pat be more successful at work. Here again, we run the risk of doing gender in this situation because we are interacting with the male client in ways that preserve societal views of men's roles and responsibilities, and perhaps our own deeply held views of a "healthy" man. Pat may leave the first therapy session feeling that the solution to his problem is to change his priorities at home and work longer hours, behaviors that would preserve the traditional societal view of what men do.

Because counseling and psychotherapy are optimal settings for gender as interpersonal process to emerge, later chapters give particular attention to the various aspects of doing gender. As illustrated in the case of Pat, we do gender:

- when we behave differently with male and female clients and attribute the difference to their "nature" and not to our own biases. For example, we question Pat, the heterosexual man, on his choices but assume Pat, the heterosexual woman, has made the right choices.
- when we hold certain views of how women and men should be, and use these views to implicitly or explicitly guide our work. For example, we assume Pat, the heterosexual man, needs to be more successful at work than he is, and Pat, the heterosexual woman, more content with her situation.
- when we ignore the gendered context of our clients' lives. For example, we neglect to ask about attitudes and values in Pat's workplace; about how roles are shared in Pat's home, and why.

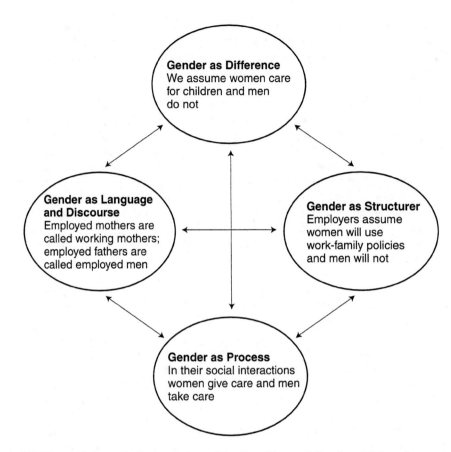

FIGURE 1.1   Schematic Presentation of the Four Faces of Gender. All four faces are mutually interactive. The schema in the figure was one of many possible sequential arrangements.

Figure 1.1 presents an interactive diagram of the faces of gender just described. These four ways of thinking about gender processes are highly correlated and mutually influencing, as depicted in the figure. For example, views of women as nurturers and men as providers (gender as difference) become associated with women's and men's abilities and their "rightful place" in the workplace or home (gender as organizer or structurer), with the internalized views both women and men bring to interactions (gender as interactional process), and with the language they use to describe their life experiences (gender as language and discourse).

Gender, Race, and Ethnicity

The faces of gender operate to varying degrees in all cultures, although how they manifest themselves may be quite different. The similarities are perhaps best reflected in the common platform developed by women from many different countries who attended the United Nations Fourth World Conference on Women in 1996. Across cultures, social systems operate in similar ways to "structure the psyches of both sexes to reproduce their desired ideal types, and they do so by controlling what can be thought and felt" (Ker Conway, 1994, p. 152). It is particularly crucial in working with clients to understand their ethnic and racial background and cultural identity, to understand how the faces of gender operate within that culture, and to understand the context of their lives in the United States.

African American individuals, for example, are faced with issues of both race and gender. Prejudicial attitudes and societal structures and practices associated with racism are normative in their lives. A crucial gender-related cultural difference between African American women and white women in the United States is the expectation of white women that men will provide for them. Employment has been normative for the African American woman; slave women worked just like slave men, and were expected to put their family needs after the needs of others (Jones, 1987). After slavery, it was often safer for African American women to be employed because of threats of lynching African American men (hooks, 1981). African American men have encountered persistent discrimination and limited educational and career opportunities. Unlike white men, societal expectations of male economic success and power have not extended to the African American male.

The pervasiveness of racism may also intensify the effects of sexism for African American women and men (Greene, 1994; Staples, 1982). In the essay, "Sexism: An American Disease in Blackface," Lorde (1984) asked, "If this society ascribes roles to Black men which they are not allowed to fulfill, is it Black women who must bend and alter our lives to compensate, or is it society that needs changing? And why should Black men accept these roles as correct ones, or anything other than a narcotic promise encouraging acceptance of other facts of their own oppression. . . . As Black women and men, we cannot hope to begin dialogue by denying the oppressive nature of male privilege" (p. 62). hooks (1995) further noted that, "contrary to popular belief, black folks have always upheld the primacy of patriarchy if only symbolically. . . . Like all other groups in this society, black families in the United States have been just as invested in structuring families so that the ideology of patriarchy and authoritarianism is reproduced even when no males are present" (pp. 71–72). Thus, African American women and men also struggle with views of gender roles and male power, privilege, and superiority vis-à-vis women, aspects of the faces of gender described. However, the context of gendered dynamics appears quite different.

Asian American clients come to therapy with still another history and cultural background. Indeed Asian Americans are a highly diverse group comprising individuals who differ in ethnicity, cultural background, acculturation, and generation of immigrants to which they belong. Often an ongoing tension in their lives is consolidating the culture of their heritage with American culture, a tension in Chinese American families Amy Tan (1989) poignantly described in *The Joy Luck Club*. However, because Asian cultures can differ significantly both in terms of customs and the history of particular Asian cultures in the United States, it is imperative that therapists have a clear understanding of a client's cultural background (see Bradshaw, 1994, for a thoughtful discussion of historical and political considerations in psychotherapy).

Asian and Asian American people also face negative ethnic stereotyping. This is particularly the case for Asian and Asian American women who are assumed to be dependent, domestic, devoted, and highly erotic (Espiritu, 1997). In Asian cultures, the socialization of women and men is somewhat similar to the processes described earlier in the chapter (Bradshaw, 1994; Espiritu, 1997). Traditional gender roles are taught assiduously from a very early age, in the home and in the school. Moreover, many Asian cultures impose devaluing sanctions against women, which reinforces the view that women are inferior and submissive to men. This cultural devaluation can cause conflicts for Asian and Asian American women developing a minority persona in a majority culture. For example, those Asian and Asian American women who prefer the freedoms and increased opportunities for personal achievement more available to women in the majority culture may not necessarily find acceptance in their culture of origin and thus may feel ambivalent about identifying with that culture. Asian and Asian American men face a different situation because male success and superiority is more consistent with their cultural norms.

In many Asian cultures women are subjected to the collective control of many, including the family and the community. There is more careful monitoring of girls' and young women's activities than of boys' and young men's, and a much lowered expectation that they will need an education or engage in life roles other than that of a family, which is considered most important.

Latino and Latina groups are also marked by diversity and include individuals of varying backgrounds from Central and South America, Puerto Rico, Cuba, and the Dominican Republic. Overall Hispanics represent approximately 10 percent of the U.S. population and are the fastest growing ethnic group in the United States, with the largest proportion being those of Mexican descent (61 percent) and Puerto Rican descent (12 percent) (Castaneda, 1996). A very large portion of these individuals was born in the United States, which makes issues of cultural identity and assimilation salient for those individuals and families in counseling. Although there is no question that traditional gender role socialization, patriarchy, and gender oppression exist in Hispanic families and societies, current research indicates that the image of the machismo man who dominates his submissive wife and family is a stereotype that serves to obscure the multidimensionality and dynamic quality of gender roles among this group (Castaneda, 1996; Vasquez, 1994). Social class in particular is an important factor that influences Latina women's ability to redefine aspects of their gender role. Poor and working-class women and men are reported to have more traditional attitudes about women's place in the home than professional women and men. At the same time, among Mexican Americans as a group, cultural traditions continue to give men greater authority over women in the Mexican American community, and discrimination based on gender and ethnicity in the workplace constrains women's efforts to redefine their work and public roles. Sandra Cisneros's (1989) highly acclaimed book, *The House on Mango Street*, illuminates many of the gendered aspects of a young girl growing up in the Hispanic quarter of Chicago—romantic story lines, pervasive gender socialization, strong family ties and friendships, and limited educational opportunity. Also described is the common stereotype that Mexican Americans are less competent than other ethnic and racial groups, a stereotype that particularly affects Latina women who, as a group, are the lowest paid workers in the United States.

Thus, gender considerations are integral aspects of race and ethnicity, and are crucial to doing effective work with clients from diverse backgrounds. Those working with diverse populations may wish to consult pertinent readings recommended at the end of each chapter and references provided throughout the book. Effectively working with clients from diverse populations requires taking many factors associated with culture into account (Comas-Diaz & Greene, 1994; Fouad & Bingham, 1995).

- Values about therapy and seeking help (especially if seeking treatment is not usual in the client's culture)
- Place of birth
- Length of time client and client's family of origin have lived in the United States
- Level or stage of acculturation or assimilation
- Values of culture of origin and adherence to those values at the present time
- Social class or socioeconomic status and education
- Religious beliefs
- Beliefs about expressing feelings and discussing family matters

Useful models for cross-cultural counseling and therapy include Fouad and Bingham's (1995) "culturally appropriate career counseling model," and Leong's (1996) "integrative model for cross-cultural counseling and psychotherapy."

Concluding Remarks

As this first chapter makes clear, we all engage in behaviors prompted by gender-related beliefs and constraints, probably much more often than we realize.

Moreover, this occurs across ethnic and racial groups. Key to this book is encouraging change through awareness and example. A first step in encouraging change is to use the terms sex and gender correctly: "By using 'gender' as a synonym for 'sex,' we confuse the language and perpetuate the myth that biology is destiny" (Pearson, 1996, p. 329). Sex refers to biology and is located "inside" the person; gender refers to cultural roles and practices and is located "outside" the person, but is often internalized in the process of living.

A second step is to understand the complexity of gender. The chapter described four faces of gender. We ask that readers use the four faces of gender as a conceptual tool or guide for exploring the complex map of gender. Later chapters use these four faces in the gender analysis of several therapy cases.

Once we as therapists and counselors can see things differently, we will then be in a position to work with our clients in their search for alternate ways of constructing a life and a sense of self. In Chapter 2 the discussion of sex differences and gender socialization continues the explanation of how gender processes influence personal and counseling relationships, both directly and indirectly.

Discussion Questions

1. These questions ask that you draw from your own experiences with a country or culture other than the United States and/or discussions you have had with individuals who have experiences with another country or culture. Be sure to indicate which country or culture you are referencing in responding to this question.

   a. Compare United States norms and values to those of the other society in terms of issues concerning women and men.

   b. To what extent does feminization and masculinization take place similarly or differently in these two cultures?

   c. To what extent does the process of gender socialization influence women's and men's perceptions and attitudes in the culture?

   d. As best you can, identify examples of how the four faces of gender are apparent in the culture.

   e. Discuss the possible implications of your responses to questions a, b, c, and d for therapy with men from this culture who seek, or are requested to seek, therapy in the United States.

2. A woman presents for therapy complaining of depression. She is having a difficult time finishing junior college. She is also experiencing difficulty with her boyfriend and her parents, whom she believes are not supportive of her being in school. With an understanding that individuals identify

with their culture of origin at different levels, what information would you seek if the individual was: (a) Asian American; (b) Latina; (c) African American? What if the client identified herself as a lesbian woman of color?

Suggested Readings

Cisneros, S. (1989). *The house on Mango Street.* New York: Vintage Books. The compelling story of a young woman growing up in the Hispanic quarter of Chicago.

Hare-Mustin, R. T., & Marecek, J. (1990b). *Making a difference: Psychology and the construction of gender.* New Haven, CT: Yale University Press. This edited book looks at the construction of gender from the perspective of psychology as a field and from the vantage points of various areas within psychology including counseling and developmental processes.

Martinez, D. (1994). *Mother tongue.* Tempe, AZ: Bilingual Press. This book tells the story of a woman and a man and their attempts to go beyond the gendered structures of their cultures.

2

Sex Differences, Sex Roles, and Gender Socialization

Eric comes to you for counseling. He is concerned with how to respond to the parents of his young daughters' friends. Several incidents over the past month have infuriated him and he wants to discuss ways to respond to these kinds of incidents in the future. In the first incident, his 5-year-old daughter Nicole had been the winner of a race at a neighborhood Fourth of July party and thus was eligible for a prize. The woman running the party picked out a tiny baby doll as her prize. When Eric suggested that perhaps his daughter select her own prize, the woman running the party said a bit sarcastically, "Oh, am I being sexist? I have a son and a daughter. If you had a son, you'd know. It's genetic." A few days later Eric was explaining to another friend that they had moved his younger daughter Anna into Nicole's room so that the small room that had been Anna's could be used as a place to do homework. Nicole was entering the first grade in the fall and they wanted to start this tradition from the beginning of her formal schooling. He reported to his friend that both girls seemed to like the arrangement just fine. His friend responded that that was a good solution for girls, but not for boys. "Boys are so active and need a lot more space."

Eric reports also being disturbed in seeing the parents of many of his daughters' friends emphasizing, reinforcing, and sometimes even boasting about supposed sex differences in their 2- and 3-year-old children. Comments such as "girls are so much easier," "girls are more fun because they love to be dressed up," "boys are more coordinated," or he or she is "all boy" or "all girl" are common, he reports. The straw that broke the camel's back occurred at a birthday party for another 5-year-old the previous week. The parents had arranged different activities for the girls and the boys. The girls were to stay at the house and play dress-up and the boys were to go to a neighborhood park to play ball. "No complaints allowed." The client mentioned something about this to another parent at the party and the response was, "There's plenty of time when the kids get bigger for things to even out. You are just too sensitive."

Eric wonders when exactly do things even out and whether insisting from a very young age that boys and girls are fundamentally different influences children's development. His reasons for seeking counseling are twofold. First, he wants to know from an "expert," if he is overreacting. Are boys more coordinated? Are his daughters destined to be sweet and compliant? Does this kind of apparently sexist behavior influence children's development and their sense of self? Does it all even out as they get older? Second, he wants help in finding a way to respond that would be heard, and that would be heard as legitimate. Now he feels either silenced or that he is overreacting because no one shares his concern. Understandably, neither behavior feels comfortable to him.

In this chapter we first describe the conventional socialization of boys and girls, highlighting dynamics associated with their differential gender role socialization. We next turn to the vast literature on gender-related differences and summarize in some detail the findings from studies comparing women and men in a number of areas. We also briefly indicate how this material is crucial to counseling and therapy. Finally, at the end of the chapter we again raise the question, "If you were the counselor or therapist to whom Eric was speaking, how would you respond to the questions raised by this father?"

Gender and Socialization

Gender is central to all theories of personality and development. The major developmental theories used in working with clients are the psychoanalytic, social learning, cognitive-developmental, and symbolic interactionist–role learning. Common to all these theories are implicit and explicit societal views of what it means to be a woman or a man and what roles are viewed as appropriate for each sex. To varying degrees these societal views and experiences become part of an individual's intrapsychic life and external social life, as we make clear in later chapters. This is true for clients and therapists, alike.

The Subtleties of Gender Socialization

Gender socialization is ongoing and begins at birth. Parents hold certain expectations for daughters and sons, as Eric's experiences illustrate. Because they want their child to be accepted by other children, parents may encourage their child to conform to the expectations of friends of the same sex, expectations that they themselves may not particularly hold. See Box 2.1 for an example.

The rigidity of gender socialization is certainly less than in previous generations. Yet, still today, studies show a surprising amount of consistency in how socializing forces shape gendered behaviors in children (Beal, 1994; Jacklin, 1989). The observable changes in women's and men's lives, such as women's greater participation in paid work and athletics, and men's greater participation in household work and parenting, make recognizing the subtleties of traditional socialization practices more difficult.

BOX 2.1   "When Is It OK for a Girl to Begin Shaving Her Legs?"

A couple came to counseling with a dilemma. Among their daughter's peer group, girls began shaving their legs in the fifth grade, a practice they very much opposed. The counselor encouraged the parents to talk with their daughter about their values and reasoning and to find out more about what she was experiencing at school. In these conversations the parents talked with their daughter about the importance of girls deciding about their own bodies, and not succumbing to pressure from boys or the culture about how girls should look. They also pointed out the realities of the situation—when leg hair grows back, it feels rough and requires shaving again. The process is unending. After a good deal of discussion about her peer group, ways to deal with peer pressure, and each of their feelings, the girl and her parents reached a compromise. For one year, each time a boy in her class commented on her "disgustingly hairy legs," she would challenge the boy, saying she would shave her legs as soon he would shave his. (No girls had commented about the hair on her legs.) At the end of the year, she could do whatever she wanted to do.

A somewhat humorous but quite illuminating example comes from an article in the *Wall Street Journal* which indicated that boys in the fourth grade earned more in allowances than girls (Nomani, 1995). In fact, the "gender gap" in allowance earnings for the sample of fourth graders paralleled the gender gap in the real world, in which women earn 69 to 74 percent of what men earn. To add insult to injury, the fourth-grade girl who had surveyed her friends to find out whether she deserved an increase in her allowance before approaching her parents, also discovered that girls reported doing 12 chores on average for their allowance but boys reported doing at most 3 chores.

It is interesting to speculate how this example fits gender stereotypes. Is male labor worth more? Do parents view boys as needing more money than girls? Are chores associated with the home more likely to be assigned to girls? Subtle dynamics about the future roles and rights of children may become embedded in how parents apply societal customs such as allowances.

As this situation illustrates, it is crucial to think through the underlying assumptions guiding interactions with children. A study by Bigler (1995), for example, found that elementary school children whose teachers consistently assigned them by their sex to various activities (e.g., "Let's alternate by boy and girl; girls on this side, boys on the other side") were much more likely to think about themselves and other children in sex-role stereotypic ways than children whose teachers made assignments by color (e.g., "Reds on this side and blues on the other").

Socialization occurs in many ways and involves parents, teachers, peers, and other adults, as well as the media, which include books, magazines, movies, and television (Duke, 1995). Block (1984) was among the first researchers to document how, from an early age, parents and teachers socialize girls and boys to hold different life expectations and different self-schemas: Girls are socialized to have "roots," or a sense of relatedness, and boys to have "wings" or a sense of freedom and self-direction.

Moreover, the stereotypic "gender" scripts from other parents that infuriated our client, Eric, are evident in popular children's books and movies such as *Aladdin, Snow White,* and *Pocohantas* as well as in magazine depictions of female and male children and adults. In a study conducted for Children Now, the Kaiser Family Foundation reported that across a broad range of media, including films, teen magazines, top-rated television shows, music videos, and movies, women are far more likely to be shown preoccupied with romantic relationships and personal appearance than concerned with jobs, educational pursuits, or social issues (Smith, 1997). Thus the images that surround children, adolescents, and adults remain quite gender stereotypic, although the report does provide some evidence of change. The study noted that 69 percent of women in movies and 34 percent on television were shown using their intelligence. Also, self-reliance was emphasized in 35 percent of female characters on television and in movies and in 28 percent of the characters portrayed in teen magazines.

In the next section we look in greater detail at modal patterns of women's and men's socialization. We will see that key to the socialization of children is the assumption that girls and boys are opposite and different—the "differences in kind" described in Chapter 1. Girls and boys are assumed to have opposite motivations, abilities, interests, and eventual life goals. Gender socialization encourages difference, not sameness, as our client Eric pointed out.

Conventional Female Socialization

Girls are portrayed in the media and in real life as needing to be pretty, wanting to please, helping the world through their goodness, being objects of men's sexual desire, and relying on others. In contrast to men whom tradition expects to make something out of their lives, women are expected to accommodate their lives to their husbands', children's, or employers' needs, regardless of their own talents and abilities.

Within traditional ideology, caring for others arises from women's "natural capacity" for childbearing and childrearing. Two other important dimensions are inextricably intertwined with women's special role and virtue within their home and family—invisibility and voicelessness in the world beyond their private roles of wife and mother. Our culture's traditional conception of women's natural place in society identifies them as suited to having influence on a limited and individual basis, not on a collective and institutional basis (Belensky, Clinchy, Goldberger, & Tarule, 1986). Historically, women had no voice or presence in the public forums that constructed the laws of our society. (This situation is somewhat different today with two women sitting on the Supreme Court and approximately 10 percent of the members of Congress being women.)

Women's efforts to act autonomously and to broaden their interests beyond the sphere of the family were met with great skepticism mostly because such actions ran counter to "women's nature." Ibsen (1879/1959) poignantly brought this to our attention in *The Doll's House*. Nora's husband, Torvald, tells her that her most sacred duty is to her husband and children.

Nora stuns Torvald (and the audience) when she responds that she has other duties that she considers just as sacred—duties to herself. Torvald, appearing unable to comprehend Nora's words, reiterates that a woman is a wife and mother before all else, she is not a person in her own right. In what has become a classic response in literature, Nora is able for the first time to disagree with her husband and to see herself as a human being who is a woman and who is capable of rational thought. She realizes that not only is she capable of thinking things over for herself, but is also capable of making her own decisions and defining who she is.

Women such as Nora who sought self-definition typically had to leave their marriages or choose not to marry. Marriage, as mentioned in Chapter 1, was for many years a legal contract that required women, in becoming someone's wife, to give up their names and their personhood. This aspect of marriage remains somewhat true today. Few if any men worry about having to give up their occupational work, or their family name, should they marry. Nor do many men feel pressured to choose between having occupational work and having a family. Within the personal world of relationships, caregiving and self-sacrifice for others is still viewed as a female domain. As we see later, women more than men worry about how to combine occupational work and family demands, usually altering occupational goals and paths to accommodate those demands.

Historically being valued and desired by men was central to a woman's status in her culture; a woman's worth to men was usually seen in terms of her physical characteristics and ability to please, satisfy, and serve men (Holland & Eisenhart, 1990; Westkott, 1986). One consequence of these realities is heterosexual women's overvaluing the importance of relationships with men, looking to these relationships as a way to feel important or worthwhile, and placing a great deal of importance on appearing attractive and feminine (Heilbrun, 1988; Lerner, 1983; Westkott, 1986; Wolf, 1992). The societal pressure to be valued by men may also result in adolescent girls feeling that they need to disconnect from their real personhood to be desirable to boys (Brown & Gilligan, 1992). Acting independently and not engaging in gendered behaviors that supposedly attract men may bring up fears of turning off men and never being in a committed relationship with a man.

Although the vast majority of women today are employed, women are still confronted with constant messages about marriage and having children as first priorities in life. Culturally, achieving financial independence and career success are granted far less attention than taking care of children, despite the facts that increasing numbers of women are achieving occupational success and that many single women are the major financial providers for families. Thus, women's lives being given meaning through their attachment to men, and men taking care of women economically in return, remain powerful standards for many women and men today. (As noted in Chapter 1, a clear exception is African American women who expect to be employed regardless of their marital status.)

Traditionally a young woman's status becomes tied to popularity and demands by men for exclusivity, and not to how well she does in school or in her work (Holland & Eisenhart, 1990). A woman is expected to narrow her professional and personal options once she has a serious boyfriend and to accommodate her life to his. Bradshaw (1994) described an interesting case in which a very bright third-generation Japanese American student, a senior in college, came to counseling with her American boyfriend, who was somewhat older and already professionally established. Difficulties emerged in the relationship when the woman, who had assumed he would be supportive of her career ambitions and her desire to attend graduate school, learned that he was not willing to negotiate the compromises necessary for her to continue her education. Several important issues related to gender emerged in the therapy. The first issue was the boyfriend's unexamined racial and sexist stereotype that she would center her life around his and not make any demands that would require him to change his well-established and comfortable life. The second was how the woman did

gender in the relationship—she not only often was passive and agreeable, behaviors that reinforced the stereotype held by her boyfriend, but she also assumed that because he was American he would want to promote her equality
and freedom in the relationship, something she was sure most Asian men would
be unwilling or unable to do because of family pressures. This dynamic of her
being passive and accommodating and assuming that her boyfriend would
make the best decisions for her had operated unnoticed in the relationship until
it became time for her to make firm plans for her graduate work.

Having a voice and being visible remains a concern for girls and women
(Brown & Gilligan, 1992; Gilligan, 1982). Many girls are still socialized to "know
their place" and to doubt their own knowledge and authority. Adrienne Rich's
(1979) essay, "Taking Women Students Seriously," instructs us:

> Listen to the small, soft voices, often courageously trying to speak up, voices of
> women taught early that tones of confidence, challenge, anger, or assertiveness,
> are strident and unfeminine. Listen to the voices of the women and the voices of
> the men; observe the space men allow themselves, physically and verbally, the
> male assumption that people will listen, even when the majority of the group is
> female. (p. 243)

Women today are taken more seriously than in early times, but likely not
seriously enough. Research indicates that compared with male peers, adolescent
girls develop less confidence in their capabilities, especially in math and science,
and believe less in their ability to successfully perform in these fields (Seymour
& Hewitt, 1997; Sonnert, 1995–1996). "Confident at 11, confused at 16" characterizes these findings (American Association of University Women [AAUW],
1991; Prose, 1990). Girls aged 8 and 9 as a group are confident, assertive, and feel
authoritative about themselves. By 15 or 16 the findings show less confidence
and lowered self-esteem, compared with male peers.

Shortchanging Girls, Shortchanging America (AAUW, 1991) summarizes the
results of a nationwide survey designed to assess self-esteem, educational experiences, interest in science and mathematics, and career aspirations of girls and
boys, aged 9 to 15. Key findings from the 3,000 ethnically and racially diverse
students surveyed were the gender differences in self-esteem and the indication
that girls emerge from adolescence with a poorer self-image, more constrained
views of the future and their place in society, and less confidence in their abilities in comparison with their male peers. The lowering of self-confidence in
girls, as they move from childhood to adolescence, is particularly troubling.
Consistent with the observations of Amanda and Mara reported in Chapter 1, a
large body of research indicates that classroom teachers give significantly more
attention, esteem-building encouragement, praise, critical feedback, and support for assertive behavior to boys than girls. Further, images of women as contributors to knowledge are still marginalized or ignored in textbooks and classroom activities, and sexual harassment of girls by boys is an accepted practice
(AAUW, 1991; Sadker & Sadker, 1994; Seymour & Hewitt, 1997).

In summary, traditional gender ideology asks the conventionally socialized woman to:

- Please men
- Not be competitive with men
- Act inferior to men intellectually
- Restrict personal ambitions
- Be silent
- Accommodate to the needs of others
- Be dependent on men
- Enhance one's status through associations with men
- Be a desired sexual object
- Give priority to marriage and children

As should be expected, there is a good deal of variability among cultural and ethnic groups and among women, but most women grow up in a cultural milieu in which these characteristics are presented as the desirable ones for girls and women.

Conventional Male Socialization

Traditionally, boys are portrayed as wanting to explore, seeking dominance, fighting for what they need, and preparing to make their mark in the world. As men they are expected to become socially and politically active, to provide for women and children, and to engage in masculine affirming activities that often involve danger, risk, sexuality, or competition with other men (Pleck, 1981a, 1995). The stereotypic ideology of masculinity requires men to see themselves as highly independent and self-sufficient and to seek ways of gaining and maintaining power in their world. Education, achievement, sexual prowess, and athletic ability all contribute to men's power. Indeed women are stereotypically the prizes of heterosexual men's rivalry with each other (Pleck 1981b).

The Brannon Masculinity Scale (BMS) was developed to measure individuals' approval of the norms and values that define the male role. The BMS is based on Brannon's analysis of the American "blueprint" of what a man is supposed to be and supposed to want to be (Brannon, 1985). From his studies of men, Brannon (1985) identified four dimensions or themes of masculinity: not being feminine (what Brannon calls "no sissy stuff"); being respected and admired for successful achievement ("the big wheel"); never showing uncertainty and weakness ("the sturdy oak"); and seeking adventure and risk, including the acceptance of violence if necessary ("give 'em hell"). Examples of items from the BMS appear in Box 2.2 on page 32.

Most pivotal, according to Brannon, is the no-sissy-stuff standard, which involves *avoiding femininity* (e.g., "It bothers me when a man does something that I consider 'feminine.' ") and *concealing emotions* (e.g., "When a man is feeling a

---

BOX 2.2   Items from the Brannon Masculinity Scale (BMS)

- "No sissy stuff"

   It bothers me when a man does something that I consider "feminine."

   When a man is feeling a little pain, he should try not to let it show too much.

- "The big wheel"

   Success in his work has to be a man's central goal in his life.

   It is essential for a man to have the respect and admiration of everyone who knows him.

- "The sturdy oak"

   I like for a man to look somewhat tough.

   A man should always try to project an air of confidence even if he doesn't feel confident inside.

- "Give 'em hell"

   A real man enjoys a bit of danger now and then.

Source: Brannon, R. (1985). A scale for measuring attitudes about masculinity. In A. Sargent (Ed.), *Beyond sex roles* (pp. 110–116). St. Paul, MN: West Publishing. Reprinted by permission of Dr. Robert Brannon.

---

little pain, he should try not to let it show too much"). The big wheel theme concerns *being the breadwinner* (e.g., "Success in his work has to be a man's central goal in his life") and *being admired and respected* (e.g., "It is essential for a man to have the respect and admiration of everyone who knows him"). The sturdy oak theme is described by *toughness* (e.g., "I like for a man to look somewhat tough") and *the male machine* ("A man should always try to project an air of confidence even if he doesn't feel confident inside"). The give' em hell theme has two interrelated aspects—*adventure* and *violence* (e.g., "A real man enjoys a bit of danger now and then").

Other researchers have identified two additional aspects of masculinity ideology. The first concerns views of male sexuality (Levant & Brooks, 1997; Thompson & Pleck, 1995); and the second, views of male privilege and men's rights. Understanding the relationship between male sexuality, male privilege, and traditional masculinity is particularly important for counseling.

In most cultures sexuality is viewed as central to male power. Men must be big where it counts, powerful, and able to take charge successfully (Zilbergeld, 1978). Depending on the culture, men may also be socialized to feel a privileged access to, or an ownership of, women and their bodies (e.g., accounts of the spoils of war often include raping the women and girls of the defeated). Pleck (1981b) described how this aspect of masculinity socialization leads men to look to women to validate them as men. That is, through sexual relations with women, any women, men look for validation of themselves as men. This kind of nonrelational sexual expression has no requirements for relational intimacy or emotional attachment (Brooks, 1997). Targets of sexual desire are instead objectified and pursued not only to release sexual tension but also to nurture and affirm a sense of adequacy (Levant & Brooks, 1997; Pleck, 1981b). Many scholars believe that this close association between sexual power and manliness pervades the American culture (Brod, 1987).

Homophobia, or the irrational fear and extreme hatred and intolerance of homosexuality, is also related to views of male sexuality and its centrality to male power, particularly male power over women (Pleck, 1995). The threat of being labeled gay becomes a powerful mechanism for social control and for protecting and reinforcing threats to what is perceived as central to men's traditional sex role with women.

Attitudes about men's *rights and privileges* is also crucial to male development (Pleck, 1995). A *New York Times* telephone poll indicated that 77 percent of male respondents aged 18 to 44 agreed with the statement, "Men's attitudes toward women have changed for the better in the past 20 years"; however, 53 percent also agreed with the statement, "Most men they know think they are better than women" (Belkin, 1989). Many men in our culture, particularly white men, characteristically grow up with feelings of confidence and specialness granted them simply because they are born male. This specialness becomes an essential aspect of male entitlement, which encourages men to feel that what they do or want takes precedence over the needs of women and that their prerogatives should not be questioned. Men may view even small losses of advantage or deference as large threats because their sense of self is so closely tied to their entitlement, especially in relation to women (Brooks, 1990; Goode, 1982).

In summary, traditional gender ideology asks the conventionally socialized man to:

- Avoid all things feminine
- Feel superior to women
- Believe men's prerogatives should not be questioned
- Restrict emotional feelings, with the exception of anger
- Act tough, aggressive, and competitive
- Be self-reliant
- Enhance one's status in relation to other men
- Engage in nonrelational sex
- Fear and hate homosexuals

Despite the pressure to do so, however, not all men adhere to these "standards" of masculinity. Moreover, the extent to which any particular man subscribes to and internalizes these characteristics varies a great deal. Many men, for example, are gentle, caring, egalitarian, and cooperative in their interpersonal relationships, and both African American and Asian American men come from a cultural heritage that values communal world views. Nonetheless, most men across various racial and ethnic groups are socialized to view a number of these characteristics as desirable for themselves and other men.

Relevance to Counseling and Therapy

Some may think gender stereotyping does not matter early on in life because the children are so young. Contrary to the views of Eric's friends mentioned earlier, it does matter (Beal, 1994). The gendered themes of socialization have profound implications for girls' and boys' development. The stereotypic view that relationships are important to girls, and not to boys, for example, leads us to believe that girls should possess the emotional skills of interpersonal sensitivity, empathy, and compassion, but not boys. Indeed, traditional socialization practices assume it is OK for men to be less competent than women in achieving close relations, a practice that can cause serious problems in relationships with partners, friends, and children. Pogrebin (1983) noted some time ago that traditional socialization atrophies men's ability to "give care" to others, and increases their need to "take care" from others.

Many men have difficulty in expressing their emotions constructively and they feel isolated and alone, yet these attributes are among the hallmarks of desirable masculinity (Brod, 1987). Many women feel overwhelmed with their responsibility for the maintenance and care of relationships and with the emotional barrenness of their relationships with male partners (e.g., Cancian, 1987; Pogrebin, 1983).

Women may fear upsetting their partners with too many demands or complaints and instead silence themselves. In individual counseling, women may present with feelings of low confidence that do not appear consistent with their academic or work performance or they may feel marginalized in their place of work.

These dynamics are seen all too often in counseling. Men more than women seek help with emotional expressiveness and violent behavior (Goodman, Koss, & Russo, 1993). Women are more likely than men to seek individual or couples counseling because of problems in a romantic relationship or with a child (Hare-Mustin, 1983). Moreover, it is not unusual for clients and counselors to view women as more able than men to make the changes needed to make relationships work, and more at fault if there are problems with relationships (Fitzgerald & Nutt, 1986; Hare-Mustin, 1983). A case in point is a woman who sought counseling for premarital conflicts. She and her partner both enjoyed their work and worked hard although his salary was much greater than hers and she worked longer hours. Most of their arguments involved his wanting her to be available to be with him when he finished work and on the weekends, times when she was often busy preparing for the next day. It infuriated him that she did not change her behavior to be with him—either quit her job or put less energy into it. She loved her work, felt torn between feeling competent in her work and pleasing him, and was at a loss for what to do.

Other dynamics that emerge in therapy, and that are addressed later in the book, include:

- *Feelings of entitlement.* Potential pitfalls include male counselors feeling annoyed when female clients question their judgments or opinions, and feeling competitive with male clients who do so; using their own discomfort in working with clients' emotions to refocus the therapy on problem solving; and unconsciously using the counseling process to affirm their masculinity.
- *Resistance to women's autonomy.* Therapists, male or female, may focus more on a female client's reports of anxiety and fear, and on her personal inadequacies, than on what may be happening in her relationship or job that makes her not feel heard or appropriately recognized. In working with a male client, a female therapist would be more likely to shy away from confronting a client who does most of the talking and interrupts her when she tries to make a comment, ignoring her own feelings of being unheard and invisible session after session because such feelings are so consistent with her own cultural experiences.

We now turn to the research on sex differences, to what motivated this body of research, and to what we can conclude from the large number of studies conducted over the years. This body of research concerns the face of gender identified in Chapter 1 as "gender as difference."

Gender-Related Differences: An Overview of Research

Given the emphasis in our culture on how women and men differ, it is not surprising that gender as difference became a main focus in research studying women and men. In this section we summarize the body of literature on what used to be referred to as the psychology of sex differences, or sex-related differences. Understanding the results of the many studies comparing boys and girls and women and men, will prove valuable in working with clients such as Eric and helping him to decide whether he is overreacting to the parents of his daughters' friends.

We explained in Chapter 1 that the term sex is now reserved for describing behaviors or characteristics actually tied to biological sex, such as hormone levels. The term gender pertains to what we *assume* is true or will be true of someone who is born biologically female or male. Gender concerns societal beliefs, stereotypes, and ingrained views about the fundamental nature of girls and boys, women and men, and thus is a broader and more inclusive term referring to the context of growing up as a female or male person in a particular culture.

Accordingly, research on what used to be called sex differences is now referred to as gender or gender-related differences.

Researchers' focus on differences between women and men appears to be due to two factors. The first relates to the cultural assumption that women and men are intrinsically different. Because women and men are assumed to be different, comparing them on various dimensions is considered useful and important regardless of the purposes of a study.

The second factor relates to the kinds of assumptions, hypothesis testing, and statistical tests commonly used by social scientists. Historically in psychology, areas of assumed difference were considered worthy of study. Thus, social scientists typically pose a null hypothesis of no difference between two groups and then use various statistical procedures to test for the difference between the two groups. If the groups being compared do not differ, the findings are considered not significant and thus not worthy of publication. Thus, the psychology of sex differences has been constructed around those characteristics researchers assumed would differentiate the sexes. Moreover, what was published was that subset of research which showed statistical differences between the scores of women and men. Another result of these normative procedures within the field is that similarities between the sexes were downplayed or ignored.

Introduction to the "Iron Rule"

There are literally thousands of studies investigating psychological sex (gender) differences. Typically these studies report that girls are more or less "Y" than boys. That is, on average girls scored lower or higher than boys on some observational measure. Because differences in "degree" on gender-related traits and abilities are often misreported as differences in kind, let's look more closely at what the results of these studies actually tell us.

Suppose the attribute under study is aggression, and researchers observe the number of times girls and boys pushed a peer away from a play area so they could play with a particular toy. Let's also suppose that on average boys pushed a greater number of times than girls—what we earlier called a difference in degree. Boys pushed on average 4.3 times in a 2-hour period, and girls pushed an average of 3.8 times in the same time frame. The standard deviation for the boys pushing was 0.4 and the standard deviation for the girls was 0.5. A test comparing the two means shows that the means differ statistically. What does this finding portray and not portray?

The finding *does not mean* that all the males pushed more (i.e., were more aggressive) than all the girls—what we called "a difference in kind" in Chapter 1. The standard deviation (SD) tells us there are some girls who pushed more than some boys (3.8 + 2 [the SD of 0.5] = 4.8), which is higher than the boys mean of 4.3. There are some boys, as well, who pushed less than some girls (4.3 − 2 [the

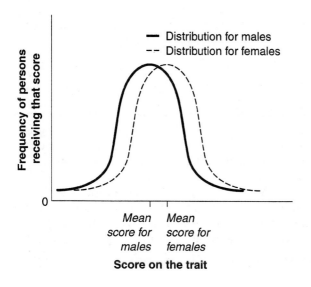

FIGURE 2.1   **Overlapping Distributions for Girls and Boys That Might Lead to a Statistical Difference**

Source: Hyde, J. S. (1991). *Half the human experience: The psychology of women* (5th ed.). Boston: Heath. Copyright © 1996 by D.C. Heath and Company. Used with permission of Houghton Mifflin Company.

SD of 0.4] = 3.5), which is lower than the girls' mean of 3.8. The distributions depicted in Figure 2.1 help make this clear. Although there is a mean gender-related difference in the number of times boys and girls pushed to get access to the toy, the two distributions overlap considerably. What we can conclude is that in this situation on average boys pushed more than girls, but some girls pushed more than some boys, and some boys pushed less than some girls.

What is the iron rule? The iron rule in social science research says that for any psychological or cognitive variable studied by psychologists, the differences within each sex are always greater than the differences between the two sexes. That is, there is more difference in pushing behavior within the group of boys and within the group of girls in our hypothetical study than between the boys and girls. Girls and boys differed on average by 4.3 – 3.8 = 0.5 pushes in a 2-hour period. However, the number of pushes within the group of boys, or within the group of girls, was at least as large as 2 × SD for each group, which would be 2 × 0.4, or 0.8 for the boys, and 2 × 0.5, or 1.0 for the girls. The numbers 0.8 and 1.0 are larger than the mean difference of 0.5.

Physical height presents another common example. It was mentioned in Chapter 1 that we typically assume men are taller than women and that observations of women and men in heterosexual romantic relationships would confirm this assumption. On average, men are about 4 inches taller than women. Height for women ranges from approximately 4'8" to approximately 6'4", and men's height from 5'2" to 7'. Thus the difference in height within women (6'4" to

4'8" = 1'8") or within men (7' to 5'2" = 1'10") is much greater than the 4-inch difference between the means of women's and men's height.

Meta-Analytical Techniques

One means psychologists have used to make sense of the large number of studies reporting sex differences is to use a statistical technique called *meta-analysis*. Meta-analysis is essentially a statistical method for literature reviewing (Hyde, 1994). This method or technique allows researchers to statistically combine the results from a number of different studies on the same topic.

In conducting a meta-analysis on studies in the area of sex differences, one first locates all the previous studies on a particular question such as, Are men more aggressive than women. For each study, the researcher computes a statistic that measures how big the difference between male and female participants was and what the direction of the difference was. This statistic is called a *d*, calculated as follows:

$$d = \frac{(\text{Mean for men} - \text{Mean for women})}{(\text{average standard deviation of male and female scores})}$$

If *d* is a positive score, men score higher; if *d* is a negative score, women score higher.

The values of *d* for each of the studies are then averaged. This averaged *d* value reflects what the direction of the difference between women and men is and how large the difference is. If the *d* is a positive number, males scored higher and if the *d* is a negative number, females scored higher.

A general guide in interpreting *d* values is to view a *d* of .20 as a small difference, a *d* of .50 as a moderate difference, and a *d* of .80 as a large difference (Hyde, 1994). A summary of effect sizes appears in Box 2.3. The meaning of these effect sizes will become clearer when we look at particular traits and abilities studied by psychologists.

BOX 2.3   Summary of Effect Sizes Indicating the Size of a Difference Detected by a Meta-Analytic Technique

Close to zero: $d = 0$ to 0.10

Small: $d = 0.11$ to 0.35

Moderate: $d = 0.36$ to 0.65

Large: $d = 0.66$ to 1.00

Very large: $d > 1.00$

Source: Hyde, J. S. (1994). Can meta-analysis make feminist transformations in psychology? *Psychology of Women Quarterly, 18,* 451–462.

Results of Meta-Analyses on Gender Differences

Meta-analyses of gender differences have been conducted in the areas of verbal ability, mathematical performance, helping behavior, spatial abilities, and sexuality. Meta-analyses have also been conducted in areas other than those concerned with gender differences, such as effects of psychotherapy with children and adolescents (Weisz, Weiss, Han, Granger, & Morton, 1995) and marital quality and stability (Karney & Bradbury, 1995).

Let's turn first to meta-analyses focused on studies reporting gender differences. The two areas in which we have long assumed that women and men differ are verbal ability and mathematics, with gender differences favoring women in verbal ability, and favoring men in mathematics ability (Maccoby & Jacklin, 1974). Other areas conceptually related to views of gender, and thus studied extensively, are helping behavior, aggression, leadership abilities, and sexuality.

Verbal Ability.   Hyde (1994) reports that contrary to the "textbook fact" that women outscore men on measures of verbal ability, a meta-analysis by her and her colleagues, which included 165 studies and 1,400,000 people, resulted in a $d = -0.11$, a value which she views as representing a tiny difference. When the studies were grouped according to year of publication, there was a decline over time in magnitude of the gender difference.

Spatial Abilities.   A meta-analysis on gender differences in spatial abilities was conducted by Voyer, Voyer, and Bryden (1995). These researchers found that any differences depended on the type of spatial ability assessed in a particular study and the test used. The largest effect size was found for the mental rotation category ($d = 0.56$), and the smallest effect size for the spatial visualization category ($d = 0.19$). The spatial perception category was intermediate with an effect size of 0.44. This study also provided some support for the hypotheses that gender differences in spatial skills have decreased in magnitude from past years to the present time. The decrease in the magnitude argues for the fact that attitudes concerning sex-related cognitive differences have changed. This attitude change is likely to have affected the way children are raised and the way women and men approach different tasks" (Voyer et al., 1995, p. 265).

Mathematics Performance.   Another common assumption in our culture is that boys are better at math than girls. Results from meta-analysis help illuminate the erroneous nature of this assumption. A meta-analysis based on 254 studies and over 3,000,000 people resulted in a $d = 0.15$, a tiny difference (Hyde, 1994). We have reproduced in Figure 2.2 a depiction of two normal distributions that are 0.15 SD apart; this is what the female and male distributions on mathematics performance would look like. As can be seen from the figure, the two distributions overlap a great deal, indicating the high degree of similarity in the distributions of girls and boys scores.

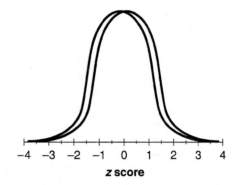

FIGURE 2.2   Two Normal Distributions That Are 0.15 Standard Deviations Apart

Source: Hyde, J. S., Fennema, E., & Lamon, S. J. (1990). Gender differences in mathematics performance: A meta-analysis. *Psychological Bulletin, 107,* 139–155. Copyright © 1990 by the American Psychological Association. Reprinted with permission.

Other findings reported by Hyde, Fennema, and Lamon (1990) counter conventional stereotypes. There were no gender differences in understanding of mathematical concepts at any age. Also the size of the difference changed with year of publication with an effect size of $d = 0.31$ for studies published before 1973 and an effect size of $d = 0.14$ for later studies. The decrease in the effect sizes again seems to parallel changes in the culture and girls' greater access to and encouragement to learn math.

Helping Behavior.   Both women and men are expected to engage in helping behavior, but the context of appropriate helping behavior relates to gender socialization. Men more than women are expected to help in times of emergency, which place them at risk and danger and require physical strength. Women more than men are expected to help in situations calling for ongoing care taking, such as care of children and elderly parents. Meta-analyses of studies in which the self-reported helping was public resulted in a $d = 0.74$ and for helping in private a $d = .02$. Averaged over all the studies, $d = 0.13$. These findings fit gender socialization in that there was a greater difference in men's and women's helping behavior in public situations involving physical danger and strength, such as pulling someone from a burning car or stopping at night to help someone change a flat tire, a $d = 0.74$, which represents a large difference. However, the $d = .02$ reflects essentially no difference in the private area of care taking.

Sexuality.   A meta-analysis on aspects of sexual attitudes and behavior was conducted on 1239 separate samples representing 128,363 respondents (Oliver & Hyde, 1993). Twenty-three different variables were included in the analysis; d values close to zero were found on most of these, including attitudes about the civil liberties of homosexuals, masturbation, and sexual satisfaction. The largest difference was found in the incidence of masturbation ($d = 0.96$), and the second largest difference in attitudes about casual sex ($d = 0.81$). Men report masturbating more than women and they hold a more liberal attitude about casual sex. It should be noted that the magnitude of these two differences is considerably larger than any of those reported with regard to cognitive abilities such as verbal and math ability, which ranged from 0.11 to 0.56. Thus, areas closely tied to socialization practices, such as frequency of masturbation and attitudes about casual sex, show much larger differences between women and men than do areas reflecting women's and men's abilities.

Aggression. Perhaps the most consistent gender difference is in aggressive behavior, with males acting more aggressively or reporting more aggressive behavior than females. In a meta-analysis of 143 studies, an effect size of $d = 0.50$ was reported, which is a moderate difference (Hyde, 1994). The causes of gender differences in aggression have been the subject of considerable debate, with some viewing it as biologically caused and others viewing it as more environmentally related. Recent reports on the lack of relationship between testosterone and male aggression has added fuel to the debate. At the same time, it is important to note that the effect size is quite moderate.

Leadership. A large-scale meta-analysis of studies of leadership behaviors found a d of .03, indicating that there are no overall gender differences (Eagly & Johnson, 1990). The only small difference was in the use of autocratic versus democratic leadership styles, $d = -0.22$. Women more than men are likely to use democratic leadership styles. Context would be important in understanding the kind of leadership style used and the reactions of those being led to that style. Overall, democratic styles are likely more effective and thus more used by leaders regardless of their biological sex. However, men more than women are likely to get away with an autocratic style in leadership settings because men may be assumed to be the rightful leaders. Women, in contrast, may have learned that democratic styles are more effective, especially in situations predominantly involving men.

What to Conclude. These results indicate that men's and women's cognitive abilities such as math and verbal ability and prosocial skills such as helping behavior and leadership skills are more similar than they are different. Meta-analyses have shown with very conclusive evidence that the gender difference in tested verbal abilities is now negligible, as are the differences in mathematics performance, with the exception, beginning in high school, of problem solving. However, much of this difference in problem-solving is explained by girls' lesser likelihood of taking advanced mathematical courses (Hyde, 1994). Gender differences in spatial ability are sizable only in the area of three-dimensional mental rotation. By far the largest effect sizes were in the area of sexuality, with men reporting a greater frequency of masturbation and a more permissive view toward casual sex.

What happens when we compare the meta-analytical findings in the area of sex/gender differences and the meta-analytic findings reported for other effects in psychology? Table 2.1 on page 42 reproduces the findings reported by

TABLE 2.1   Effect Sizes for Psychological Gender Differences and Other Effects in Social Science Research

Falling into Different Ranges of Magnitude	Effect Size				
	0–0.10	0.11–0.35	0.36–0.65	0.66–1.0	Over 1.0
Gender differences	43	60	46	17	5
(n = 171)	25%	35%	27%	10%	3%
Other Effects in Psychology	17	89	116	60	20
(n = 302)	6%	29%	38%	20%	7%

Note: $\chi 2 = 47.37$, p < .0001.

Source: Hyde, J. S., & Plant, E. A. (1995). Magnitude of psychological gender differences: Another side of the story. *American Psychologist, 50,* 159–161. Copyright © 1995 by the American Psychological Association. Reprinted with permission.

Hyde and Plant (1995). Using the established guidelines that a *d* of 0.20 is small, 0.50 moderate, and 0.80 large, we can see from the table that most effect sizes for gender differences fall in the small to moderate range, with only 13 percent being above an effect size of 0.66. Also observable from the table is the large variability in the magnitude of gender differences across different behaviors, and the large percentage of effect sizes that are negligible. In fact, the effect sizes tend to be greater for other effects in psychology, with only 6 percent being negligible and 27 percent being above an effect size of 0.66. Other effects in social science research refer to the meta-analysis of various psychological, educational, and behavioral treatments (Lipsey & Wilson, 1993).

Concluding Remarks

At this point you may have already made some educated guesses about the possible connections between gender socialization, the meaning of gender differences, and the process and goals of counseling. Many of us, not unlike our client Eric's friends, have assumed that the sexes are "opposite" and may even have a vested interest in seeing men in one way and women in another. Indeed, some of our clients may hold this view as well.

What issues related to gender socialization, and to what women or men are supposed to be like, can we expect clients to bring to counseling? What issues will you yourself bring to counseling in these areas? What attributes and assumptions may be projected on to you because of other people's stereotypes about someone of your sex? Later chapters provide reasons for these kinds of questions.

We see three specific issues inextricably tied to gender as particularly central to counseling's commitment to facilitating human development across the life cycle. These topics, which we call power, nurturance, and context, weave through the themes of later chapters. Power and nurturance represent important descriptors of the counseling process—therapists empower and provide care—yet within our culture power and nurturance can take on very different and often gendered meanings. The larger social meaning of these terms, and how this meaning may determine individual behavior, relate to the domain of context.

We also focus on context because traditional theories ignored or minimized the influence of context on individual behavior, and on behavior in the therapeutic setting (Gilbert, 1994; Hare-Mustin & Marecek, 1990). As was mentioned in Chapter 1, the change of focus from sex to gender was extraordinarily important for counseling and psychotherapeutic theory and practice because it made possible new explanations for human behavior—explanations that differed from the biological determinism central to traditional theories. It allowed our thinking to move away from internally determined women and men, to women and men developing in social and cultural contexts. It allowed us to consider how views of one's biological sex can be influential in the manner in which individuals are treated and in the opportunities and constraints they experience in their day-to-day life.

Living in a particular society at a particular time is the larger context or frame of one's life. Because views of gender vastly influence all aspects of most societies, from socialization practices to implicit and explicit laws and policies, we cannot ignore the power of context in gendered human development and in counseling and therapeutic settings.

This now said, we return to the earlier question: What would you say to our client Eric who wants to know from an "expert," if he is overreacting?

Discussion Questions

1. How do stereotypes about women and men affect the way therapists work with female and male clients?
   a. Discuss some common stereotypes people you know hold about women and men and heterosexual relationships.
   b. Identify two misperceptions you yourself may have held about men's and women's abilities and personal attributes.

2. Describe your own gender socialization, and where possible, identify aspects of your socialization that are consistent with the material presented in the chapter.

Suggested Readings

Doyle, J. A. (1984). *The male experience.* Dubuque, IA: William C. Brown. An exceptionally readable book on the male role in American society, particularly its problematic aspects.

Levant, R. F., & Pollack, W. S. (Eds.). (1995). *A new psychology of men.* New York: Basic Books. A comprehensive in-depth coverage of various aspects of men's traditional socialization and the lives of contemporary men.

Westkott, M. (1986). *The feminist legacy of Karen Horney.* New Haven: Yale University Press. This highly informative book traces female gendered socialization from the perspective of a prominent theorist, Karen Horney.

Fundamentals

This part of the book is concerned with the application of gender theory to various aspects of practice. In Chapter 3 we provide a framework for understanding and developing an ability to detect gender bias in therapeutic practice. Then in Chapter 4 we describe gender-informed theories of therapy including several forms of feminist therapy as well as gender-aware therapy.

Earlier chapters looked at different ways in which theories guide counseling and therapy. In Chapter 5 we look at a somewhat different aspect of theory. We consider the language used in theories and in describing client concerns and everyday behavior. We also look at language in the form of dominant discourse. Dominant discourses can guide and shape our thinking about client concerns and what we say and do in counseling. Chapter 6 continues this discussion, but in the area of sexuality. We discuss the place of sexuality in the life and psyche of clients and how gender socialization shapes women's and men's sexual experiences and their beliefs about those experiences. Also considered is how views of sexuality relate to the many faces of gender and to gendered processes in counseling.

Finally Chapter 7 describes in some detail a number of gender issues male and female clients commonly bring to therapeutic settings. Included are discussions of male gender role strain, sexual harassment and rape, and issues facing dual-earner families.

3

Identifying Gender Bias in Practice

You are a male therapist or counselor, and Susanna, a 31-year-old divorced woman, has made an appointment with you. She is a small woman, attractive and stylishly dressed. Susanna's divorce was approximately 6 months ago. During this first session she periodically cries. She talks of her 5-year marriage, her dreams of being the perfect wife when she first married, her two miscarriages, her fears of not being able to please her husband including sexually, her knowledge of affairs her husband had, and her "falling apart" when he left.

She describes her husband Dennis as her "pillar . . . he was what held me together." When he left her, she said her life fell apart. For the first 2 weeks, she stayed in bed most of the time. Finally, with help from a sister and a friend, she was able to apply for and be hired as a full-time teacher assistant at the elementary school in her neighborhood.

She concludes by saying that over the past 3 months there are times when she feels better, but there are also times (like the present) when her depressed feelings return in full force. She says she needs someone to talk with, or to call, when she feels so low. She is relieved to be talking to a man whom she knows can help her. She wants to come and see you on a weekly basis until she feels better and wants permission to call in between meetings if she is feeling desperate and alone. (Adapted from Gregory & Gilbert, 1992)

Before reading further, take a few minutes to think about your reactions to Susanna, what your initial thoughts are about the nature of her concerns, and what the possible goals for treatment might include. Be as honest as you can. The practicing professionals who responded to this vignette reported a number of different feelings, ranging from intrigue to irritation, and a variety of ideas about possible core concerns and treatment goals (Gregory & Gilbert, 1992).

The concerns Susanna brings to counseling are quite poignant—her world has fallen apart around her and she wants help in overcoming her feelings of desperation, failure, and loneliness. The long-term and short-term goals of counseling for Susanna will differ depending on what one sees as the basic issues that need to be addressed. These might include: (1) Susanna is going through the trauma of an unexpected divorce and needs support to work through her loss; (2) Susanna is an overly dependent person who will transfer her dependent needs from Dennis to the male therapist; (3) Susanna is underfunctioning in order to feel acceptable and desirable as a heterosexual woman.

What one might view as the issues underlying Susanna's distress has a lot to do with the theories informing one's work. Some theories give more emphasis to intrapsychic factors such as dependence and female seductiveness; other theories give more emphasis to contextual variables such as life events and societal norms and practices. In either case, the conceptualizations used would likely have a lot to do with gender, as earlier chapters made clear, because gender has implicitly or explicitly formed the foundation of nearly all psychological theories of personality.

The chapters in Part I of this book described the many faces of gender and how they are ever-present in counseling and therapy. This chapter begins the process of relating contemporary thinking about gender to therapeutic practice.

We first provide a brief historical context and then summarize areas of documented gender bias for women and for men. The ability to detect bias in one's own work and in the work of others is essential to effective counseling and therapy.

Historical Context

Profound criticisms of psychotherapy in the late 1960s and early 1970s prompted a reevaluation of the field. Three publications in particular stimulated this criticism. The first was the classic paper, "Psychology Constructs the Female," describing how psychology as a field could say nothing about women because women had not been studied (Weisstein, 1968). Weisstein cogently demonstrated that women were assumed to fit the theories developed to describe men's behavior, and were viewed as deviant if they did not fit the theories. The second publication was Chesler's (1972) book, *Women and Madness,* a disturbing account of how women were treated by mental health professionals. Using data reflecting the large numbers of women prescribed medication or hospitalized for depression, Chesler concluded that women who were not happy with the constraints of the traditional sex role assigned to them were viewed as pathological. Consistent with the psychodynamic theories of the time, clients' feelings of dissatisfaction with the female role were interpreted by mental health professionals as intrapsychic problems associated with "penis envy" and their feelings of inadequacy as women.

Chesler further concluded that the female role was itself viewed as a model for pathology, a situation which placed women in a double bind. On the one hand, women were viewed as disturbed because they engaged in behaviors consistent with the traditional female role, such as acting passive and submissive or living their lives through others. They were also viewed as disturbed if they engaged in behaviors outside of the female traditional role, such as promoting their own interests and abilities and not centering their lives around men's wishes and desires. Although similar kinds of constraints were placed on male behaviors, men were viewed as healthy as long as they adhered to conventional male roles. Only by engaging in roles and behaviors stereotypically associated with women and the female role did men become liable for being judged disordered.

The third important publication was the paper by Broverman, Broverman, Clarkson, Rosenkrantz, and Vogel (1970), "Sex-Role Stereotypes and Clinical Judgments of Mental Health." In their study, practicing mental health professionals in a number of different fields were asked to describe either a healthy woman, a healthy man, or a healthy adult, sex unspecified. Results from the study provided evidence for what the researchers called an implicit "double standard of mental health" for women and men. Mental health professionals described the healthy woman as less independent and rational and more submissive and childlike than the healthy man or the healthy adult, sex unspecified. Moreover, descriptions of the healthy man and the healthy adult, sex unspecified, were nearly identical, in contrast to the significant discrepancies between descriptions of the healthy woman and the healthy adult, sex unspecified.

These early studies, which coincided with the burgeoning feminist movement in the United States, prompted investigations of bias in the treatment women received from providers of mental health services. One particularly important study was the Report of the Task Force on Sex Bias and Sex-Role Stereotyping in Psychotherapeutic Practice of the American Psychological Association (1975). The Task Force was instructed to examine "the extent and manner of sex bias and sex-role stereotyping in psychotherapeutic practice as they directly affect women as students, practitioners, and consumers." Findings from the study are incorporated with later studies in this area and appear in the following sections of the chapter.

Understanding Gender Bias in Counseling and Psychotherapy

That gender bias occurs in the therapeutic setting is well established (Gilbert, 1992). Indeed, sexism and gender bias often easily enter into theory and practice, as the case of Susanna will help illustrate.

The Case of Susanna

This case example at the beginning of the chapter depicts the female client often portrayed in the therapeutic literature and described by Chesler (1972) in her book, *Women and Madness.* As you will recall, the women Chesler studied were often viewed as disturbed if they engaged in behaviors consistent with the traditional female role and if they were unhappy with their prescribed role.

Box 3.1 on page 50 summarizes ways in which bias commonly enters counseling and therapy. The first of these four ways is using unexamined assumptions about women and men to guide one's work with clients. In the case of Susanna, unexamined assumptions might include that women are naturally dependent on men, or that for men to stay in a marriage they must feel satisfied sexually. These assumptions are tied to beliefs about women's and men's nature. Should these beliefs guide therapeutic treatment, Susanna would not be expected to use therapy to change her feelings of dependence. Indeed, her male therapist may feel irritated by her dependence and at the same time fearful of being saddled with it. In addition, Susanna would be held responsible for her husband's leaving her. These unexamined assumptions might prevent explorations of other possibilities such as encouraging the client to challenge some of her beliefs about herself, clarifying what she means by her need to call if she is feeling desperate and alone, working with her to broaden her base of support, and exploring her experiences of loss through miscarriages and divorce.

BOX 3.1   **Factors Contributing to Gender Bias in Counseling and Therapy**

- The use of unexamined assumptions about women and men to guide work with clients

  Example: Viewing men as more competent than women in work settings or as more psychologically healthy than women

- The separation of a client's concerns from the context in which they occur, including the context of the counseling relationship

  Example: Conceptualizing a client's anger as transference when the therapist has acted in ways to silence the client

- The focus on intrapsychic dynamics as the basis for explaining and working through a client's concerns

  Example: Focusing on what clients did to bring on their sexual abuse

- The use of gender stereotypic models as the standard for adaptive or healthy behavior and psychological functioning

  Example: Assessing clients' level of functioning on the basis of how well their behavior fits conventional roles for women and men

Bias is also likely to enter therapy and counseling when the concerns of the client are isolated or separated from the circumstances in which these concerns occur, including the context of the counseling relationship. Because counseling and therapy can be such a personal experience, it is not uncommon to focus exclusively on what clients are feeling and to ignore the context of clients' feelings, including one's own behavior as a therapist. In the case of Susanna, her feelings of falling apart may be due to her profound dependence. Alternately, they may stem from the assumption that a man would make her life complete, an assumption tied to a value system or context that both her husband and family of origin may have shared and reinforced. Moreover, should the therapist hold this same view and reinforce her looking to him to solve her problems and make her feel better, he may begin to experience her dependence on him as her being seductive—a common response by male therapists in the study (Gregory & Gilbert, 1992).

Susanna's way of presenting her difficulties may make her treatment prone to bias in still other ways. Because she experiences herself in ways associated with conventional views of women, counselors or therapists who hold the belief that women need men for strength and a sense of purpose would likely focus the counseling on intrapsychic dynamics associated with poor self-image and an inability to enjoy sex. Moreover, they might use gender stereotypic models of mental health to guide the goals of treatment. Using such models would be problematic in working with this client because these models traditionally view dependence on men as a sign of healthy psychological functioning for women.

Research efforts have helped identify underlying themes and general areas of sexist bias in counseling and psychotherapy with women (American Psychological Association, 1975; Fitzgerald & Nutt, 1986) and to a lesser degree with men (Good & Mintz, 1993; Robertson & Fitzgerald, 1992). Not surprisingly, central to the problems of bias are therapists' and counselors' sexist attitudes and lack of knowledge about women, men, and gender.

Bias in Counseling Women

Bias in counseling women has received much more attention than bias in counseling men. Women more than men have expressed concern with how patriarchy and sexism have limited their lives, and in some cases, have been extremely harmful. Three general areas of bias are well documented: fostering traditional sex roles, having bias in expectations and at the same time devaluing women, and responding to women as sex objects, including the seduction of female clients (American Psychological Association, 1975). The first two general areas are addressed in this chapter. Later chapters discuss aspects of bias in the third area: responding to women as sex objects.

Fostering Traditional Sex Roles.   This area remains one of the key biases affecting the counseling of women today. Women's normative roles have changed dramatically since 1960 and now clearly include occupational work. Meanwhile, attitudes about "what women want" and who holds primary responsibility for childrearing have changed much less. Theories of child development are just beginning to include mothers and fathers as primary caregivers. The many studies on day care indicate that day care is not harmful to children and in many cases provides children with more resources and opportunities than traditional care (Scarr & Eisenberg, 1993). Nonetheless, female parents feel tremendous pressure to be the primary care-giving parent and to be the one responsible for childrearing and for marital happiness.

What might represent an example of this form of gender bias in therapy? In family therapy, a therapist supports the idea that childrearing, and therefore any children's problems, are mostly the responsibility of the mother. In this situation the counselor might work to support the husband's power in the family as the breadwinner and minimize his responsibilities in childrearing, and thus legitimize his minimal involvement in any problems associated with the children. The wife, in contrast, might be viewed as "controlling" or "demanding" if she desired more participation from her spouse or suggested he change his work schedule somewhat to accommodate childrearing needs.

This type of gender bias can take still another common form. In our discussion of gender socialization in Chapter 2 we mentioned that, traditionally, being valued and desired by men was assumed to be central to women's identity; a woman's worth, and her life script, was usually seen in terms of her physical characteristics and ability to please, satisfy, and serve men (Westkott, 1986). The view that women need men to feel complete not only guides some theories used in counseling but also reflects stereotypic attitudes counselors may hold. Examples in counseling could take the form of a therapist assuming that problem resolution and self-actualization for women come from marriage or perfecting the role of wife. A counselor, for instance, might use Erikson's theory of identity development to suggest to young adult female clients that their identity problems would be resolved by marrying and having children.

Bias in Expectations and Devaluation of Women.   This area of bias has received a good deal of attention in the public schools. Myra and David Sadker (1994) describe how public education has "failed at fairness" and shortchanges girls. Girls' learning problems are not identified as often as boys, boys receive more of their teachers' attention, and girls outperform boys in most subjects but are viewed as less able. This failure has to do with bias in expectations of women and devaluing women's abilities and potential contributions in areas of academic achievement. Similar kinds of biases can occur in counseling. The therapist may foster views of women as passive and dependent and react negatively to female clients who are active, assertive, and aggressive in their real lives or in the counseling situation. Such clients may become labeled as "difficult," "castrating," or " bitchy."

Another aspect of bias in expectations has to do with women's assumed dependence and its relation to female sexuality. In Westkott's (1986) examination of Karen Horney's writings on girlhood sexualization, she illuminated the relation between women's dependence behavior and the sexualization and devaluation they experience growing up in a society that views women as essentially sexual beings (Box 3.2). Westkott theorized that the core of what appears to be characterological dependence in women is instead a need to confirm that one has a self and that that self is lovable in a culture that views women as having no self apart from men's needs for them as sexual objects and bearers and caretakers of their children.

Lerner (1983) further states that many theorists and counselors fail to distinguish between women's overt passive-dependent behavior and the functions it serves. She maintains that women's passive displays of dependence frequently have a protective function for them. By underfunctioning with significant men in her life—a spouse, employer, or counselor—the woman avoids any

---

BOX 3.2   A Student's Personal Awareness of Devaluation

"When males in my life joked about how to tell if a woman was a virgin by looking at the way she walked, I was uncomfortable but silent. When Pat (another person in her class) made a comment about most guys are usually only interested in having sex with a woman, not necessarily in her personality or who she is as a person, I agreed with his statement. Now that I realize that it is a way of devaluing and sexualizing women, I am angry and am beginning to confront the assumptions behind these jokes and comments."

threats to a man's presumed superiority and strength, and remains safe from the negative consequences of overstepping her bounds as a woman. In other words, she protects the male ego from the fact that she is capable of taking care of herself, a characteristic she believes would put the relationship at risk and make her unlovable and undesirable in a man's eyes.

As mentioned earlier, it is not unusual for counselors to describe attractive dependent clients, such as the client Susanna, as seductive, histrionic, or manipulative (Gregory & Gilbert, 1992). Because a woman's all-encompassing dependence on men is often associated with her attractiveness and desirability, an essential part of sexual attractiveness became a female's "meekness, submissiveness, and resignation of all individual will into the hands of a man" (Mill, 1869/1970, p. 233). As noted earlier, a possible basic issue we identified in this case was, "Susanna is underfunctioning in order to feel acceptable and desirable as a heterosexual woman."

The extensive documentation of the sexist treatment of women by mental health professionals resulted in the development of guidelines for counseling women. Box 3.3 on pages 54–55 summarizes the "Principles Concerning the Counseling and Psychotherapy of Women," developed by the Division 17 (Counseling Psychology) Committee on Women and subsequently endorsed by many other national groups concerned with counseling and therapy with women (Ad Hoc Committee on Women, 1979; Fitzgerald & Nutt, 1986).

Bias in Counseling Men

Sexism in the psychotherapeutic treatment of men has received much less attention than bias in the treatment of women. Men have sought counseling less than women and are more hesitant to do so (Good, Wallace, & Borst, 1994; Robertson & Fitzgerald, 1992). Traditional male socialization encourages power, domination, competition, and control, as well as proving masculinity through nonrelational sex; vulnerabilities and awareness of feelings and emotions are considered signs of weakness appropriate for women but not for men (Good & Mintz, 1993; O'Neil, 1981; O'Neil, Good, & Holmes, 1995; Scher, 1981). Moreover, therapy processes rely on clients engaging in self-awareness and reflection, expressing feelings and vulnerabilities, discussing problem areas, and trusting in the helping relationship, characteristics that are largely antithetical to the modal male experience (Scher, 1990). Finally, as a group men have felt less constrained by definitions of healthy male functioning and by their prescribed roles. Recall that in the classic Broverman study in which counselors rated the characteristics of either a healthy woman, a healthy man, or a healthy person, sex unspecified (Broverman et al., 1970), mental health professionals described the healthy adult as similar to the healthy man.

Nonetheless, gender biases and processes are as likely to occur with men as with women. Constraints traditionally placed on how men should act became integral to theories and assumptions about "normal" male development, just as they did in theories about "normal" female development (Levant &

BOX 3.3   **Principles Concerning the Counseling and Psychotherapy of Women**

Preamble

Although competent counseling/therapy processes are essentially the same for all counselor/therapist interactions, special subgroups require specialized skills, attitudes and knowledge. Women constitute a special subgroup.

Competent counseling/therapy requires recognition and appreciation that contemporary society is not sex fair. Many institutions, test standards and attitudes of mental health professionals limit the options of women clients. Counselors/therapists should sensitize women clients to these real-world limitations, confront them with both the external and their own internalized limitations and explore with them their reactions to these constraints.

The principles presented here are considered essential for the competent counseling/therapy of women.

1. Counselors/therapists are knowledgeable about women, particularly with regard to biological, psychological and social issues which have impact on women in general or on particular groups of women in our society.
2. Counselors/therapists are aware that the assumptions and precepts of theories relevant to their practice may apply differently to men and women. Counselors/therapists are aware of those theories and models that proscribe or limit the potential of women clients, as well as those that may have particular usefulness for women clients.
3. After formal training, counselors/therapists continue to explore and learn of issues related to women, including the special problems of female subgroups, throughout their professional careers.
4. Counselors/therapists recognize and are aware of all forms of oppression and how these interact with sexism.
5. Counselors/therapists recognize and are aware of verbal and nonverbal process variables (particularly with regard to power in the relationship) as these affect women in counseling/therapy so that the counselor/therapist-client interactions are not adversely affected. The need for shared responsibility between clients and counselors/therapists is acknowledged and implemented.
6. Counselors/therapists have the capability of utilizing skills that are particularly facilitative to women in general and to particular subgroups of women.
7. Counselors/therapists ascribe no pre-conceived limitations on the direction or nature of potential changes or goals in counseling/therapy for women.
8. Counselors/therapists are sensitive to circumstances where it is more desirable for a woman client to be seen by a female or male counselor/therapist.
9. Counselors/therapists use non-sexist language in counseling/therapy, supervision, teaching and journal publications.
10. Counselors/therapists do not engage in sexual activity with their women clients under any circumstances.
11. Counselors/therapists are aware of and continually review their own values and biases and the effects of these on their women clients. Counselors/therapists understand the effects of sex-role socialization upon their own development and functioning and the consequent values and attitudes they hold

for themselves and others. They recognize that behaviors and roles need not be sex based.

12. Counselors/therapists are aware of how their personal functioning may influence their effectiveness in counseling/therapy with women clients. They monitor their functioning through consultation, supervision or therapy so that it does not adversely affect their work with women clients.
13. Counselors/therapists support the elimination of sex biases within institutions and individuals.

Developed by the Division of Counseling Psychology's Task Force on Women. Counseling Psychology is a Division of the American Psychological Association. See Ad Hoc Committee on Women (Division 17). (1979). Principles concerning the counseling and psychotherapy of women. *The Counseling Psychologist, 8,* 21. Reprinted by permission of Sage Publications, Inc.

Brooks, 1997; Levant & Pollack, 1995; Scher, Stevens, Good, & Eichenfield, 1987). There has yet to be a comprehensive study investigating gender-related bias in counseling and psychotherapy with men. Studies such as Robertson and Fitzgerald (1990), however, provide evidence for viewing men who engage in roles and behavior associated with the conventional female role as less healthy than men who do not assume such roles. In their study practicing counselors and therapists were randomly assigned to view one of two versions of a videotaped simulation of a depressed white male client. The tapes included nine segments taken from counseling sessions that spanned a period of 6 weeks. The tapes were identical except that in one version the man was portrayed as gender-traditional (i.e., the male client was an engineer and his spouse a full-time homemaker) and in the other version the man was portrayed as gender-nontraditional (i.e., the man had the major responsibility for domestic matters including child care, and his wife, who was an engineer, was the family provider). This information was embedded in the first videotaped segment.

Results from their study indicated that in comparison with the man in the traditional situation, mental health professionals rated the man in the nontraditional situation as less instrumental, using a scale similar to the Personal Attributes Questionnaire scale reproduced in Chapter 1. This finding illustrates the common tendency to assume that men who choose other than traditional masculine roles are lacking in personality characteristics typically associated with being a healthy man. The mental health professionals in the study were also more likely to attribute the man's depression to his marriage and children when he was in a nontraditional marriage. Furthermore, not one counselor or therapist questioned whether the man and his spouse in the traditional situation had discussed their marital role arrangement but many raised this issue for the man in the nontraditional situation.

Thus, fostering traditional gender roles is one area of bias in therapy with men. Other likely themes of gender bias in counseling men are:

- Encouraging a stance of independence and a distancing of emotions and feelings in personal relationships with women and men

- Failing to recognize the personal costs to men, and the damage to women, when men equate personal power with sexual power over women
- Alienating men from their children by associating the ability to give care with weakness
- Encouraging and modeling autonomy, success, and competition
- Leaving unchallenged the exaggerated relationship between male sexual power and feelings of personal meaning and importance in one's life

A final area of bias related to several of those already mentioned is therapists failing to challenge in themselves beliefs associated with homophobia, a variation of men's fear of being vulnerable with other men.

Markowitz (1993) provides a thoughtful account of the experiences of a straight male therapist working with a gay male couple. Initially the therapist thought he would have no difficulties working with the couple, who had sought counseling about some difficulty in their sex life, and was pleased that they had been referred to him. However, during the second session he found his stomach churning when one man in the couple put his arm around his partner in a natural gesture. Then he reports, "Every homophobic stereotype I had ever heard about 'queers' and 'fags' came to the fore in my mind when Ralph and Bill started to tell me about their sex life" (p. 15). The therapist thought that he had been quite successful in hiding his feelings of discomfort from his clients but in the sixth session, Ralph asked very directly if the therapist was having a problem with the couple's homosexuality. Ralph mentioned the importance of being able to trust that he was comfortable working with them before they could go further in therapy. The therapist was struck by the contrast between Ralph's sincerity and his own hidden feelings. He did admit in the same session some modicum of anxiety around the couple's physical intimacy, but clearly realized that he needed to seek supervision. "The truth was, he could not handle the details of the lovemaking which were shared in the context of their presenting problem" (p. 15).

The person from whom he sought supervision, a gay therapist, first recommended that he read gay fiction so he could understand aspects of gay life based on the experiences of gay people, not homophobic stereotypes. The supervisor also helped the therapist to recognize his own homoerotic feelings as well as his history of being disconcerted by the sight of gay men being physically affectionate. Slowly but surely the therapist, through supervision, was able to accept his own occasional homoerotic feelings as normal and to work through his homophobia. The slow gathering of information about himself and the messages he had received from society about gay men enabled him to eventually feel comfortable with the couple and free to confront them on aspects of their relationship, such as why one partner always needs to be the one to initiate sex.

This therapist feels grateful that he was able to work effectively with Ralph and Bill and they offered him the chance to learn more about himself. "The inevitable result of such an internal journey is the insight that all of our ideas about what is "normal" and "abnormal" sex are culturally derived" (Markowitz, 1993, p. 16).

One of the most important personal issues a therapist must deal with in the area of working with gay or lesbian clients is admitting to his or her own internalized homophobia (Harrison, 1987). This type of "heterosexual bias" is subtle and can take the form of valuing heterosexuality as superior and of using heterosexual relationships as the standard for understanding and judging gay relationships (Eldridge, 1987). Gender biases become apparent when therapists find themselves assigning gender or sex roles to the partners as a way to understand their interactions, perhaps even going so far as to ask clients which "role" they play in the relationship.

Concluding Remarks

Understanding sources of gender bias in counseling and therapy are central to effective therapeutic work. In this chapter we identified characteristics that make the counseling process vulnerable to gender bias and described common areas of bias in counseling women and men. The next chapter describes several feminist theories of practice that grew out of attempts to address the gender bias inherent in existing theories and how those theories were applied in counseling and therapy.

Discussion Questions

1. Box 3.3 summarizes principles concerning the counseling and psychotherapy of women. What principles do you think should appear on a similar list concerning the counseling and psychotherapy of men?

2. Imagine going to counseling with a concern that either you have or invent. What kinds of gender bias might you experience with a female therapist? a male therapist?

Suggested Readings

Chesler, P. (1972). *Women and madness.* New York: Doubleday. An engrossing book providing an important historical perspective on gender bias in the field of mental health.

Savin-Williams, R. C., & Cohen, K. M. (Eds.). (1996). *The lives of lesbians, gays, and bisexuals: Children to adults.* Fort Worth, TX: Harcourt Brace. An excellent overview and introduction to the topic, which captures well a broad spectrum of voices on current understandings and issues.

See Unger, R., & Crawford, M. (1996). *Women and gender: A feminist psychology.* New York: McGraw-Hill; and Hyde, J. S. (1996). *Half the human experience: The psychology of women.* Lexington, MA: D. C. Heath. These two books present an overview of the extensive literature that has developed since 1970 on the psychology of women, including various theories of female development across the life cycle.

4 Gender-Informed Theories of Counseling and Psychotherapy

Mikel, a thoughtful, sensitive man in his late twenties, seeks counseling about a rela-
tionship with a woman, Monika, who is about his age. They have similar ethnic and ed-
ucational backgrounds, share many interests, get along well, and have a very satisfying
sexual relationship. They have been dating for a little over 6 months, and although the
relationship is going well, Mikel knows that Monika is not the person he wants to even-
tually marry. She has never brought this up with him, but Mikel, who holds a deep be-
lief in egalitarian relations with women, felt more comfortable communicating to her
that, as much as he enjoys and likes her, he does not feel about her the way he wants to
feel about a woman to whom he would commit himself for life. Monika seems fine with
this and sees no reason for him to be so apologetic and concerned. She said that she too
was enjoying their time together, especially the physical aspects of the relationship. Mikel
still feels confused and wants to meet for a few sessions to discuss the situation and
whether he should suggest they break up. A particular concern he has is that Monika
may not be aware that she hopes he will eventually feel differently about her as a future
life partner. He likes Monika a great deal and does not want the relationship to end badly.

How would you work with Mikel? What may be key issues to address? We leave
discussion of Mikel until a later place in the chapter and ask that you keep his
presenting concern in mind as you consider the material presented here.

This chapter continues on the theme of providing therapeutic interventions
free of gender bias. We describe several gender-informed theories of practice in
some detail. Approaches informed by gender, it will become clear, ask that we
rethink traditional assumptions about what is needed for therapy and counseling to be effective.

Feminism and Feminist Practices in Counseling and Therapy

I believe that we have to start seeing sexism and racism as practices that are profoundly antispirit and antilove. For me feminism is not a movement of women
against men. It's a way of thinking that allows *all* of us to examine the harmful
role sexism plays in our personal lives and public world and to figure out what
we can do to change this. It's a movement that creates space for the spirit and for
being a whole person. (hooks, 1995, p. 188)

Many people incorrectly assume feminism refers to bra burners, radicals,
and man haters. Feminism, in reality, refers to "the principle that women should
have political, economic, and social rights equal to those of men." The feminist
movement is "the movement to win such rights for women." Feminists are
"those individuals who advocate for the social, political, and economic equality

between women and men and between groups of women and men." These definitions come from Webster's New World Dictionary (1978).

Feminist perspectives have profoundly influenced counseling theory and practice (Gilbert, 1992; Gilbert & Osipow, 1991). Moreover, feminist therapists and counselors embrace a number of different theoretical orientations, including person-centered, gestalt, cognitive-behavioral, and psychodynamic. Our discussion centers around the importance of gender perspectives in feminist therapy and the importance of feminist perspectives in gender-aware counseling.

It is important to note that although feminist therapies developed in response to society's treatment of women, feminist practices are of inestimable value to men and in therapy with men. Similarly, gender-aware counseling and therapy combines the principles of feminist therapy with emerging knowledge about gender and presents integrated principles of counseling for working with women and men.

What Are Feminist Therapies?

Feminist therapies represent attempts to incorporate the principles of feminism into the practice of counseling and therapy. The various feminist therapies developed within somewhat differing times and social contexts. They also differ in their conceptions of gender and in the focus of the counseling. Three important feminist therapies are:

- Empowerment feminist therapy
- Androgyny and assertiveness training
- Relational models of therapy

Empowerment feminist therapy, the first form of feminist therapy, was initially developed in the 1960s and 1970s (Gilbert, 1980; Lerman, 1976; Sturdivant, 1980), and further developed in the 1980s and 1990s (Brown, 1994; Worell & Remer, 1992). Two other models or forms of feminist therapy are *androgyny and assertiveness training,* popular in the late 1970s and 1980s and not much used today, and *relational reframing models,* initially referred to as a self-in-relation model, and developed by Jean Baker Miller, Judith Jordan, and other theorists at the Stone Center in the late 1970s to the present time (Enns, 1993; Marecek & Hare-Mustin, 1987).

Empowerment Feminist Therapy. Empowerment feminist therapy was innovative in two important ways:

1. It shifted the focus of the therapy away from the client's intrapsychic life to the context of a client's life. That is, counseling was shifted to focus on the actual problems and difficulties experienced by clients and to the ways that women's social inequality contributes to their problems. This change in focus

challenged the medicalization of women's problems, particularly the treatment of women's depression (Chesler, 1972), as well as the validity of psychoanalytic-based theories about women. Increasing numbers of women in the 1950s and 1960s were medicated for depression and anxiety because it was assumed that there could be no "external" reason for their condition (Chesler, 1972). The origin of their difficulties was presumed to be biological or physiological in nature.

Similar assumptions guided psychoanalytic-based theories of women's discontent. Concepts such as "penis envy" were commonly used to describe women who were not content with their role as wife and mother and their status as a woman. The goals of analysis at that time included neither helping women recognize the real-world reasons for why they felt the way they did (e.g., many women were denied educational, athletic, and career opportunities solely on the basis of their biological sex and regardless of their interests, talents, and abilities) nor questioning the oppression they felt in their lives.

2. It attempted to reconstruct the therapy relationship on the basis of mutuality by granting the client autonomy and authority. Clients were encouraged to ask questions of therapists before entering into treatment and to trust their own assessment of the usefulness of treatment. Clients, for example, were encouraged to ask counselors about their training and education as well as the depth of their experience with populations and issues pertinent to the client, such as the extent of the therapist's experience working with dual-earner families, lesbian and gay couples, adolescent boys or with issues such as sexual abuse, grief, or marital difficulties. Clients were also encouraged to ask counselors personal questions that might bear on their counseling, such as whether they had reared children or had knowledge of particular cultures.

These changes were important in "demystifying" the therapist as a person of unique power and knowledge who knows clients better than clients know themselves, and who is competent to work with any client, regardless of issues and culture. These changes also allowed for a therapeutic environment that inspired and enhanced a client's sense of personal power and self-knowledge. Consistent with these views, clients were encouraged to find a counselor or therapist with whom they felt comfortable and whom they considered helpful.

Androgyny and Assertion Training.   Androgyny and assertion training as a form of feminist therapy grew out of Bem's early work on androgyny and gender schema theory (1993). These forms of therapy, very popular in the late 1970s and much of the 1980s, were based on the belief that if people could learn to be more androgynous in their personal behavior, that is, possess both feminine expressive personality characteristics and masculine instrumental characteristics, we could resocialize individuals to go beyond socialized sex roles. By so doing it was assumed we could eventually eliminate sexism and thus accomplish the feminist goals of equality. (Scales assessing expressive and instrumental traits, which at that time were incorrectly labeled scales of femininity and masculinity, appear in Box 1.3.)

Counseling focused on skills building, particularly assertiveness training for women, but with some emphasis on expressivity training for men. The initial excitement regarding androgyny as a solution for eradicating sexism was tempered by the limitations of the theory and hence of the treatment goals consistent with the theory. This form of feminist therapy focuses on the individual—on personal growth and the acquisition of skills—and largely ignores the social context of clients' lives and ways in which behavior is embedded in a social system, a perspective crucial for a feminist approach to therapy. Moreover, empirical research using Bem's concept and measure of androgyny revealed that gender was far more complex than androgyny models postulated (Spence, 1991, 1993).

Relational Models of Therapy.   Relational perspectives, which developed from Miller's (1976) book, *Toward A New Psychology of Women*, initially argued for a uniquely female "core self-structure" and female developmental path based on the centrality of relationships and emotional connectedness to others in women's lives (Jordan, Kaplan, Miller, Stiver, & Surrey, 1991; Miller, 1976). Living in a patriarchy was assumed to cause women to develop an orientation toward caring for others, a heightened sensitivity to others' emotions, and a sense of self that is fundamentally tied to relations. Referred to as self-in-relation, these perspectives were highly influenced by Gilligan's work, *In a Different Voice* (1982), in which she postulated that women acted out of a morality of care, as well as by Belensky, Clinchy, Goldberger, and Tarule's (1986) research and theory on women's ways of knowing.

Criticisms of core assumptions of the self-in-relation model have resulted in reformulations of the underlying theory (Jordan, 1997). A key criticism focused on the model's assumption of essential differences between women's and men's personality and behavior, differences not supported by a very extensive research literature (see Chapter 2 for a summary of this research). Such assumptions not only reinforced traditional stereotypes about women's nature but also could be interpreted as support for maintaining women's oppression (Mednick, 1989). Research also indicated that Gilligan's (1982) model of ethical decision making applied equally well to women and men. That is, in making decisions about ethical dilemmas, both women and men use justice and caring perspectives to a similar extent (Friedman, Robinson, & Friedman, 1987). A second concern was the scant attention given to issues of race, ethnicity, and culture or to contextual factors associated with gender processes.

Now presented as a "relational model of therapy" (Jordan, 1997), this feminist approach to therapy uses the term *relational self* rather than the term *self-in-relation*. Central to the therapeutic model is the theme of connection and disconnection, which is presented as a guiding principle for the therapist (Miller & Stiver, 1997). When therapists are empathic with both sides of the connection-disconnection paradox of clients, they can better understand client resistance to relinquishing strategies for avoiding connections and then can express their desire for connections. According to the model, developing the capacity for relational awareness allows one to acknowledge, explore, and transform patterns of disconnection. Patterns of violence and trauma in a culture can create a context of disconnection for both clients and therapists. Racism and sexism, for example, are viewed as the result of chronic disconnections stemming from many instances of empathic failure that have remained unacknowledged (Jordan, 1997). Patterns of disconnection typical for therapists include acting out of defensiveness rather than out of authenticity and using controlling response patterns rather than empathic ones.

Key concepts in this approach to feminist therapy are reframing human attributes traditionally associated with women's nature and roles as positive human strengths (e.g., viewing sensitivity to others as a human strength women have developed rather than a weakness associated with women's nature) and viewing the therapist or counselor as providing care and nurturance to clients.

Differences among the Various Feminist Therapies

These forms of feminist therapy differ in several ways. For example, empowerment feminist therapists offer a relationship to clients that emphasizes clients' autonomy and equality; this contrasts with the traditional therapeutic relationship in which the therapist is assumed to have special power and knowledge (Marecek & Hare-Mustin, 1987). Relational feminist therapists offer a counseling relationship that offers clients care and nurturing, which contrasts with the distance and emotional detachment of the traditional therapeutic stance (Jordan et al., 1991).

The forms of feminist therapy also differ in their conceptions of gender and in the goals of counseling. Empowerment feminist therapists explicitly incorporate all the faces of gender we have discussed. They acknowledge the importance of acquiring traits and skills discouraged by conventional gender socialization and valuing and embracing aspects of the female and male experience devalued in a sexist culture. In addition, this approach also focuses on changing gendered relations and gendered institutional structures. The goals of therapy center around self-understanding, empowerment, and change in the context of a gendered society. Clients are viewed as empowered to change not only themselves but also to bring about change in situational and societal conditions that they or other individuals in the culture experience as oppressive (e.g., a female client empowered through counseling to request a salary increase may also be empowered to raise the issue of gender bias in salaries among her co-workers.) The androgyny and relational approaches, in contrast, while also emphasizing socialization practices, give much less theoretical attention to how differences in power and status relate to socialization practices or to how these differences serve to maintain the practices or create the differences. Instead the goals of therapy center around individual changes such as increased self-acceptance and personal courage.

Despite their differences, there is also a good deal of commonality among the various feminist therapies. It is to this commonality in feminist therapy approaches that we now turn.

Core Components of Feminist Therapies

Feminist therapy takes a number of forms and can be incorporated into a variety of theoretical approaches to counseling and psychotherapy, including the behavioral and person-centered. However, its practice is invariably informed by feminist political philosophy and analysis and a commitment to bring about social change "that creates space for the spirit and for being a whole person" (hooks, 1995). Three principles are important to the practice of feminist therapy: the personal is political, the therapist-client relationship is egalitarian, and women are valued.

"Recognizing That the Personal Is Political" (or the Importance of Sociocultural Context).   Bernard (1975) helps make clear what is meant by the phrase, "the personal is political." She pointed out that changes at the individual level do little if the structures of a society remain unchanged: "So long as the institutional structure of our society favors men, the question arises as to can women, no matter how well prepared psychologically and intellectually, expect to be dealt with on the basis of their merits rather than on the basis of their sex?" (pp. 17–18).

Intrapsychic counseling theories often view clients as being *without* a culture, personal history, or gender that might have anything to do with their responses in a particular situation (Sherif, 1979). Feminist approaches take exception to this practice and believe that we must always consider individuals within their social context and acknowledge societal contributions to women's and men's individual problems (see Scher, 1981). Because sexism is institutionalized within our culture, and maintained through formal and informal practices, it is central to the context of normal personal development and experience.

An example of "the personal is political" principle comes from the case of a young woman who sought counseling in the 1950s to deal with the depression that ensued when she was forced to resign her teaching position because she was pregnant. She was counseled to count her blessings, and not to expect an exception to be made for her; it was within the school's legal rights to dismiss her as incompetent for teaching and as a negative role model for students because she was pregnant. She lost her job, however, not for personal reasons—she was still a good teacher and she loved her work, but for political and societal reasons codified by law—pregnant women belong in the home, not the workplace.

Several well-established counseling practices and goals are associated with the principle that the personal is political (Gilbert, 1980; Worell & Remer, 1992), for example, separating the internal from the external, reframing pathology, and emphasizing societal change, rather than "adjustment."

Separating the internal from the external refers to counselors working with clients to differentiate between what clients have been taught and accepted as socially appropriate behavior and goals for themselves (i.e., the external) from what they personally consider as appropriate for themselves (i.e., the internal). Thus, counselors encourage clients to evaluate the influences of social roles and norms on their personal experiences and to recognize the relationship between societal, external factors and psychological or intrapsychic internal factors. Separating out what has been taught and accepted, and becoming clear on one's own sense of self, is central to the process of empowerment.

A counseling example is the process one would go through in working with new parents struggling with the decision to take a 6-month unpaid leave from their employment. The issues for a new mother might be guilt at wanting to continue her work or hesitation at asking a spouse to be more involved in the care taking; issues for a new father might be fear of what his peers would think or concern that it would ruin his career opportunities.

Reframing pathology refers to counselors not blaming clients for thinking, acting, and feeling in ways that are consistent with living in a sexist society but rather understanding that they are adapting to it. The counseling process helps clients come to understand the role of society in shaping all individuals, including themselves. Clients may begin to see certain past and present behaviors as understandable efforts to respond adaptively to oppressive, sexist conditions, including those for which they feel shame. Thus, for women, anger at how one was psychologically battered in a marriage or anger at the experience of sexual abuse is framed as an adaptive response to an oppressive situation in which one had little power. For male clients, feelings of failure associated with being physically overpowered by male peers or at being abused sexually is similarly framed as an adaptive response in a situation in which one has little power.

Emphasizing societal change rather than "adjustment" refers to the feminist belief that healthy functioning cannot be achieved solely through individual changes. As Bernard's earlier quote indicates, societal changes are necessary to bring about true egalitarianism. This need for social change in order to create less gender-biased conditions perhaps most directly pertains to the relationship between the personal and the political. For example, it may take the form of clients suggesting family leave policies to employers, giving teachers feedback about sexist practices in the classroom, or helping sons and daughters recognize sexist messages in the media.

In summary, the personal and political can be conceptualized as two coexisting dimensions that occur in tandem. One of the processes in feminist therapies, for example, is separating the internal from the external, separating what is true of a person, or describes a person as an individual, apart from societal constructions of that person as a woman or a man.

Viewing the Therapist-Client Relationship as Egalitarian. Feminist therapy strives toward an egalitarian and nonauthoritarian relationship based on mutual respect. Moreover, the goals, direction, and pace of feminist therapy are developed in a collaborative process. These processes directly counter aspects of traditional socialization in which women were viewed as the lesser sex, expected to listen to authorities, and looked to others, especially men, to set their life goals; and men were expected to act independently, not need help, and use their power to determine relationships.

The often-cited case of Dora, in retrospect, provides an example of a tragic therapeutic relationship that was basically a nonegalitarian, noncollaborative therapeutic relationship (Hare-Mustin, 1983).

Dora is brought by her father to Freud when she is 18 years old and suffering from what today might be called depression. Her story is a drama of betrayal, played out between two unhappy families, hers, and the "shadow" K family. Freud regards Dora as vengeful because she has confronted the K family with Mr. K's propositioning her as well as her father's affair with Mrs. K. Both of these are emphatically denied by the adults involved, and Freud (who believes the adults and not Dora) views Dora as a disagreeable creature who consistently put revenge before love. Dora breaks off treatment with Freud, an act which he and later biographers further attributed to her nasty and revengeful nature.

What Dora needs most is confirmation of the truthfulness of her perceptions and thus confirmation of herself. However, the stereotypes are in place: women are not to be believed, women are like children. The adults involved ultimately admitted that her accusations were true—but only much later (and too late for Dora) (Hare-Mustin, 1983, p. 593).

Two therapeutic practices are particularly associated with viewing the counseling relationship as egalitarian, neither of which was present in the case of Dora. The first is establishing a therapeutic relationship that the client experiences as empowering and affirming. The second is counselors' continual monitoring their own biases, distortions, and limitations, especially with respect to gender processes and knowledge about women's and men's gendered experiences (Gilbert, 1980; Worell & Remer, 1992).

As with person-centered therapy (Rogers, 1961), through the process of counseling, clients learn to be the experts on themselves; it is the counselor's role to support clients' movement to confidence in their own perceptions and judgments. Counselors recognize their power to facilitate transformation, and accordingly convey their own valuing of the change process to their clients. They are ever mindful of their influence on clients and the potential power of their privileged position vis-à-vis individuals who seek their help. Finally, clients are not only encouraged to find a therapist with whom they are comfortable but also to question therapists' assumptions and interpretations.

Valuing Women and Valuing the Female Perspective. Feminist therapists work with clients in ways that value women's contributions to society and women's traditional and emerging characteristics and roles. Historically women have been less valued than men in our society and were primarily considered in relation to men. Rarely was it asked, "What are women for themselves?" We described in an earlier chapter how women were objects in other people's dramas and had no personal story, no separateness from the fabric of men's lives. In her book, *Writing a Woman's Life,* Heilbrun (1988) reminds us that "women have long been nameless. They have not been persons. Handed by a father to another man, the husband, they have been objects for circulation, exchanging one name for another" (p. 121). In literary works, as in real life, death and marriage were the only two possible ends for women, and were frequently the same end—for the young woman ceased to be an entity, a person in her own right.

This principle of feminist therapy addresses the importance of countering pervasive traditional images that devalue women and the effects of these images on women and men. For example, women are bombarded with messages that their value is tied to their attractiveness and ability to please others, yet they are devalued for being that way. The cartoon strip *Cathy* informs us almost daily that single career women are obsessed with getting a man and fight a losing battle to control their eating and maintain their beauty.

This principle also has important implications for counseling with men. Many men have learned to devalue women's contributions in the home and the workplace. Through counseling, men can come to recognize how they devalue women—their spouse, their daughter, or their female employees. Such a process could involve examining their own nonconscious ideology about gender and then working to bring about changes consistent with a more positive view.

Feminist counseling practices and goals associated with this principle include appreciating female-related values such as cooperation and affiliation, valuing women and relationships with women, accepting and liking one's body as a woman, trusting women's perceptions, and giving voice to women's experiences (Worell & Remer, 1992). Particularly crucial in this regard is giving voice to women's experience of their own sexuality.

The Cases of Mikel and Camilla

Mikel.   Mikel, it will be recalled, wants to meet for a few sessions to discuss the situation with Monika and whether he should suggest to Monika that they break off their relationship. A particular concern he has is that Monika may not be aware that she hopes he will eventually feel differently about her as a future life partner. Mikel likes Monika a great deal and does not want the relationship to end badly. He is confused about what he is feeling and mentions early on in the session that he senses that what he is feeling may be related to his socialization as a man.

Two aspects of male socialization would be particularly important to consider in counseling Mikel. First, part of Mikel's concern is that he will hurt

Monika because she does not really believe him. Although his concern could possibly be warranted, it appears that Monika is comfortable with the situation, and it is her comfort that is causing Mikel's discomfort. His concern about possibly hurting her, or perhaps using her, is likely tied to gender stereotypic notions of women needing a man to feel secure and using her sexuality to entice and hold on to a man. We describe in Chapter 6 how women's sexuality is traditionally defined in terms of men's desire, not women's own desire. A woman is typically viewed as an object of a man's sexual desires rather than a person who enjoys "sex," experiences herself as sexual, or has sexual desires.

A second important issue to consider in counseling Mikel concerns the valuing of women and the trusting of women's perspectives and experiences. Mikel's own sense of male prerogative and entitlement, associated with normative male socialization, not only may make it hard for him to view Monika as not needing him but also make it difficult for him to really listen to and hear her. Traditionally men have defined women's needs and wants and served as experts on what women were feeling. Some of that may be occurring here as well. In a sense Mikel is acting in a patronizing manner toward Monica, assuming that she does not know herself or that he knows her better than she knows herself.

Camilla.   Espin (1994) views feminist therapy as valuable in working with women of color because of the importance it places on sociocultural factors, the validation of clients' experiences, and clients' empowerment. "Because women of color are the most invisible and unknown among women," she believes it is crucial to use therapeutic approaches that give voice to the unheard and embody the invisible (p. 270). Espin (1994) shared a moving case of a young woman age 20 who came to the United States with her family from Central America when she was 15 years old. Camilla was particularly close to her grandmother, who still lived in her country of origin, and was distressed by problems in their relationship caused by her grandmother learning of Camilla's sexual preferences.

> She came to therapy wanting to speak in Spanish because, according to her, 'her problems were in Spanish,' and she also wanted a feminist therapist who would not reject her lesbianism. She actually was not sure that such a therapist really existed because she thought all feminist therapists were white. [Unlike a previous male therapist who was Latino] she was pleased to see that rather than trying to encourage her to change her sexual orientation, I was interested in ways of helping her be happier in her relationships by choosing more appropriate partners. We worked intensely on self-esteem issues and also on her relationship with her grandmother.

When Camilla terminated therapy she returned to her home country for an extended visit with her grandmother. At her own initiative Camilla's grandmother invited Camilla's partner of the past 2 years to stay at her home for part of the visit (Espin, 1994, p. 278–279).

Gender-Aware Therapy

Gender subsumes individuals' behaviors within their social context. An understanding of gender within context requires more than the absence of sexism. Gender awareness includes a sensitivity to a person's present and past life context with its attendant sex-role constraints, expectations, and prescriptions, as well as a theoretical understanding of the complex processes of gender construction and performance. The importance of gender processes to counseling relationships is central to what has come to be known as gender-aware therapy (GAT) (Good, Gilbert, & Scher, 1990).

Gender-aware therapy is an approach to counseling that brings together gender processes and feminist approaches. GAT, like feminist therapies, conceptualizes change as personal, contextual, and systemic. The five central principles of GAT are as follows:

1. Regard conceptions of gender as integral aspects of counseling and mental health.
2. Consider problems within their sociocultural context.
3. Actively seek to change gender injustices experienced by women and men.
4. Emphasize development of collaborative therapeutic relationships.
5. Respect clients' freedom to choose in collaboration.

According to gender-aware therapy, women and men need to be understood and treated as living within a societal and environmental context that not only holds stereotypic assumptions and expectations about what is desirable for women and men, but also uses differential reward systems and policies associated with these stereotypic views. Gender-related constraints such as discrimination in the workplace are to be considered actual barriers to self-expression rather than forms of intrapsychic weakness. Likewise, psychological pain resulting from the sexualization of women or the fostering of male inexpressiveness is recognized as internalized psychological conflict occurring within the larger context of gender-role socialization and societal biases concerning women and men. In gaining this kind of recognition and reframing, the client may begin to feel less shame and self-blame.

The gender-aware therapist works to challenge and encourage clients to explore the desires of their inner self while at the same time recognizing societal assumptions, expectations, and interpersonal situations that create gendered processes in them. Clients are assisted in recognizing "the doing of gender," helped in viewing other options, and supported in considering a broader set of alternatives for themselves. In addition, gender-aware therapists recognize the power inherent in the therapist's role.

Box 4.1 on page 70 summarizes key aspects of these therapies. Later chapters describe common gender issues brought to counseling and gendered dynamics

---

BOX 4.1   Key Aspects of Feminist and Gender-Aware Approaches to Counseling and Therapy

1. Recognition of oppressions based on gender, race, and class
2. Centrality of sociocultural context
3. Demystification of therapist power in the therapeutic relationship
4. Ongoing self-examination of values on the part of the therapist
5. Reframing pathology
6. Separation of intrapsychic dynamics from external contexts
7. Emphasis on change both in therapy and in society
8. Valuing the female perspective
9. Focus on women's empowerment

---

that emerge in the process of counseling. In considering these issues and dynamics we also provide further discussion of the processes and goals of gender-aware approaches to counseling and therapy.

Concluding Remarks

In this chapter we traced the evolution of approaches to counseling that demonstrate contemporary thinking about gender, namely feminist therapies and gender-aware therapy. These approaches can be incorporated into a variety of other theoretical approaches to counseling, such as behavioral and person-centered. Informed gender-aware therapists rethink traditional assumptions about the processes and goals of counseling and they continually question what is needed for counseling to be effective. Principles presented in this chapter are *essential* to counseling. These principles include regarding conceptions of gender as integral aspects of counseling and mental health, considering client problems within their social context, and developing collaborative counseling relationships with clients.

The remaining three chapters in Part II consider gender processes in two other contexts: sexuality, and the language and discourse of the counseling process itself.

Discussion Questions

1. Think about the theoretical orientations that currently guide your counseling and therapeutic work with clients. Select a particular client (real or

imaginary) and describe how you will incorporate what we have learned about gender into the treatment of that individual.

2. You are working as an intake consultant at a university counseling center. A heterosexual undergraduate comes in requesting to work with a therapist on relationship issues. Assuming that you have the opportunity to recommend the client to therapists of equal ability and experience, what might be some advantages and disadvantages associated with referring the client to a female counselor? To a male counselor? Would you recommend the client work with a female or a male counselor? Discuss your rationale. Respond first for a client of the female sex, and then respond for a client of the male sex.

Suggested Readings

Betz, N. E. & Fitzgerald, L. F. (1993). Individuality and diversity: Theory and research in counseling and psychotherapy. *Annual Review of Psychology, 44,* 343–381. A comprehensive and well-written analysis of contemporary research about therapy with diverse populations; specifically addressing issues associated with gender, cultural diversity, and gay and lesbian lifestyles.

Lorde, A. (1982). *Zami: A new spelling of my name.* Freedom, CA: The Crossing Press. This "biomythography," which provides a chronicle of the late Audre Lorde's life from her childhood in Harlem to her coming of age in the late 1950s, describes with personal honesty the evolution of a strong and remarkable character.

For an in-depth understanding of feminist therapies the reader is referred to Brown (1994), Enns (1993), Gilbert (1980), Worell & Johnson (1997), and Worell & Remer (1992).

Gender, Language, and Dominant Discourse

Maria, a 34-year-old homemaker, has two healthy children and an ambitious, successful, and concerned husband. She is a tall woman with an air of confidence about her. Maria tells herself that she "has everything," yet she seeks an appointment with you because of feelings of depression and malaise as well as a growing anger and resentment toward her children and husband. During the appointment, she appears distraught and confused. From her perspective, her dissatisfaction is entirely irrational. She says, "I have nothing to be angry and depressed about." She is concerned that her feelings are beginning to have a negative effect on her marriage. She tells you that her goal for seeking help is to be a better and more satisfied wife and mother. (Rossman, 1994)

Maria is very disappointed in herself and comes to you for advice about what she is doing wrong. Once again, the long-term and short-term goals of counseling for Maria depend on the theories the counselor uses to identify basic issues that might need to be addressed. Possible issues for this client include: (1) Maria has some unresolved childhood issues that need to be identified and addressed. For example, Maria may have psychological concerns from her childhood that are affecting her capacity to nurture and care for others without resentment; (2) Maria's marriage is not as happy as she presents it. Her husband may be away from home a lot and she may be feeling lonely and unloved; and (3) Maria has defined herself in terms of other people's needs and beliefs. For instance, her assumption that she "has everything" may need to be explored and challenged.

Earlier chapters looked at different ways in which theories guide counseling and therapy. In this chapter we look at a somewhat different aspect of theory. We consider the language used in theories and in describing client concerns and everyday behavior. We also look at language in the form of dominant discourse. Dominant discourses can guide and shape our thinking about client concerns and what we say and do in counseling.

Gender and Language

Language matters, perhaps in more ways than we typically realize. As will become clear in the chapter, language can assert traditional assumptions about gender and thus play a powerful role in maintaining nonconscious views about women's and men's nature as well as how they should behave. Assumptions about women's and men's differing psychological natures have become embedded in the everyday language we use to describe or explain our own behavior and our observations of others' behavior.

We often use one language when describing women's behavior and a different language to describe the same behavior in men. Excellent examples are the words *slut* and *stud*. These two words have different connotations but describe the same behavior—individuals who engage in sex with a number of different partners. The word *slut* is derisive and personally demeaning; the word *stud*, complimentary and personally enhancing. Many men may secretly want to be called studs but few if any women aspire to being called sluts.

We use adjectives stereotypically associated with women or men to discourage certain behaviors in female or male children. Male children are often instructed not to act like girls—which means not to show emotions that would indicate a sensitivity to others, not to engage in such activities as sewing, playing with dolls, or domestic work, and not to create visions for themselves as teachers, nurses, child care workers, or secretaries. Female children are often instructed to be "ladylike"—which means to be polite, quiet, and sensitive to others and concerned with how they appear to others. We use this language to keep boys from behaving like girls and girls from behaving like boys.

Keller (1992) describes how language, especially the language of science, plays a powerful role in maintaining stereotypic views about women and men and "true nature." In Chapter 1 some examples from science were described including the view that a woman's egg passively waits while a man's sperm compete with each other, as if in a 100-yard dash, to fertilize the waiting egg. (In actuality, the two cells fuse, a process in which both the egg and the sperm participate actively.)

How language is used to describe aspects of family life provides another example. We are now well familiar with the term "working mothers." Women who are employed outside the home and rear children are considered working mothers; this is the term one would use in locating research articles on the topic. Should you want to locate research articles on men who are employed outside the home and rear children, the parallel term "working father" would be of no help. No resource lists working fathers in its index. The fact that no study we know of refers to working fathers as a normative group tells us a great deal about gender ideology with regard to the family: Women who work outside the home are identified by their parental roles; men who work outside the home are not—they are simply employed. Notice how the language, "employed men" rather than "working fathers," keeps invisible men's connection to their children and helps maintain stereotypic views about the separation of employment and family in men's lives.

Common Themes

In Chapter 2 we cited a passage from Adrienne Rich (1979) about the need to listen to the voices of women. Historically women's voices were not granted much authority and were typically not listened to or heeded. Men were supposed to speak for women. As Rich explains, the voices of women are "taught early that tones of confidence, challenge, anger, or assertiveness, are strident and unfeminine." She makes the further observation that men are allowed, and allow themselves, more space, physically and verbally, and that they assume other people will listen to them, even when the majority of the group is female. These observations are consistent with male and female socialization practices that encourage men to be forceful and dominant and women quiet and demure.

A good deal of research concerns gender and the use of language (Aries, 1987; Crawford, 1995; Tannen, 1990, 1994). Are there common themes when women and men talk? As we shall see, Rich's observations are accurate.

Interruption: Patterns of interruption depend on who is talking to whom. Across a number of situations and studies, in conversations between women and men, men on average interrupt women significantly more than women interrupt men. In same-sex conversations, interruptions are about equally divided.

Topic control: The few studies on this issue indicate that women introduce more topics into the conversation than men and that men were more likely to decide which topics would be picked up and elaborated on.

Talking time: This theme has received a good deal of research attention. Contrary to the stereotype that women are the talkers, this body of research indicates that in mixed-sex groups or pairs, men take up much more of the air time than women do. This appears to be the case in dating situations, classroom settings, and work settings. (No research to date reports on counseling settings.)

Use of silence: Silence in conversations can be used as a device to control the interaction, depending on the context. Leaders who say little in group discussions can exert control by withholding approval or not sharing their views and leaving others uncomfortable. In dyads in which individuals take turns talking, the person who remains silent controls the conversation, particularly when the other person in the dyad makes a request for or expects the courtesy of a response. Overall, studies indicate that men more than women use silence to control conversations.

Crawford (1995) uses the body of research on gender differences in language to reframe women's and men's use of language within the broader concept of the *doing* or *making of gender*, a concept we introduced in Chapter 1. According to Crawford, using certain speech patterns "does gender" because those patterns serve to preserve deeply ingrained views of how women and men relate, which in turn are tied to societal assumptions about women's and men's essential nature. From this perspective, the differences observed between women and men in conversation are tied to assumptions about power and status, with those of higher status and greater power interrupting more, talking more, and so forth. In our society men as a group are granted greater power and status than women as a group and this difference gets reproduced in patterns of verbal communication.

Tannen (1990) also has been intrigued by these patterns of differences in men's and women's language in conversations. Her explanation is similar to Crawford's, in that she posits that men see themselves in a hierarchical social order in which they are either one-up or one-down. In the world as men construe it, according to Tannen, conversations are negotiations in which people either try to achieve the upper hand or protect themselves from others' attempts to have the upper hand and put them down. Women, in contrast, she argues, perceive themselves as part of a network of connections. For women more than men, conversations are negotiations in which people try to "seek and give confirmation and support, and to reach consensus" (p. 25).

Pleck (1981b; 1995) also sees these patterns as doing gender, but he provides a somewhat different view than Crawford or Tannen. According to Pleck, a key aspect of male socialization is the notion that men are independent and need no one. Although illusionary, this nonconscious view serves to obfuscate men's normal dependence needs on women and other men. From this perspective, men's withholding themselves from relations with women by the use of silence, topic control, and so forth not only provides men with the illusion of an independent stance but also reinforces their dominant position. As Pleck (1981b) also points out, by engaging in these kinds of interactions, men give women the ability to make men feel like men, since maintaining their dominant position depends on women seeing men as superior to them. This kind of dynamic between women and men is another example of doing gender initially presented in Chapter 1.

Relevance to Counseling and Therapy

These same dynamics are likely to occur between clients and counselors, and can be problematic, as later chapters further illustrate. Female counselors who feel hesitant to interrupt male clients may hold back from redirecting the process of counseling to perceived client problems. Male counselors who feel more comfortable when they control and dominate interactions with women would have difficulty establishing close working or equitable relations with female clients. Moreover, female clients who are accustomed to letting men control the topic of conversation may find counseling moving in directions that meet the counselors' needs more than their own needs. Pope and Bouhoutsos (1986), for example, describe situations in which counselors' voyeuristic needs are met by asking female clients unaccustomed to challenging male authority to provide details about their sexual behavior.

Counselors' awareness of these kinds of dynamics can also assist clients in understanding and making sense of their own experiences outside of therapy. Female clients who feel unheard at work could be helped by understanding gendered patterns and developing strategies to change these patterns. One woman teacher, for example, was totally demoralized by her principal interrupting her every time she tried to make suggestions in meetings. Counseling with her focused on understanding the gendered context of her work, a male elementary school principal and mostly female teachers, and how her soft-spoken manner and indirect way of speaking contributed to her being more easily interrupted. With this new awareness, the client was in a good position to develop effective strategies to change the situation.

Couples seeking marital counseling often engage in patterns of communication that leave one of the partners feeling unheard. Counselors sensitive to gendered themes of communication can quickly point out these dynamics and move the counseling to deeper levels. In the case of Maria, for instance, she may have brought up some of her unhappiness with her spouse but it may have been met mostly with her husband's silence or with his changing the topic and then doing most of the talking. Such an unempathic response would likely leave her feeling unheard and alone, and add to her feelings of unhappiness. Maria's spouse, on the other hand, may sense that she is not happy and feel helpless about what to do to change the situation, and thus may avoid talking about it.

Because the same pattern is certain to emerge in the session with the couple, counselors sensitive to gendered communication patterns can use these patterns to move the counseling to deeper levels. In this instance, for example, a counselor can share her or his observation with the couple, and use it as an opportunity to encourage both partners to share what they feel when their responses are met with silence. A next step would be to work with the partners to listen to each other and to help them identify emotional barriers to really hearing what the other partner has to say (e.g., he may fear she will leave him). These kinds of discussions can deepen the partners' mutual understanding and respect, and put them in a better position to address issues in the marriage. Maria's unhappiness, it may turn out, is more tied to her husband's unwillingness to share himself emotionally and spiritually, than to decisions the couple made about their work and family roles.

Nonverbal Communication

In her book *Body Politics,* Henley (1977) was among the first to describe the relationship between gender and nonverbal communication. Her analysis of research comparing nonverbal behavior in situations of equal and unequal status concluded that nonverbal behaviors often reflect the micropolitical structure of a society or culture—in the case of gender, the micropolitical structure between women and men. In particular, Henley's work drew parallels between the nonverbal patterns observed in male–female interactions and those observed in interactions between status equals and between status unequals. Table 5.1 on page 78, which is reproduced from her book, shows these parallels.

As can be seen from Table 5.1, there are striking similarities in the nonverbal behaviors observed between status nonequals and the nonverbal behaviors observed between women and men. For example, between status nonequals, the superior does not disclose and the subordinate does, a pattern similar to what stereotypically occurs in male–female interactions. For the behavior touching, superiors may engage in touching but subordinates do not; in nonintimate male–female interactions men touch women much more than women touch men.

TABLE 5.1   Gestures of Power and Privilege: Examples of Some Nonverbal Behaviors with Usage Differing for Status Equals and Nonequals, and for Women and Men

Behavior	Between Status Equals		Between Status Nonequals		Between Men and Women	
	Intimate	Nonintimate	Used by Superior	Used by Subordinate	Used by Men	Used by Women
1. Address	Familiar	Polite	Familiar	Polite	Familiar?*	Polite?*
2. Demeanor	Informal	Circumspect	Informal	Circumspect	Informal	Circumspect
3. Posture	Relaxed	Tense (less relaxed)	Relaxed	Tense	Relaxed	Tense
4. Personal space	Closeness	Distance	Closeness (option)	Distance	Closeness	Distance
5. Time	Long	Short	Long (option)	Short	Long?*	Short?*
6. Touching	Touch	Don't touch	Touch (option)	Don't touch	Touch	Don't touch
7. Eye contact	Established	Avoid	Stare, ignore	Avert eyes, watch	Stare, ignore	Avert eyes, watch
8. Facial expression	Smile?*	Don't smile?*	Don't smile	Smile	Don't smile	Smile
9. Emotional expression	Show	Hide	Hide	Show	Hide	Show
10. Self-disclosure	Disclose	Don't disclose	Don't disclose	Disclose	Don't disclose	Disclose

*No studies available on behavior.

Reprinted with permission of Simon & Schuster from Henley, N. M. (1977). *Body politics: Power, sex, and nonverbal communication.* Copyright © 1977 by Prentice-Hall, Inc.

Common Themes

In revisiting and updating her 1977 research, Henley (1995) concludes that "the duality of function of nonverbal behaviors for dominance or intimacy, and their parallel use in situations involving gender and other power dimensions, have been well established" (p. 55). Areas she updated that have particular importance for counseling are space, touch, and facial positivity or smiling.

Space. Considerable research indicates that women's personal space is smaller than men's. That is, both women and men are observed in greater proximity to women than they are to men. Henley (1995) believes that the most compelling explanation for this consistent observation is that females are approached more closely than males are. In situations in which women are in control of their own spacing, as in choosing their own seating, women make choices that provide them with greater personal space (Henley & LaFrance, 1984).

Touch.   Touching between women and men has also received considerable study. Factors important in these studies are the intentionality of the touching, the age of the participants, the nature of the relationship between participants, and the setting or context in which touch is observed. Overall, research findings indicate that women are touched more than men and that men are more likely to touch women than women are to touch men. Men are more likely to initiate touch in cross-sex encounters but not in same-sex encounters. These findings characterize adult touching. Little evidence of gender asymmetry has been reported for children.

Facial Positivity or Smiling.   Smiling is an important aspect of attractiveness (Langlois, Roggman, & Musselman, 1994). It is well established that women smile somewhat more than men and that there is an inverse association in the culture between smiling and power, with those who have less power smiling more often. Interestingly, media portrayals of smiling, when compared with actual smiling recorded in naturalistic observation of public behavior, describe the sexes as more different in their smiling behavior than occurs naturally. Women are portrayed in the media as smiling more than they do in naturalistic observation, and men are seen as smiling less than they do in naturalistic observation.

Relevance to Counseling and Therapy

These gendered nonverbal patterns occur in counseling settings. For example, both female and male counselors may anticipate more facial positivity and smiling behavior from female clients than male clients and may feel more free to touch and hug female clients. These expectancies would not only reflect the power differential in counseling, but also the power differential associated with gender detailed by Henley.

Male therapists who touch and hug female clients may be eroticizing the counseling with female clients under the guise of providing warmth and support, and thus using the power of their gender to nonverbally direct the counseling to meet their own needs. Female counselors who are in the habit of hugging female clients at the end of a counseling session may be forcing a closeness that makes it more difficult for female clients to feel that autonomy, self-definition, and disagreement are permissible. Moreover, hugging and other forms of touching associated with personal space suggest an intimate relationship between status equals (see Table 5.1). Counseling is a professional relationship, not a personal relationship. Any nonverbal or verbal behaviors that blur this distinction are confusing to clients and interfere with the counseling process. Later chapters provide further discussion of these issues.

Dominant Discourse

Language also becomes important in understanding how clients and counselors interact in ways that reproduce conventional assumptions about gender within the counseling process and become apparent as "dominant discourses." Hare-Mustin (1994) informs us, "The therapy room is like a room lined with mirrors. It reflects back only what is voiced within it" (p. 22). In other words, if both the client and the counselor hold a certain set of beliefs about what it means to be a woman or a man, these are the only beliefs that can get voiced within the counseling session.

When counselors lack awareness of gendered processes, and of how language can proclaim these processes, alternate views remain outside of the therapy room. In the case of Maria, for example, her language reflects the stereotypic view or discourse that she "has everything" because she has a successful husband and healthy children. Imbedded in this discourse is the assumption that women's identity is defined by marriage and children. If both Maria and her counselor assume she has everything, the process and goals of counseling can only reflect back what is voiced within it—she has everything and is not happy, so there must be something wrong with Maria. For other possible explanations and goals to emerge, the language, "has everything," and the discourse associated with the "accepted female plot" (described in Chapter 2) would need to be challenged. The "accepted female plot," it will be recalled, requires that women conceal a sense of personal agency and a sense of self separate from the needs of others.

Definition of Dominant Discourse

Dominant discourse refers to "a system of statements, practices, and institutional structures that share common values. A discourse . . . is the medium that provides the words and ideas for thought and speech, as well as the cultural practices involving related concepts and behaviors" (Hare-Mustin, 1994, p. 19). Stereotypic assumptions about women's and men's differing psychological natures are embedded in the everyday discourse used to describe or explain one's own behavior and observations of others' behavior. A woman who offers to help someone is often described as "being mothering," regardless of the kind of relationship between the two people and the kind of help offered. What is conveyed by this language is the larger, powerful discourse that whatever women do, their motivations are ultimately tied to their biological role of mother.

Basically discourses shape how we think about things and how we talk about them. Discourses both reflect and sustain certain world views such as the "nature" of female and male sexuality, motherhood, and masculinity. Discourses allow certain phenomena attention and voice, and disallow or obscure other phenomena. Dominant discourses appear "natural" and self-evident, and thus act to preserve and perpetuate existing practices, beliefs, and power relationships. Thus, having only one dominant discourse not only results in doing gender, but also doing gender creates the dominant discourse. An illustrative example is the constellation of behaviors now identified as sexual harassment. For many decades, employed women assumed that certain behaviors and attitudes came along with the turf of employment or wanting employment; men held a similar view. There was no public or private outcry because there was no other discourse to describe these interactions in employment settings. It appeared self-evident that men in positions of power over women have the prerogative of sexualizing those relationships. Women and men who engaged in these interpersonal dynamics, regardless of whether the woman was flattered and dated a boss, was fearful and left her job, or said no, and was subtly punished, were acting as women and men were expected to act in such situations (i.e., doing gender). In acting in these ways, they were also creating dominant discourses associated with men's entitlement to women's bodies.

Because discourses are so embedded in custom and culture, how they shape individual choices is not readily apparent (Marecek & Hare-Mustin, 1990). We mentioned in Chapter 1 in the discussion of the teen article, "Fresh Voices" that the seemingly benign conventional dating practices, in which men ask women out and pay for the date, can have negative consequences for women. In the survey we cited (Gandara, 1995), a sizable percentage of male and female college students indicated that women owe male dating partners sex when the men had spent a lot of money on a date, and that under these conditions it was "OK" for guys to force themselves sexually on their female dates. In this example, what women and men see as their "choices" in dating situations are shaped by the societal view that men are entitled to women's bodies if they pay enough. It is a view perpetuated by the behaviors of the dating partners that gives ownership of women's bodies to someone other than women themselves.

As this example of prevailing dating practices well illustrates, Hare-Mustin's (1994) comment about the mirrors in the therapy room also applies to society. Conversations in real life often reflect the dominant discourses of the society, making it more difficult for individuals to engage in conversations that could provide alternative meanings or disrupt conventional practices. In retrospect, we realize that we provided an alternate discourse for our teenage daughters when we questioned why men should always pay on dates. We suggested that women could pay their own way, a practice our daughters and many of their friends have adopted and like (Box 5.1).

BOX 5.1   Changing Gendered Discourses: One Example

Parents can provide an important alternative for teenage daughters and sons when they question why men should always pay on dates. We suggested to our daughters that women should pay their own way, and they, in turn, convinced some of their friends. It is a practice they find they very much like.

Common Dominant Discourse Themes

Hare-Mustin (1994) identifies two dominant discourses especially relevant to issues that clients bring to therapy. These are the "male sexual drive" discourse and "women and men as equals" discourse. Next we describe these two discourses and their relevance to client concerns and counseling goals. In a later chapter we show their relevance to dynamics that emerge in counseling and therapy.

The "Male Sexual Drive" Discourse.   Our earlier example about dating illustrated the powerful role language and discourse play in shaping ideas and views about normal sexual experience. In Chapter 6 on sexuality and gender, we describe some of the stereotypic assumptions about male sexuality that guide some men's sexual behavior. Some of that material is relevant to our present discussion of the "male sexual drive" discourse.

The "male sexual drive discourse" is a derivative of a sociobiological myth: In the animal kingdom, there exists a male imperative to pursue and procreate and a complementary female role to be acquiescent and receptive (Crawford, Kippax, & Waldby, 1994). As defined by Hare-Mustin (1994), in this discourse "the woman is seen as the object that arouses and precipitates men's sexual urges. Men's sexual urges are assumed to be natural and compelling; thus the male is expected to be pushy and aggressive in seeking to satisfy them" (p. 24). In the context of the male sexual drive discourse, not only are men entitled to sex with women, but also male sexual conquest and domination become eroticized and thus central to "sexiness" and arousal (Hare-Mustin, 1994). Moreover, women who do not accede to male arousal risk being viewed negatively and labeled as "uptight" or "frigid."

The assumption that male sexuality is "uncontrollable" can have an impact on the perception of appropriateness of using force in sexual relationships. For centuries a woman's status as wife implied consent to sexual intercourse, regardless of level of force used to attain sex. Studies of adolescents reflect a similar view. Goodchilds, Zellman, Johnson, and Giarrusso (1988), for example, polled a sample of 432 adolescents regarding their judgments of the acceptability of using force during sexual situations: 21 percent of girls and 36 percent of boys felt force was appropriate if "he's so turned on he can't stop"; and 42 percent of girls and 51 percent of boys felt force was acceptable if "she gets him sexually excited."

Prevalent views of male and female sexual behavior are consistent with their differential gender role socialization (see Chapter 2). It is assumed that men are active initiators and pursuers in sexual situations and that masculinity is confirmed through sex with women (MacCorquodale, 1989; Pleck, 1981b). In contrast, the traditional female role's emphasis on the concealment of both personal agency and a separate sense of self becomes manifest in sexual situations as women being submissive to male desires and acquiescing to male needs. Studies of male adolescents by Pleck, Sonnenstein, and Ku (1993) indicated that the acceptance of traditional male role attitudes emphasizing status, toughness, and not having any characteristics traditionally ascribed to women is associated with having more sexual partners, a less intimate relationship with a partner

---

BOX 5.2   Illustration from a Study of Heterosexual Dating Relationships

We designed a study to investigate the male sexual drive dominant discourse in heterosexual dating relationships. A main purpose of the study was to see if we could set up situations in a laboratory setting in which dominant discourses about heterosexual dating could be reproduced and in which they could be disrupted and changed (Gilbert, Walker, Goss, & Snell, 1997). Young single heterosexual adults were asked to role-play a series of dating scenarios starting with a first date and developing into an intimate relationship. In half the dyads, the man was instructed to initiate greater sexual intimacy and the woman was instructed to say she was not ready; in the other half, the instructions for the male and female partners were reversed so that the woman was asked to initiate greater sexual intimacy and the man was instructed to say he was not ready.

We expected dialogues in which the man was the initiator to reproduce the male sexual drive discourse and those in which the woman was the initiator to disrupt it and allow alternative discourses to emerge. The discourses we coded in these studies appear in Box 5.3. Before looking at Box 5.3, jot down what you would have said in these two situations. Then underline those parts of your response that you think do or do not reproduce the male sexual drive dominant discourse.

---

when sex first occurs, an adversarial view of close relationships with women, less acceptance by males of responsibility to prevent pregnancy, and lower condom use (see also Box 5.2).

"Women and Men as Equals" Discourse.   This discourse concerns how narratives associated with cultural views can preserve gender inequality. Basically, the "women and men are equals" discourse serves to obscure patriarchal views of male preeminence and female subordination within any male–female relationship. By focusing on women and men as free agents, the discourse ignores the context of women's and men's lives, and the greater status, power, and privilege generally ascribed to men than women. (This has not been the case for African American men in the United States, however.)

Earlier in the chapter we mentioned that until the 1980s sexual harassment was viewed as a "natural" dynamic that occurred between individual women and men in employment and educational settings. Within the "women and men as equals discourse," male bosses pressuring female employees for dates or sex would be considered a matter between the individuals involved. If the woman says yes, it is her business and her life. Obscured and ignored by the discourse is the fact that the request for a date occurs in the context of a power relationship in which the boss has greater power. A woman who refuses runs the risk of losing job security and throwing away advancement opportunities. The woman and man in this situation are not equals.

Marriage provides another good example. Within our culture we assume that individuals marry for love and are free to create whatever kind of marital relationship they so choose. In actuality, relationships develop within a cultural and societal context. Both partners, and the intimate relationships they form, are embedded in and constrained by formal and informal laws and practices (Aldous, 1990; Gilbert, 1994). Marriage, for example, is a legal contract typically reserved for heterosexual partners, not a personal agreement. Typically, however, it is only when heterosexual partners wish to break or dissolve the contract that the stark reality of its legal aspects become evident.

Are women and men in marriage "equals"? Historically they were not. Husbands' power over wives was regarded as natural, altruistic, or necessary for family harmony (Okin, 1989). The law also closed off married women to paying jobs and educational pursuits.

Although these laws no longer apply, informal practices within our society continue to expect the female partner to alter or give up her employment to care for the family, to depend on the male partner economically, to put the man's needs before her own, and look to him for security. These informal practices profoundly influence female–male equality in marriages (Sanchez & Kane, 1996; Thompson & Walker, 1989). Often clients we see in counseling entered a marriage based on presumed equality, only to find themselves years later in a "contract that operates to deepen the inequality between the male partner and the female partner" (Okin, 1989, p. 128).

Relevance to Counseling and Therapy

Acceptance of the "male sexual drive" and "women and men as equals" discourses, by both women and men, influences the expectations that individuals bring to heterosexual dating, committed relationships, and marital relationships (Gilbert & Walker, 1998). In particular, the male sexual drive discourse influences views of what is normal sexuality for women and men.

The "Male Sexual Drive" Discourse.   The male sexual drive discourse focuses on male needs and entitlements and sees women as an object of male arousal. Consequently verbal and nonverbal communication and behavior within the relationship may result in women deferring to men's desires and both women and men acting in ways that satisfy men's sexual entitlement and dominant stance. In the case of Susanna described in Chapter 3, a counselor who accepts the male sexual drive discourse would likely assume that her sexual difficulties caused her husband's seeking sex elsewhere; Susanna's sexual problems would be included among the goals for her counseling. Adherence to the male sexual drive discourse would obscure other possible dynamics, such as Susanna's consent to unwanted sex or her husband's use of forced sex, both of which would have profound implications for her self-esteem and for both partners' marital happiness. Such adherence would also obscure the possibility of her husband's engaging in nonrelational sex with her.

The male sexual drive discourse encourages nonrelational sex as the most desirable form of sex. Thus, even within a committed relationship, some men may be unable to engage their partners both emotionally and sexually. Instead, their assumptions about male sexuality result in their denying the humanity of their partners, objectifying, and perhaps even violating their partners in their efforts to meet what they consider to be normal male needs (Brooks, 1997). As Shotland and Hunter (1995) concluded, women may engage in compliant, unwanted sex early in a relationship, so that their partners perceive them as sexually normal and remain in the relationship. Later in the relationship, they continue compliant sexual behavior to avoid disappointing their partners, but not without risking damage to the relationship. When these kinds of dynamics become characteristic of a relationship, the partners not only would be playing out the dominant discourse of male sexual arousal, but also would be considering the woman's compliance to unwanted sex as facilitating relationship stability.

Gender issues associated with the male sexual drive discourse are addressed in Chapter 7. These issues include gender role strain, male emotional inexpressivity, and rape. Later chapters also discuss issues pertinent to the counseling relationship, such as the eroticization of the counseling relationship and sexual relations with clients.

"Women and Men as Equals" Discourse.

The unquestioned acceptance of the women and men as equals discourse by both women and men also profoundly affects relationships. Particularly important in counseling couples is recognizing the various forms of the women and men as equals discourse and how doing gender by partners recreates the discourse.

Sharing family work is a problematic area for many couples. Female partners who feel overburdened and resentful, yet see themselves as choosing to do much more than their spouse, may be unaware of or hesitant to challenge the power relations in the marriage. Couples who come in unhappy with the traditional arrangement that developed over the years may be acting on the assumption that women and men have different abilities; counseling could help them to recognize that the abilities of women and men are more similar than they are different and that sharing or exchanging roles is possible. A case in point is a partner who felt overly burdened by the provider role and disappointed that the other partner had no interest in being employed. In counseling it became clear that both partners felt stuck because neither one thought he or she was capable of doing what the other one was doing. Through a series of homework assignments, they recognized abilities in themselves and each other that freed them to move beyond their stereotypic assumptions.

Dominant discourse themes noted in a study of heterosexual dating are presented in Box 5.3 on page 86.

In summary, counselors can work to sustain or to challenge dominant discourses about gender. Counselors can give salience to one part of a client's story and use the counseling to reproduce conventional assumptions about gender. On the other hand, counselors can give salience to other parts of a client's story and work with her or him to disrupt those discourses and allow alternative discourses to emerge. A female client traumatized by her husband's verbal attacks on her character and abilities talks about her feelings of responsibility for the

---

BOX 5.3 Dominant Discourse Themes Detected in the Study of Heterosexual Dating Relationships

Themes coded in situations in which male partner initiates greater intimacy and female partner says she is not ready:

- Woman reassures man/acknowledges man's sexual needs, and her role in causing him frustration.
- If sexual needs are not met within a period of time, a man has the right to look elsewhere.
- Sex will bring the couple closer together.

Themes coded in situations in which female partner initiates greater intimacy and male partner says he is not ready:

- Woman questions her own desirability.
- Women are supposed to set limits on sexual advances.

Conclusions from the Study

Our results clearly support the idea that women and men share a nonconscious assumption about the powerful nature of male sexuality and female acquiescence. Dominant discourse themes were readily prevalent even when an attempt was made to change or confound the discourse by providing the alternative context in which women were instructed to initiate intimate scenarios. However, focused group discussions with participants from both experimental conditions resulted in some questioning of the male sexual drive discourse and the emergence of new possibilities and choices such as the idea that women do not owe men sex, that women can act on their own sexual desire, that men do not have to have sex, and that reciprocity in relationships is freeing. Thus these findings underscored the pervasive nature of certain dominant discourses yet pointed to possible ways to make visible alternate ways of relating.

---

rages and the toll these rages have taken on her self-esteem. An intervention that focused on her feelings of responsibility, and at what she does to bring on his rages, would sustain the dominant discourse of women and men as equals, and view her as part of the problem. An intervention that focused on her feelings and the appropriateness of these feelings in what is an abusive situation can empower the client with the knowledge that this is abuse and that it is harmful to her. The latter intervention challenges the discourse that she is "equally" responsible or to blame and encourages the client to consider other options such as the husband seeking counseling for his rages or simply not putting up with his rages, even if this means leaving the relationship.

Concluding Remarks

This chapter identified three areas associated with gender and communication. We first looked at the importance of language in preserving certain views of women and men and how communication between women and men can reflect and reproduce conventional socialization patterns. For example, contrary to popular views, in mixed-sex dyads men take more of the air time than women. Nonverbal communication patterns also can reflect status and gender-related patterns that become manifest in areas such as touching and personal space. Finally, language in the form of dominant discourse was described and the importance of two prevalent discourses was illustrated—the "male sexual drive discourse" and the "women and men as equals discourse." These concepts are central to understanding clients' concerns and experiences as well as aspects of the counseling process itself.

The chapters in Part II of the book concern the application of gender theory to various aspects of practice. We now turn our attention to another important aspect of gender, namely, sexuality, and to its crucial role in therapeutic practice.

Discussion Questions

1. Select a friend of the same sex and a person of the other sex whom you see and converse with on a regular basis. For 1 week, use the categories described in the chapter and note what characterizes your conversations with each person. At the end of the week, read over your notes and think back over the many conversations. What themes can you identify? What conclusions can you draw about possible gendered patterns in your conversations?

2. Ask a person in your class to observe your conversation with a third person and to give you feedback on the patterns of verbal and nonverbal communication observed.

3. One way we continuously do gender is through what is articulated in dominant discourses. Often, subordinate discourses are lost or excluded from the classroom, the therapy setting, and the political arena because they arouse discomfort and fall outside of accepted ways of thinking and acting. What strategies or techniques could encourage these voices to be heard, tolerated, and valued in these different settings?

Suggested Readings

Crawford, M. (1995). *Talking difference: On gender and language.* Thousand Hills, CA: Sage. A thoughtful and concise assessment of the study of gender and language.

Tannen, D. (1990). *You just don't understand: Women and men in conversation.* New York: William Morrow. A bestseller that describes stereotypic ways women and men converse.

6 Sexuality and Gender

Frank, having recently begun an internship at a university counseling center, was not quite prepared for the presenting problem of Hal, a senior at the university. Hal's problem was that he rarely ejaculated during intercourse. He had no difficulty with achieving and maintaining erections but in almost all sexual encounters no matter how prolonged the intercourse, which was pleasurable, he experienced neither orgasm nor ejaculation. This was not the case with masturbation. Frank had difficulty seeing this as a problem when many men Hal's age had difficulty with premature ejaculation. In supervision, however, Frank came to understand the distress that Hal experienced.

Frank initially had fallen into a gender-stereotyped trap in counseling this young man. The trap is related to the myth that a man who can endlessly have intercourse without orgasm is a real man and the most desired object of women. (We talk about the myths of male sexuality in a later section of the chapter.) We cannot be sure what effect Frank's initial reaction of disbelief at Hal's distress had on Hal, or the development of the counseling relationship, as Hal did continue to work with Frank for several months.

Sexuality in our culture is so heavily laden with meanings and repercussions that many clients have a sexual concern when they begin therapy. This concern, coupled with the intimate nature of the counseling process, in a society that often confuses intimacy with sexuality makes an understanding of the connection between sexuality and gender crucial for effective counseling.

It would be easy to ignore or even deny the issue of sexuality in the counseling interaction. In fact, in discussing sexual concerns, therapists often use the power of their role to shield themselves from their own discomfort and perceived shortcomings, hiding behind their power. Because sexuality is an area that is fraught with discomfort in our culture, despite our obsession with it, we find that clients too are often reluctant and uncomfortable in bringing up matters related to sexuality. Taking the client's sexuality into consideration does not mean exploring its details, but rather being aware of the implications and determinants of the client's sexuality, and its relation to conceptions of gender.

In order to understand the place of sexuality in the life and psyche of clients, in this chapter we explore how gender socialization shapes women's and men's sexual experiences and their beliefs about those experiences. Also considered in the chapter is how views of sexuality relate to the many faces of gender and to gendered processes in counseling.

What Is Sexuality?

Sexuality is the total expression of the attempt to discharge energy from sexual drives. The way we dress, the way we talk, the way we flirt or don't flirt, the smells that excite us, the memories that impel us, and the rush of anticipation

---

BOX 6.1   What Exactly Is Sexuality?

1. When you ask someone about sexuality are you asking about:
   - Intimacy?
   - Eroticism?
   - Sexual activities?
2. When you think about your sexuality and its expression, do you think about it as a quality of yourself or as emerging out of or within a relationship?
3. How are you aware of displaying your sexuality (e.g., wearing certain clothes)? What needs are met by your behavior?
4. What are the characteristics of individuals whom you find sexually attractive (e.g., age, physical attributes, and so on)? What is the youngest and oldest person you would consider as a sexual partner? Would you consider a person of the same sex as yourself as a sexual partner?

---

when we hear a certain voice are all expressions of our sexuality. Who attracts us and how and the content of our fantasies are all a product of who we are sexually. Ultimately, who we are sexually is determined by our history, the circumstances of our life, and our biology (Box 6.1).

It is now generally accepted that our sexual object choice is biologically determined and there are fewer attempts to change that choice by the mental health profession (Morin, 1977). Homosexuality was removed from the *Diagnostic and Statistical Manual of Mental Disorders* (DSM) as a mental disorder in 1975. Rather, the emphasis in counseling is on helping people to accept their sexuality and to find contentment and satisfaction with it. Attempting to change sexual orientation frequently causes guilt and sets impossible goals for the client. (This is not to suggest that counselors should accept every behavior but rather should avoid attempting to press their values on clients.)

That sexuality is expressed in many ways is a fact. Its expression varies with age, sex, socioeconomic status, religion, ethnic or cultural background, geographical area, education, and likely a host of other factors. The questions in Box 6.1 underscore the complexities of sexuality. Being able to answer these questions for oneself as a therapist or counselor will facilitate bringing clarity to discussions of intimacy, eroticism, and sexual activity in therapeutic work with clients.

Gender Socialization and Sexual Expression

Gender and sexuality are intimately connected. How we wish to be sexually and how we express our sexual desires and inclinations are powerfully tied up with our gender socialization as women and men and what we perceive as important to social acceptance and reward. Examining the relationship between gender socialization and sexuality helps illuminate the close relationship between gender and sexuality.

Our sexual behavior is so intimately tied up with gender roles and expectations that it is very difficult to separate them. How we express our sexuality is a function of what we learn our culture expects from us as sexual beings. Women are usually expected to be comforting and nondemanding and thus are not supposed to be initiators in sexual matters. Men are supposed to be competitive and winners and therefore are often obsessed with being better and bigger in sexual matters. What our natural inclinations are often get overshadowed by what we believe our sexual expression "should be."

Gender socialization is subtle, insidious and far-reaching, influencing all of what we do and are. Frequently when individuals wish to behave contrary to their gender socialization, they are beset by a kind of gender angst or guilt. For example, the man who would like to be made love to, who wants to be taken, so to speak, often hides this wish because it would represent embracing a traditionally feminine role and that is unacceptable to him. The same is true of a woman who would like to be the aggressor and find her sexual prey but winds up following the usual rules and expectations. Even when she is not aware of following the rules, she is likely not acting out of her wishes but instead out of gender angst or guilt.

What Do Women and Men Experience?

What most of us experience with our sexuality is *pressure:* pressure to have sex, pressure not to have sex, pressure to perform spectacularly, pressure to be whatever our partners want or need, pressure to enjoy sex, pressure to desire sex, pressure to be responsible, pressure to be irresponsible, pressure to have and realize our fantasies, and pressure to do it right in a whole host of ways.

Ours is a culture obsessed with sex and sexual expression. From the selling of toothpaste to the blatantly sexual words and activities on MTV to the latest novel published, sex is big business (Tiefer, 1995). In the process of this exposure to sexual messages our internal set of guidelines for sexual expression is formed and rooted. Counselors do well to listen carefully so they understand the rules and expectations of their clients and can thus work with their clients' expectations when that is necessary.

In our overly sexualized culture it has become virtually impossible for people to grow up in the kind of virginal, naive, innocent, and charmingly natural way that once was the expectation. Children are warned, often at very tender ages, to be careful of predators; the news media and all its outlets are filled with sexual information; men and women are pictured in a variety of states of undress on posters, in magazines, on TV, and in the movies. Sex is constantly before us and we are usually unable to avoid it or its effect.

Romance is also constantly before us and we are urged to be romantic and flirtatious and seductive. This pressure to be romantic gets confused with sexual expression and is another element in the sexual difficulties in which our society finds itself. Many clients, usually women, complain that their partners are not romantic enough but rather are only interested in sex. Men are raised to see sex as a self-validation. For men, romance is presented as a way to get the sexual trophy rather than being presented as a way of life that is rewarding in and of itself, something women are pressured to accept as their life plot (Brooks, 1997; Ker Conway, 1995). The resulting difficulties are obvious and often are rooted in pervasive myths about female and male sexuality.

Women and Sexual Myths

To surrender in and to sex is the obligation if not the destiny of women. This myth is at the root of a great deal of the behavior of women in relation to men. Closely intertwined with the myth of surrender is the belief that sex is the province of men and that women are responsible for male sexuality, responsible for surrendering, and responsible for creating desire. A sexy woman, a heterosexual object, turns on men by how she looks and presents herself. Whether she enjoys "sex," experiences herself as sexual, has sexual desires, or prefers men as sexual partners appears mostly irrelevant. Both Marilyn Monroe and Lana Turner confessed in their biographies that they were not great companions in bed, and that sex was not that important to them. With the exception of Madonna, our culture has few positive examples of women who are sexual for themselves. Women who show sexual desire are labeled negatively and viewed as loose or insatiable—exaggerations that help limit women's sexuality to sex object, which is relatively safe on the one hand, or out of control, which is risky, on the other hand. Furthermore, a woman who demonstrates good sexual knowledge may be labeled promiscuous, even today (Wyatt & Riederle, 1994).

"Sex equals currency." Recall the example in Chapter 1 about dating and the assumption that if a man spends enough on a date, a woman owes him a sexual encounter in return. This myth perpetuates the view that women's bodies are objects for exchange and sex is a way that women get what they want or make themselves salable and marketable. Unfortunately, these stereotypic conceptions of women's sexuality influence some women's and men's sexual expression.

Women's knowledge of sexuality often is "constructed by ignorance and shame" (Tiefer, 1995, p. 129). For most women, learning about sexuality and sexual attractiveness comes from peers, from the covers of teen and women's magazines, and from the media. Many women learn from an early age that they are responded to as sexual, but they are not to act sexual (Westkott, 1986). To be an object, rather than a subject, means that many young girls are denied choice, intention, and the freedom to develop their own sense of their sexuality. Girls are often valued first as sexually attractive beings, an object that is chosen for its sexual desirability. Girls must be pretty and attractive to obtain love and happiness (Westkott, 1986).

This cultural situation presents a number of dilemmas for women. They are not socialized to verbalize their sexual intentions openly or to instruct their partners on what pleases them. Instead, as we explained in the previous chapter, women are taught that men orchestrate sex and initiate sexual contact. Many depend on male knowledge about safe sex or accept the male sexual drive discourse described in Chapter 5 and put themselves at risk for sexually transmitted diseases and pregnancy (Wyatt & Riederle, 1994). It is not unusual for women to come to counseling discouraged about their sex lives with partners, blaming themselves, and at a loss for what to do about it.

Often important in counseling is providing information, suggesting or lending out resources such as *The New Our Bodies, Ourselves* (Boston Women's Health Collective, 1996), *Lesbian Sex* (Loulan, 1984), or *Woman's Experience of Sex* (Kitzinger, 1985), providing a climate for dialogue, and encouraging self-knowledge. This process is particularly important for women such as Susanna, the client described in Chapter 3, who are socialized to be sexually passive and receptive and to look to relations with men for meaning in their life. Adolescents and young women, in particular, may need help in defining their own sexuality. Many consent to unwanted sex for such reasons as ignorance, the need to survive, to be accepted and nurtured, fear if they refused, and material gain, real or hoped for (Walker, 1997; Wyatt & Riederle, 1994). Once empowered, these young women can choose from other ways of sexual expression.

Although there is ferment and change and many women and girls are organizing their sexual lives in a manner that they deem satisfying to themselves, the power of the above myths is so pervasive that it will take generations before they are rooted out and a clear nonsexist sexuality will be present for women, and for men. It is essential for counselors to support women who seek ownership of their bodies and the right to express their sexual desires without shame and fear. Understanding how myths have kept women in a subservient position to men will be crucial in offering that support.

Men and Sexual Myths

As one would suspect, myths for women have to do with how to please men, whereas myths for men have to do with how men act. If one believes the ads, men are obsessed with sex and are constantly striving to measure up to some mythical standard. In the first edition of his book on male sexuality Zilbergeld (1978) described 10 beliefs guiding male sexuality to which a large percentage of women and men still subscribed despite overwhelming evidence to the contrary. These beliefs are presented in Box 6.2 on page 94. We strongly suggest that readers honestly respond to these assumptions and discuss their responses with

BOX 6.2   Sexuality Questionnaire

Please respond to the following items in three different ways. First, indicate the extent to which you agree with each statement by marking a number ranging from 1 to 5 using the definitions below. Second, if you marked a 3, 4, or 5, indicate with a "yes" or "no" whether your behavior has been influenced in some way by the belief that the statement is true. Think about your entire life, not just your current life and sexual experiences. Finally, indicate the extent to which *you think* others agree with the statement. Use the same scale, shown below.

1 = Strongly disagree
2 = Disagree
3 = Neutral or not sure
4 = Agree
5 = Strongly agree

Statements	(1) You agree?	(2) Influenced by?	(3) Others agree?
1. Men shouldn't express certain feelings.	_____	_____	_____
2. Sex is a performance.	_____	_____	_____
3. The man is responsible for orchestrating sex.	_____	_____	_____
4. A man always wants and is always ready to have sex.	_____	_____	_____
5. All physical contact must lead to sex.	_____	_____	_____
6. Real sex includes intercourse.	_____	_____	_____
7. Sex requires erection.	_____	_____	_____
8. Good sex involves increasing excitement terminated only by orgasm.	_____	_____	_____
9. Sex should be natural and spontaneous; you shouldn't have to learn.	_____	_____	_____
10. Birth control is the woman's responsibility.	_____	_____	_____

Items are adapted from Zilbergeld, B. (1978). *Male sexuality.* New York: Bantam Books.

their friends and other students. It is harmful to clients to perpetuate these myths in counseling.

Men are socialized to view sex as a performance. Therefore, how often, how much, how long, how loud, how overpowering, and how cosmic is of primary concern, particularly to their self-concept and to the stories they relate to male peers. You can imagine the shame many men carry around when they believe these myths and their sexual "performance" falls far short of what they think it should be. In these situations, obsessions about sex with women, any woman, results from needing to prove their masculinity.

Another male sexual myth is that it is "two feet long, hard as a rock, and can go all night" (Zilbergeld, 1978, p. 26). Not surprisingly, the reverse is typically the case. Moreover, after the age of 40, many men, at times, have problems getting and maintaining erections, particularly in times of stress or if they smoke and drink alcohol regularly. Coming to counseling with these kinds of issues is often difficult for men because all men are assumed to be sexually potent.

Sex is not supposed to be tied up with men's self-image or self-worth, but it is. Many young men are deeply concerned about who and what they are because they are not measuring up to the mythical standards of male sexuality. Seeing sex only as intercourse, men attempt to disconnect from their emotions. Consequently, many men are destined to be in a quandary when they undergo a variety of feelings and emotions as a result of their sexual experiences. The suppression of tender feelings of love and concern, which surface as a relationship develops, as well as of the timidity, fear, and reluctance surrounding such relationships, may cause a chain reaction often ending in anger and rage as the man is unable to adequately integrate all that he is feeling. (This may be the case for our client Rolando described in the next chapter.)

Suppression of emotions makes achieving intimacy through sexual interactions difficult. Intimacy gets detached from sex in the male mythic construct. This difficulty is further underscored by the belief that sex is a means for conquering another person and that such a conquest is somehow enhancing for the man (Good, Heppner, Hillenbrand-Gunn, & Wang, 1995; Truman, Tokar, & Fischer, 1996). It is thus somewhat plausible to see how sex and violent feelings could become connected, a topic we consider in the next chapter.

Counselors can help debunk these myths by offering information and by listening carefully. Often simply providing basic information of a statistical or sociological nature will help. Mentioning that the vast majority of American men believe their penises are too small can help give a client perspective on his self-perceptions. Also helpful is providing information on what is pleasurable for women sexually or what are usual problem areas for men. Suggesting books can be useful, in both providing clients with information and bringing discussions of sexuality and gender into the counseling. The first edition of *Male Sexuality* (Zilbergeld, 1978) and *Intimacy Between Men: How to Find and Keep Gay Love Relationships* (Driggs & Finn, 1990) may be useful in this regard. Frequently clients (and counselors) have many questions and too much shame or discomfort to attempt to get answers from their friends or parents. Encouraging clients to bring questions to sessions may be a way for the therapist to help the client realize how rare and how difficult these discussions may be.

What Is Supposed to Be Experienced?

Women and men, the sexual myths tell us, are supposed to experience breathtaking, groundbreaking cosmic sex. The earth is supposed to move, actually heave and catapult us heavenward. Nice image. Does it happen? Sometimes probably, maybe all the time for some, and never for others. The problem is in the expectation, not in the reality. If we were satisfied with our sexuality that would be tantamount to finding the Holy Grail. Unfortunately, a great many people are not satisfied nor content with their sexual expression. Moreover, many hold the belief that good sex comes naturally. As Tiefer (1995), a well-known sexologist, explains, "What always amazes me is people who want to have exciting and gratifying sex but who think it just comes 'naturally' without practice or knowledge. I'm sorry, but no one can play Rachmaninoff without putting in a lot of piano practice" (p. 134).

What Could Be Experienced?

What people could experience sexually is a calmer, more satisfying, and more consciously congruent sexual side of themselves. Aiding people in expressing themselves more naturally and responsibly often emerges as a therapeutic goal. In the sexual realm, this would necessitate liberation from societal demands and fantasized expectations. Demands that an individual be one way or another or only act in a particular manner may feel like rules. However, when there is informed, intelligent consent between people as to how they wish to interact sexually, it is not the prerogative of society to interfere with that expression except in cases of coercion and exploitation. Discussing the great variety of sexual expression with a client is a good way for a counselor to begin dispelling myths. Sexual intercourse is just one form of sexual expression and does not represent "sex" or the most pleasurable aspect of sex for many people. Same-sex partners consider what they do "sexual intercourse," for example, and express their sexuality in other ways. Also, few women experience orgasm through intercourse (Tiefer, 1995). Counselors empower clients through facilitating and guiding, not through policing, especially when sexuality is concerned.

Within the context of sexuality, issues of power, dependence, affection, and intimacy need to be considered, particularly how these issues are related to gender. Although important concerns in all relationships, these issues are frequently most obvious in the sexual interactions of people. Relationships can be analyzed on the dimensions of power and affection (Foa, 1961). An analysis of who is in charge and in charge of what provides significant information on what is going on and how the parties are responding. For example, after careful analysis of how power and dependence are tied together, Gilbert (1987a) postulated that an important component of male abuse of women results from a man's realizing his profound dependence on a woman; the attendant rage derives from internalized beliefs associated with the male gender role proscribing dependence of any kind. (This dynamic is similar to the male gender role dysfunction described in Chapter 7.) So, who is dependent on whom is a most important question in understanding relationships.

The affective element in relationships also needs to be examined, especially who is providing affection and whether or not it is satisfying. Finally, understanding intimacy as a product of power, dependence, affect, and affection is essential in understanding what transpires in a relationship. The delicate titration of all relationship components determines the level of intimacy.

The Dark Side of Gender and Sexuality

Just as gendered myths that surround sexuality interfere with its pleasurable expression, distorted and destructive uses of gendered sexuality create pain and distress for many people. These qualities are being referred to as the dark side of gender and sexuality.

Hostile Environment

Sexuality, a way for people to join together in an enhancing mutuality, can become a means for joining people in a hurtful if not destructive manner when the purpose of the sexual expression is the domination of one person by another. The phrase "hostile environment" covers a multitude of situations in which one person is made to feel threatened by another through the use of subtle or blatant sexual behaviors. This threatened feeling is different from feeling intimidated or uncomfortable, and it is the sense of threat to some area of well-being that defines the hostile environment (Paludi & Barickman, 1991).

Examples of how one person creates, or is in danger of creating, a hostile environment are a manager who comments excessively on an employee's appearance or suggests non–work-oriented socializing, the faculty member who reveals too much personal sexual history, or the therapist who continually asks questions about the client's sexual interactions. Such situations are characterized by disparities in power, be it financial, organizational, physical, or gender role. Power is usually abused for the benefit of the individual holding the power. An example is a male counselor having doubts about his heterosexuality who goes to a male supervisor to consult on a case involving a gay client and being subtly propositioned by that counselor to explore his homosexual feelings with a caring and concerned adult. (Further discussion on sexual harassment appears in the next chapter.)

The dark side of sexuality also subsumes injustices like date rape and consent to unwanted sex. The power of the male partner in conjunction with a sense of entitlement can cause an enforced sexual interaction. Women clients bring to counseling their experiences of date rapes and of the hostile environment perpetuated by the climate of seduction so often promoted in social interactions. This seduction is not to be confused with flirting, which can be charming and enjoyable; the hardened attempt to use another person sexually for the primary benefit of the user can often be disguised as flirting, but the user's intent is hostile and dehumanizing.

Gender socialization affects communication regarding sexuality and the negotiation of safer sex. For example, how well men subscribe to traditional beliefs is an important predictor of condom use among heterosexual men (Pleck, Sonnenstein, & Ku, 1993). In addition, two heterosexual people being committed to each other does not necessarily mean that a male partner will be committed to safe sex practices (Amaro, 1995). Women asking for safe sex may be heard by some men as a questioning of their male prerogative and of how commitment is defined in the relationship. Women who have been sexualized and who have not had a chance to have their own life are more likely to be passive and dominated.

Pornography

Pornography is not uniform and it is not unitary. However, where it maintains stereotypes and promotes inequitable power relationships it is destructive (Stock, 1997). Many believe that pornography has no redeeming social value (e.g., MacKinnon, 1995). Others contend that women would be more harmed from the repression of sexually explicit material than from their free expression (e.g., Tiefer, 1995). Individuals need to make up their own minds as to the role or acceptability of pornography in their lives. Pornography that depicts, and thus promotes, abuse and misuse of those who are most vulnerable, as in the case of children, is not a positive expression of sexuality.

Sexual Abuse of Children

The sexual abuse of children is an enormous problem. More people are reporting those committing incest and sexual abuse (Courtois, 1988). In working with adults who have been sexually abused children and in working with abusers who are currently in therapy, counselors and therapists see the enormous problems, from the stringent legal requirements to report suspected abuse in many states to the powerful issues and emotions that such abuse raises in and for them. Dealing with abuse is painful and complicated for both counselors and clients.

Sexuality has always had a dark side for reasons that are not always discernible or necessary to understand. On occasion, reasons may help in tempering a reaction that, although justified by appropriate outrage, may not lead to a positive outcome for the victim or the perpetrator. Understanding the connection between gender and sexuality in our culture is of some aid to the counselor in grasping difficult aspects of sexual expression.

The Meaning of Sexuality

Our sexuality is intimately tied up with our sense of self and our relationships with others. Even if we are not active sexually or are sexually repressed, how we see ourselves and how we interact with others is affected by who we are, which is influenced by who we are sexually. Ours is a sexually charged culture and the trappings and entrapments of sex are unavoidable. Sexual expression is an important part of gender socialization and therefore we are affected directly and indirectly by our sexuality and cultural expectations about it. It is not possible to see endless advertisements of men and women in sexualized poses in their underwear without being affected by them. Erotic arousal may not always be the result but likely invidious comparisons are frequently made. The simple presence of such sexual data gives us the message that this is important stuff and we should want more of it in all its guises.

Interestingly, it has only been during this time of HIV/AIDS that the responsibilities inherent in male sexuality have become important. To be a responsible sexual partner or responsible sexual person necessitates respect for others as well as for oneself. When this respect is demanded because of potentially odious consequences, individuals may respond with grudging compliance or with blatant disregard of their responsibilities. Without respect for oneself and for the rights of others, sexuality will create chaos and pain in relationships and in our culture.

When sexuality becomes a means toward narcissistic gratification rather than an end of joyous self-expression, the possibility of responsible behavior is startlingly diminished. This situation becomes obvious in therapy, especially in couples counseling, when partners are unable to recognize how their nonrelational sexual pattern cripples their vain attempts to connect to one another (Brooks, 1997; Levant & Brooks, 1997).

The assumed entitlement of men (Gilbert & Scher, 1992) and the assumed surrender of women prepare the way for problems in being together. This is too frequently the case in gay, lesbian, and heterosexual relationships even when sexual activity is not a part of the interaction. It is hard to connect to another person in consistently satisfying ways when one feels superior or inferior. Our sexuality and the way it is influenced by our culture suggests that dominance and submission are intimately tied up with how we are sexually and what our appropriate gender role-related sexual behaviors should be. This situation almost guarantees problems in interaction and connection.

Having an ecstatic, joyous, and fun experience is a major part of what mature and healthy sexuality can and should provide us. Sexuality has to do with life and joy. How we express it is individual and ought to be. However, relishing and using it well is a universal gift and perhaps even a right. Although being sexual can be a joyous and life-sustaining experience, this may not be everyone's experience for reasons ranging from cultural practices and individual preferences to sexual abuse and trauma. Our responsibilities toward others in our sexual expression are paramount, as far too many individuals have this right taken away from them through some form of sexual abuse. The expression of our sexuality has potential to cause pain and destruction for ourselves and for others. We must be careful and thoughtful in our understanding of our sexuality so that we behave reasonably and responsibly. In counseling we must be prepared to assist clients with achieving a deeper and more humane understanding of how and when to express their sexual selves.

Effective Counseling

Effective counseling requires knowing that the qualities of understanding, empathy, and acceptance, coupled with knowledge of the varieties of sexual behavior and experience, are key to assisting clients in exploring and satisfying their sexuality. Counselors must be comfortable with their own sexuality and as honest as possible with themselves and with their clients in appropriate ways (Scher, 1992). They must be willing to accept those different from themselves. As with Frank, the counselor introduced at the beginning of this chapter, being aware of what myths one has internalized and accepted as reality is important. Lacking knowledge of prevalent myths about sexuality puts counselors in the position of being blind-sided by clients whose presenting problems necessitate triumphing over those myths. The questions presented in Box 6.3 may be helpful for effective therapeutic work by identifying blind spots and areas that often are not sufficiently considered.

Basic to working successfully with clients in regard to their sexuality is the quality of nonjudgmental acceptance. The ways in which counselors are called on to be nonjudgmental are surprising in their variety. For example, a male therapist once counseled a male college student who, after initially getting acquainted, seemed terribly distressed. He struggled and struggled to tell the counselor a secret that made him feel terribly guilty. He became agitated, sweaty, began to hyperventilate, and was wringing his hands. The counselor was busy making all sorts of assumptions about what the secret was: being homosexual, fathering a child, committing rape, while the client continued to suffer with revealing his terrible secret. Finally, the client blurted out with a cascade of tears and sobs, "I masturbate." The counselor was literally breathless with surprise and had to recover quickly so that he did not appear to scoff at the client's concern.

How to be nonjudgmental is difficult, however. We are raised with all sorts of prescriptions and proscriptions about our sexuality. We need to examine our history, beliefs, values, and expectations in order to be as knowledgeable about

BOX 6.3 Questions about Sexuality Helpful for Counselors and Therapists to Consider

1. What sexual topics do you feel comfortable talking about with a client? Which are less comfortable? Which topics do you avoid?
2. If a client reports that a new sexual partner is not sexually satisfying, what would you suggest the client do?
3. How would you view a female client of your own age who is a virgin? A male client of your own age?
4. Do you view yourself and people you know as either heterosexual or homosexual? Does the notion of bisexuality make sense in view of your experiences, either personally or for your clients?
5. What is your personal theory as to why some people are gay?
6. A gay male couple is choosing to refrain from sex because of HIV or AIDS, and want your opinion on whether the quality of intimacy will be affected. What would you say?
7. In your experience, what factors make it more difficult for gay male partners to maintain their relationship? For lesbian partners?
8. A parent wants to know how counselors determine and explain to a child what it means to be "old enough" or mature enough to be sexually active?
   - What cultural values may be involved?
   - Would a child's biological sex make a difference in making this determination?
   - Do you think that a father would view this differently from a mother?
9. A parent wants to know if sex education or discussions of sex encourage children to engage in sexual activities. What would you say?
10. A client wants to know if most people in committed relationships are monogamous? Whether you think monogamy in committed relationships is desirable? And whether it is sustainable? What would you say?
11. Do you feel that it is necessary to have an orgasm to enjoy sex? In your opinion, what is the most enjoyable part of a sexual experience?
12. Are current discourses on gender politics in danger of "sanitizing" sex and emptying sex of eroticism?
13. In your opinion, has women's increased sense of their own sexuality influenced their experience of sex?

ourselves as possible and, in the process, about others, (see the case example on Susanna presented in Chapter 3). Fooling oneself about one's own sexuality is surprisingly easy and widespread. Reading in areas of sexual expression that are different from our own is often a helpful exercise and can help us to explore our values and judgments. Personal therapy, helpful in so many other ways, can assist in getting a better take on our sexuality. Reading the works of sex therapists, going to workshops, paying attention to the sexual expressions of one's culture, and listening carefully to all those one meets are ways of expanding, deepening, and humanizing our grasp of sexuality.

Also crucial is knowing the ins and outs of sexuality. This means doing a good deal of reading and study about sex itself, how it is expressed, what the consequences of its expression are, and what kinds of questions one may need to answer. A variety of excellent resources are available (e.g., Hyde, 1990; Tiefer, 1995). Also important is learning the contemporary, and often changing, slang about sex and contemporary mores of the young regarding dating, relationships, and sexual expression. Members of different generations may see the same things in vastly different ways. It is usually a good idea to have a variety of reading suggestions, especially for young people, which can help clients better understand their sexuality and its expression. The content of the readings might change, and one must keep up with the latest literature.

Another component of effective counseling is understanding the relationship between sexuality and gender. Gender socialization and the "doing of gender" influence and determine the expression of sexuality in both clients and therapists, including their interactions in the therapeutic setting. Counselors and therapists are as susceptible as everyone else to the dark expressions of sexuality. These issues are explored in later chapters.

Understanding the context of sexual expression and accepting it are also mandatory. There are forces in the culture that demand more stringent controls and sanctions for those who choose to be sexually active or whose choice of sexual expression does not fit restricted and limited views of what is appropriate in human behavior. Gay and lesbian adolescents especially are at risk. Archaic laws and restrictions can become weapons of hatred whose power is great and destructive impact significant.

Finally, as with most other areas of counseling, it is essential not to be afraid. If therapists fear sexuality, clients will be unable to feel comfortable and trust the counselor and the therapeutic relationship. A somewhat unusual example illustrates the value in a counselor's comfort with a client's sexual or apparent sexual behavior.

The client, a young man, arrived for his sessions wearing progressively fewer garments. First his socks disappeared, then his shoes, then his shirt, then his trousers (replaced by shorts), then his T-shirt. Then the shorts got shorter. The male counselor did not comment on the abbreviated costumes but did adjust the thermostat. Therapy appeared to be going well despite the changes in costume. At the point where nudity seemed in the offing, suddenly more garments were slowly added and the counseling ended with the client fully dressed. In later sessions it became clear that the male client was expressing his gradual psychological revelation of himself through his revealing his body, an important metaphor in his own life. In this case the counselor was able to control his discomfort with the situation and allowed it to run its course as it appeared secondary to the work that was necessary for successful completion of the counseling process. However, he might also have used the strength of the therapeutic relationship to explore sooner the dynamics that the removal of clothing represented in a manner facilitative to the client's understanding of himself.

Concluding Remarks

This chapter continued the discussion of language and dominant discourses and extended it to the language and discourses (myths) used in describing female and male sexuality. We discussed the place of sexuality in the life and psyche of clients and therapists and how gender socialization shapes women's and men's sexual experiences and their beliefs about those experiences. We also emphasized how crucial it is for counselors and therapists to be knowledgeable about sexuality and to be comfortable with their own sexuality.

Discussion Questions

1. What myths, assumptions, or personal experiences in the area of sexuality might influence the effectiveness of your work with clients? Identify at least four. Based on readings, discussion, and your own thoughts, how might you constructively work on changing this within yourself?

2. A couple comes to see you because they are having a conflict in their sexual relationship. He wants to explore and act out some bondage fantasies. She does not. They want your assistance. What are your immediate reactions? What would you say? Now imagine their desires reversed. What are your immediate reactions? What would you say? Does your gender socialization affect your responses? How?

Suggested Readings

Sprecher, S., & McKinney, K. (1993). *Sexuality.* Newbury Park, CA: Sage. A comprehensive account of current theory and research in the area of sexuality that pays close attention to sexual satisfaction and sexual coercion.

Tiefer, L. (1995). *Sex is not a natural act and other essays.* Boulder, CO: Westview Press. This highly readable book presents a basis for a more human and compassionate model of female and male sexuality, one which moves away from biomedical models of orgasm and phallocentrism.

7

Gender Issues Brought by Clients

Rolando, a stylishly dressed man, comes to see you. He complains of bouts of anger, depression, and boredom and describes a series of recent crises. His story relates an inability to sustain close personal relationships, which has persisted since early adolescence, as well as a history of inconsistent performance and acting out behavior in school and on the job. He describes himself as becoming involved quickly and often in romantic relationships, but experiencing a growing uneasiness as each relationship becomes "heavy." Prior to this feeling, he describes himself as being overly attentive. Once the uneasiness sets in, he becomes progressively irritable and demanding and picks fights, which on one occasion became physically violent. "I either drive them away or I walk away," he says, referring to the lovers in his life. "And it has been that way for as long as I can remember." (Adapted from Estrada, 1989)

Is Rolando's sex and resulting gender socialization important in understanding his presenting concerns about depression, anger, and alienation? Does it matter in counseling Rolando whether his lovers are women or men? Would therapy with Rolando be less effective if the therapist lacked an understanding of how gender issues enter counseling through this client's presenting concerns? Does the counselor need to understand Rolando's ethnic background?

Several gender issues may pertain to this case. Male socialization, it will be recalled, emphasizes concealing emotions, especially feelings of pain, being successful at work, looking to women for nurturance, and needing no one.

- Rolando's difficulty in establishing close personal relationships, for example, may relate to the stereotypic view that men should control and dominate interactions with women and other men. Withholding themselves in relationships can provide an illusion of an independent stance that reinforces a man's dominant position, but also keeps him emotionally remote and disconnected.
- Rolando may have been sexually abused as a child, an experience that he has been unable to talk about, and which leaves him feeling vulnerable, confused, depressed, and angry. If this were the case, Rolando's emotional difficulties would be compounded by the fact that repression and dissociation are common survival strategies in response to trauma.
- His poor work performance may leave Rolando feeling financially at risk. His acting out behavior, which further jeopardizes his achieving financial security, may come out of anger and rage associated with his sense of failure as a man.
- If Rolando's partners are women, he may also be looking for validation of himself as a man through his sexual relations with them. His profound sense of alienation and failure may leave him feeling needy and dependent on women for strength, on the one hand, but furious that he feels so dependent on women, on the other hand.

- If his partners are men, or mostly men, the dynamics of homophobia and heterosexism need to be considered. As mentioned in an earlier chapter, homophobia is the irrational fear, intolerance, and in its most severe form, hatred, of people who are gay or lesbian (Pharr, 1988). This prejudice leads to persistent beliefs in negative stereotypes toward gays and lesbians, and supports discriminating actions against these groups in areas such as jobs, housing, and child custody. Lesbians and gays, socialized in the same values, often internalize these negative stereotypes and develop some degree of self-hatred or low self-esteem, a form of internalized homophobia (McCarn & Fassinger, 1995), which Rolando may be experiencing.

When homophobia is combined with cultural and institutional power, the result is heterosexism, the belief in the inherent superiority of heterosexuality and its right to dominance. This is analogous to sexist and racist attitudes, which when combined with the cultural and institutional power to enforce these attitudes, results in sexism and racism. Heterosexism can have a powerful influence on a man's (or woman's) choice to envision, enter, or stay in a relationship with a same-sex partner. For gays or lesbians, being "out" with family or friends as well as being "out" on the job can have devastating repercussions for career advancement or even the right to remain employed. Yet choosing to "be discreet" can also have personal costs in terms of feeling isolated, compartmentalized, and unaffirmed (Eldridge, 1987). If this were the case for Rolando, his emotional difficulties could be compounded by coping strategies customary among gay men.

Gender Issues and Clients' Presenting Concerns

This chapter describes some of the gender issues that counselors and therapists need to understand to work effectively. In working with Rolando, for example, counselors need to know how aspects of male socialization can inform their work and facilitate this client's understanding of his own experiences.

An important goal of the chapter is to help readers understand that gender issues are not "women's issues." Both men and women experience gender issues; all gender issues relate to the context of women's and men's lives and how they are shaped and molded as gendered beings. That certain issues appear more prevalent for one sex than the other sex reflects differential socialization processes and societal expectations and practices. For example, women more than men struggle with conflict between their parenting and occupational roles, not because women are anxious and relational by nature, but because the culture expects women to be the primary caregivers regardless of their other life roles. Men more than women struggle with isolation and alienation because the culture expects "real" men to need no one and glorifies the notion of stoic, self-contained men.

We have selected a subset of gender issues that we believe are common in counseling women and men. These are divided into three broad categories. The first is a brief section on gender issues associated with women's sexual attractiveness and beauty, topics covered extensively in other sources (see Attie & Brooks-Gunn, 1989; Freedman, 1986; Johnston, 1997; Wolf, 1992). The remaining two are more extensive sections on gender issues associated with male gender role strain, and gender issues associated with integrating work and family life, respectively. Earlier chapters introduced aspects of these three gender issues, especially the discussion in Chapter 2 on gender socialization, in Chapter 5 on dominant discourse themes, and in Chapter 6 on gender and sexuality.

Gender Issues Associated with Women's Sexual Attractiveness and Beauty

A number of gender issues center around the concept of women's attractiveness and beauty. In this section we mainly focus on issues concerning dieting and staying attractive. Historically, being valued and desired by men was an important component of a woman's self-concept because women's worth to men was seen in terms of their virginity, their physical characteristics, and their ability to please, satisfy, and serve men (Westkott, 1986). One result of these gendered processes is narrow definitions of female attractiveness. Another is a good deal of shame and ignorance on the part of women about their own bodies (Tiefer, 1995).

Women's sexuality is closely tied to women's beauty and women's body image. The narrow cultural definitions of female beauty in our society, coupled with aggressive advertising campaigns, make many women feel unattractive, while at the same time striving to be more attractive. Women more than men spend a great deal of time worrying about their appearance, including their weight. Concerns about weight and thinness are now viewed as chronic stressors in women's lives, crossing lines of race, ethnicity, and class (Mintz & Betz, 1988; Rodin, Silberstein, & Striegel-Moore, 1985). Many women in the normal weight range diet as a lifestyle and nearly all women who participate in expensive liquid diets regain the weight within a year. Chronic dieting is dangerous to one's health and to one's self-esteem. The destructive effects of the ideal of female beauty include damage to women's self-concept, depression, chronic dieting, eating disorders such as bulimia and anorexia nervosa, and the misuse of medical procedures such as cosmetic surgery, liposuction, and estrogen replacement therapy (National Women's Health Network, 1989).

Male Gender Role Strain and Its Attendant Gender Issues

Clatterbaugh (1990), Levant and Brooks (1997), among others, conclude that "without question" the traditional system of male dominance affects men negatively. "Even if men themselves are not oppressed, those who assume a traditional masculine role tend to pay a price" (Clatterbaugh, 1990, p. 117). Pleck (1995) uses the paradigm of gender role strain to describe men's experiences of attempting to meet societal role definitions that are not only impossible to meet but also psychologically unhealthy and even dysfunctional. His strain paradigm, which grows out of theoretical views of gender construction, postulates that molding children to develop personality and behavioral traits prescribed by gender roles creates gender role strain in the form of male gender role "discrepancy" and male gender role dysfunction.

Discrepancy Strain, Male Emotional Restrictiveness, and Male Shame

Discrepancy strain occurs when men or women fail to live up to the standards, expectation, and norms of their traditional gender role. Not conforming to standards has negative consequences for how women or men are perceived and valued by significant others as well as for their self-esteem and internalized self-judgments (Pleck, 1995). Areas of discrepancy strain often change as the girl or boy develops and the context of the individual's life changes. For example, in our culture more strain may occur earlier in life from a boy's being small and unathletic and later in life by a man's being underemployed or unemployed, not feeling powerful in his life, or feeling trapped in a job he hates.

Normative socialization processes use many means to shape the lives of women and men. Krugman (1995) views shame, or the feelings that arise when one experiences oneself as deficient in an important feature of self-identity, as one of the more powerful socialization tools, particularly for boys and men. The author argues that the processes of normal male socialization leave many boys "shame-sensitive," a psychological state that inhibits their maturation and their ability to integrate normative shame responses. According to Krugman, because shame, or even the possibility of shame, so significantly threatens the security of a man's sense of self, boys are in danger of failing to develop a sense of self that can withstand normal threats to the ego. "Rather than being able to tolerate and modulate shame states, males are likely to react with avoidance, compensatory behaviors, and primitive fight-flight responses," such as acting cool, distancing oneself emotionally, minimizing and denying vulnerable feelings, engaging in acts of rage, and abusing drugs and alcohol (p. 100).

Male emotional restrictiveness and proneness to shame sensitivity, tied to a learned inability to deal with one's emotions, culminate in problem areas associated with discrepancy strain. Traditional standards and ideals for male development in many cultures require that boys and men restrict themselves emotionally. The characteristics associated with being emotionally sensitive and expressive, intimate, and connected interpersonally are characteristics assigned to the female role and thus stereotypically viewed as belonging exclusively to the female world. Masculine men, "real men," need no one. Recall the "sturdy oak" described in Chapter 2. In reality, male independence (and female dependence) is mainly an illusion that both women and men "do gender" to create and perpetuate. Men stereotypically depend on women to express their sensitivity for them (Pleck, 1981b) and to provide the nurturance that they themselves are often unable to give (Pogrebin, 1983). This dynamic shows itself often in counseling couples.

A husband who lacks confidence may fear that sharing his experiences and feelings with his spouse will lower her opinion of him as a man. Rather than engaging in an interdependent process with her, which might enhance mutuality in the relationship as well as his personal well-being, the man in this example may act distant, let his wife initiate contact with him, and then view the interaction as reflective of her needs. The wife may hold the same view because she needs to see her spouse as strong and confident. This example describes a familiar gender dynamic in which men look to women to give them strength but neither sex acknowledges women's role in enhancing men's well-being.

Another aspect of men viewing themselves as not needing anyone is projecting on women a need to depend on men. For example, many men who see women as wanting too much from them may, in fact, themselves desire a great deal of emotional support and understanding from women which they are not willing or able to see. A case in point is a heterosexual couple who sought counseling. They had been dating for over a year while he had been trying to get out of a marriage with "an extremely dependent wife" whose family of origin was from South America. This man had fallen in love with an independent career women "who brought him incredible happiness." After much agony and many discussions, he decided he could not leave his wife, regardless of how miserable the marriage, because she needed him too much. In hearing more about the marital relationship, however, it became clear that he was dependent on her needing him. He encouraged her to talk everything over with him and to leave all decisions to him. This talking consumed much of his time away from work and provided him with an emotional closeness and sense of well-being otherwise absent in his life.

Discrepancy strain and feelings of shame also arise with respect to men's provider role. This can occur in men who define their sense of self by the provider role, and hence to an authoritarian system in which they become controlled by the conditions of employment and see other men as their rivals (O'Neil, Good, & Holmes, 1995; Pleck, 1981b). Successful men are supposed to be successful breadwinners, despite the physical and emotional costs involved. Because society provides the definitions of "success," definitions that may be inappropriate or unattainable by most men, many men are viewed as not particularly good providers. Men who choose other paths, and who seek close and loving relations with their families and partners are viewed as suspect, and run the risk of being labeled as unambitious, househusbands, or Mr. Mom. (Chapter 1 referred to the age-old practice of keeping women and men in their "traditional" places by accusing them of becoming the "opposite sex" when they attempted to broaden their human qualities to include love and work.)

It is crucial for men who seek counseling to understand the sources of their discrepancy strain or their shame. Useful for these kinds of discussions in counseling are items from the Brannon scale reproduced in Chapter 2. Another helpful scale is the Gender Role Journey Measure (GRJM) developed by Jim O'Neil and his colleagues (O'Neil, Egan, Owen, & Murray, 1993).

The Gender Role Journey Measure (GRJM; O'Neil et al., 1993) reflects the view that an individual's internalized gender ideology can change, progressing stage by stage, from endorsing traditional, sex-segregated world views to viewing oneself and one's world in less restrictive and sexist ways. Its three stages, illustrated in Box 7.1, are acceptance of traditional gender roles, gender role am-

---

BOX 7.1   Items from the Gender Role Journey Measure

Traditional Gender Roles

1. Men should make the major money decisions for a family.
2. Feminists have caused the problems between women and men.
3. I feel upset when people don't accept men as superior to women.
4. It is not masculine for men to show weakness.

Gender Role Ambivalence

1. I sometimes feel confused about gender roles.
2. I sometimes feel confused about my role as a man or woman.
3. I am afraid to question why I am restricted from doing things because of being male or female.

Personal-Professional Activism

1. I believe that sexism hurts women and men.
2. I have taken some actions in my life to reduce sexism.
3. I feel inner strength and power because of my gender role freedom.
4. I feel less restricted because of gender role changes I am making.

Respondents use a 5-point Likert scale to report the degree to which each of the statements is 1 (not at all true for me) to 5 (very true for me). A lower score on the first two scales and a higher score on the third scale reflect greater progress on the gender role journey.

Source: O'Neil, J. M., Egan, J., Owen, S. V., & Murray, V. M. (1993). The Gender Role Journey Measure: Scale development and psychometric evaluation. *Sex Roles, 28,* (3/4), 167–185. Used with permission of the author and Plenum Publishing.

bivalence, and personal-professional activism. The GRJM can be used with men and women and thus also provides therapists with a tool for discussing important relationship issues related to gender.

Dysfunction Strain, Male Prerogative, and Violence against Women

Dysfunction strain refers to "the idea that the fulfillment of gender role standards can have negative consequences because the behaviors and characteristics these standards prescribe can be inherently dysfunctional in the sense of being associated with negative outcomes either for the male himself or for others" (Pleck, 1995, pp. 16–17). Several areas of research support this idea, particularly research concerning male entitlement to power over women, including women's bodies.

Male Prerogative.   In most cultures, boys and men are more highly valued than girls and women. The extent of this differential evaluation may vary, but its result is always to grant men more power, freedom, and privilege than women (Kahn, 1984). A clear example of this reality is reflected in the conversations with four teenagers described by Fine and Macpherson (1994): "Adolescence for these four young women was about adventures of males and the constraints on females. . . . Their version of feminism was about equal access to being men" (p. 220). (Two of these young women were African American, one Korean American, and one European American.)

Generally speaking, men in many societies grow up with feelings of confidence and specialness granted them simply because they are born male. This specialness is an essential aspect of what has become known as male prerogative and entitlement (Gilbert, 1987a). Male prerogative encourages both women and men to feel that what men do or want to do takes precedence over the needs of women and should not be questioned. The basic sentiment here is that, "Men have a right to do what they want to do and women who interfere need to learn their place." For men whose sense of self is closely tied to what they have come to believe are men's prerogatives, especially in relation to women, even small losses of advantage or deference can be experienced as large threats to men's rights and privileges (Goode, 1982).

Frank Rich (1994), commenting on the *Sports Illustrated* annual swimsuit issue, noted that men will not easily give up the old order in which men call the shots and women submit without protest. "Much as we want to believe that this hierarchy has been discredited—and despite all the laws written to dismantle it—old habits die hard. . . . Time Warner has too much invested in the message 'Women are Property' to give it up without a fight" (p. E13).

Dynamics associated with male prerogative often emerge in counseling with couples. An example is a young professional Latina woman who came to counseling with her Latino boyfriend of several years because she felt too dependent on him and wanted to live on her own for awhile and not see him on a regular basis. She carefully and lovingly explained to him how she needed to feel strong in herself before entering into a marriage with him. He had a difficult time hearing this, however. His immediate response was, "Do it if you want, but that's the end of our relationship." Later in the session he referred to her as wanting to whore around, a motivation that apparently made sense from his perspective, but it showed a profound lack of understanding of his dating partner. A woman wanting and needing to be strong in herself simply did not compute for him: "It just was not necessary for a woman." He was satisfied with the relationship and was highly suspect of her motivations to change things. He was also threatened by her wanting to develop a more independent sense of self and felt confused about these feelings and where they were coming from.

In later sessions it became clear that he equated a woman wanting to be strong for herself as a woman who did not need a man. A rule of thumb in counseling is that when a male client has a knee jerk reaction to a woman's legitimate need for independence, devalues such needs by accusing the female partner of dishonorable motivations, or uses patronizing tones, it is likely that feelings of male prerogative have surfaced and need to be recognized from his perspective and worked through.

Another crucial aspect of male prerogative must be understood by therapists. The notion that "women are men's property" relates not only to male entitlement to power over women but also to male entitlement to women's bodies, whether in a swimsuit issue of *Sports Illustrated,* the broadcast media, or real life. Earlier chapters described the strong association between sexuality and power and, in particular, the centrality of the male sexual drive discourse to views of male power. In the past 10 years sexual harassment, acquaintance rape, and sexual abuse of children have exploded into public consciousness. Romantic partners were implicated in 50 percent to 57 percent of sexual assaults reported by college-age and adult women (Koss, 1990). Movies such as *Dolores Claiborne, Priest, Prince of Tides,* and *The Spitfire Grill* have made visible the trauma of childhood sexual abuse.

Sexual Harassment. A female client comes to see you and wonders if she is being subjected to sexual harassment by her boss. He keeps asking her to go to dinner with him, corners her in the office to tell her his personal problems with his ex-wife, and just lately has started calling her at home. The client, you notice, is quite plain and unattractive. Could this be sexual harassment?

A male client you have been seeing asks your opinion about some written complaints he received from the two female students in his research group. The client, who is dealing with the aftermath of a messy divorce, teaches in a physics department. The letter from the two students states that he belittles their contributions to group discussions, excludes them from professional meetings away from campus, and attributes their research findings to other group members. Could this be sexual harassment or another form of sex discrimination?

Sexual harassment, most broadly defined, refers to the unwanted imposition of sexual requirements in the context of unequal power. Sexual harassment is about power and the need to dominate; it is not about physical attraction

(MacKinnon, 1979). It occurs in many forms—innuendo, "friendly harassment," overt sexual comments, unwanted touching, or even sexual coercion. Sexual harassment also includes subtle forms of intimidation—lingering, sexually suggestive remarks, and behaviors and attitudes that demean or exclude women—that create a "hostile environment" and unreasonably interfere with an individual's performance. As one client noted, "It's the daily little insults that wear you down. We are expected to go along with jokes about women's sexuality or stupidity, pinups in the office, demeaning attitudes, lewd remarks, and 'joking' requests for sexual intimacy."

Harassment remains a common workplace experience for women (Gutek, 1986, 1993; O'Donohue, 1997). Prevalence figures suggest that 53 percent of women have been harassed at some point in their working lives, and about 10 percent have quit a job because of sexual harassment (Gutek, 1993; O'Donohue, 1997). Women in nontraditional jobs and fields (e.g., truck drivers, neurosurgeons, military, engineers) are especially likely to be harassed (Gutek, 1993; Rose & Larwood, 1988). The figures in university settings are comparable, with approximately 30 percent of undergraduate women experiencing sexual harassment from at least one of their instructors during their college careers (Backman & Backman, 1997; Paludi & Barickman, 1991; Verba, 1983). Reports from other sources indicate that sexual harassment by male peers begins in elementary school and continues through the middle school and high school years (American Association of University Women, 1991; Pipher, 1994). Such harassing experiences have negative consequences for girls and women, dampening their creative spirit and self-esteem, and interfering with educational and career goals (Paludi & Barickman, 1991).

Few women sexually harass men, with less than 9 percent of men reporting harassment at work by men or women, and few of these reported incidents meeting definitions of sexual harassment as it is legally defined (Gutek, 1993). Men's motivations to engage in behaviors constituting sexual harassment vary and center around such nonconscious views as "women are men's property," women naturally want to accommodate to men's needs, women do not belong in their occupational area, or women are taking jobs that rightfully belong to men.

Interestingly, studies indicate that many men imagine they would be flattered if their female boss or colleagues pressured them for dates or sexual favors (Verba, 1983). Clearly the meaning of such behaviors differs for men. Men claim that they would see as flattering and related to their attractiveness what women experience as related to their "place" in society. A client mentioned during a session how upset she was about a boss who put his hands on her breast and said, "Small but nice." After working through her anger and getting clearer on her rights in this situation, she filed a complaint with the company and made an appointment with her boss to explain that his behavior was offensive. He insisted that he had not intended to harass her and had expected her to feel flattered; he also acknowledged that his behavior was inappropriate and that he needed to reassess his behavior in the work setting.

During the next session the client wondered how flattered her boss would feel if his female boss put her hand on his genitals and said, "small but nice." This

---

BOX 7.2   Techniques for Working with Female Clients Reporting Sexual Harassment or Experiencing Unwanted Sexual Advances*

- *Validation of feelings:* The client has been violated and has a right to feel afraid, angry, confused, distrustful. She is not overreacting.
- *Validation of the harassment:* The woman has experienced a form of sex discrimination. Her rights have been violated.
- *Framing the experience:* Sexual harassment is about the abuse of power; it does not concern physical attraction. She did not bring this on herself.
- *Developing effective strategies:* Strategies include documenting what has happened, keeping a diary if the behavior persists, writing letters to harassers, talking to them with a person of authority present, and taking some kind of formal legal action.

*As explained in the chapter, sexual harassment is a legal term describing either unwelcome sexual advances or requests for sexual favors, or other verbal or physical conduct of a sexual nature by someone in a person's educational or work environment. Typically, a single sexual harassing behavior such as one offensive remark is not viewed as constituting sexual harassment but patterns of such remarks or behaviors are considered sexual harassment.

---

reframing brought some humor to the situation—she got quite a chuckle out of the image—and it helped the client reclaim some of her equilibrium and power. The client, who had a child from a previous marriage, was now in a lesbian relationship but she was not "out" in her place of work. This factor was important to her counseling and to her discussion of possible strategies. She did not want to have to deal with both harassment and homophobia, and she did not want to leave her employment because of economics and because she liked her job.

In the past women were expected to, and did, absorb the various forms of sexual harassment for a variety of reasons—fear of reporting it to others, blaming themselves for the attention or for not handling the situation better, and fear they would not be believed or taken seriously. Because sexual harassment is not publicly acknowledged as a major form of sexual abuse, clients often need to rely on counselors to frame their experience as harassment. Supportive techniques for working with clients who have experienced sexual harassment appear in Box 7.2. These techniques can also be useful with clients who engage in harassing behaviors. The professor referred to earlier in this section needed help in seeing how his attitudes and behavior negatively affected his two female students. His validating these students' feelings, and acknowledging to them that his behavior was not in their best interest as students, was helpful to the students and to him (see Box 7.2, "Validation of feelings" and "Validation of the harassment").

Sexual Assault and Battering.   Sexual assault is not new. As Marge Piercy's poem suggests, rape was just another behavior that women learned to absorb and keep silent (Box 7.3). Violence against women takes many forms

BOX 7.3   Rape Poem

There is no difference between being raped
and being pushed down a flight of cement steps
except that the wounds also bleed inside.

There is no difference between being raped
and being run over by a truck
except that afterward men ask you if you enjoyed it.

There is no difference between being raped
and being bit on the ankle by a rattlesnake
except that people ask if your skirt was short
and why you were out alone anyhow.

There is no difference between being raped
and going head first through a windshield
except that afterward you are afraid
not of cars
but half the human race.

The rapist is your boyfriend's brother.
He sits beside you in the movies eating popcorn.
Rape fattens on the fantasies of the normal male
like a maggot in garbage.

Fear of rape is a cold wind blowing
all of the time on a woman's hunched back.
Never to stroll alone on a sand road through pine woods,
never to climb a trail across a bald
without that aluminum in the mouth
when I see a man climbing toward me.

Never to open the door to a knock
without that razor just grazing the throat.
The fear of the dark side of hedges,
the back seat of the car, the empty house
rattling keys like a snake's warning.
The fear of the smiling man
in whose pocket is a knife.
The fear of the serious man
in whose fist is locked hatred.

All it takes to cast a rapist is seeing your body
as jackhammer, as blowtorch, as adding-machine-gun.
All it takes is hating that body
your own, your self, your muscle that softens to flab.

All it takes is to push what you hate,
what you fear onto the soft alien flesh.
To bucket out invincible as a tank
armored with treads without senses
to possess and punish in one act,
to rip up pleasure, to murder those who dare
live in the leafy flesh open to love.

From *Circles on the Water* by Marge Piercy. Copyright © 1982 by Marge Piercy. Reprinted by permission of Alfred A. Knopf, Inc.

including physical assault and sexual assault (Goodman, Koss, & Russo, 1993).
The term physical assault includes acts of violence likely to cause injury such as
hitting, pushing, slapping, and threatening with a lethal weapon. Sexual assault
and nonconsensual sexual relationships also encompass a broad range of acts
from unwanted petting to rape. Psychological violence can also occur within
marital relations. Such violence may include coercion, degradation, intimidation, humiliation, threats to take away children or to kill oneself, and threats to
a woman's property.

Most counselors will work with women who have been physically abused
at some point in their life. A woman reports a rape to the police every 5 to 6 minutes; over 80 percent of sexual assaults reported by college-age and adult
women are perpetrated by an acquaintance (cited in Goodman et al., 1993).
These statistics cross the lines of ethnicity, race, and economic status. An estimated 1 million women each year seek medical assistance for wife battering.
Surveys indicate that approximately half of sexual assault and battering victims
eventually seek professional help, and many do so years after it occurred.

Sexual assault and battering relate to gender in a number of ways. First, aspects of male socialization patterns offer implicit approval of male violence. In
trying to understand why men rape, Brod (1987), for example, pointed to male
socialization patterns in gangs, sports, and the military, practices that not only
encourage fighting but also view women as the spoils of battle.

Second, many men who rape or batter, particularly within ongoing relationships with women they know, are viewed as good guys who make mistakes.
This interpretation and attitude distances male violence from the fabric of
women's daily experience, making it appear rare and unusual when in fact it is
quite customary and usual. Thus, we are shocked when we learn that a high-
level male official beats his spouse, and has for years, but we view this as unusual and newsworthy rather than as another example of what happens in a
large number of relationships. By pretending it does not happen very much,
what is an ongoing reality for many women and men stays hidden and invisible, and for many it is a shameful reality beyond their control.

These kinds of societal and individual dynamics make the situation more
resistant to change. Rolando, the client introduced at the beginning of the chapter, was horrified that he became physically violent on that one occasion and
feared this would happen again. His rage and alienation felt so strong that he
was afraid to be in relationships, yet he needed some safe place to express what
felt like overwhelming feelings. Coming to counseling was a last resort; he could
not get himself to tell anyone about his feelings or behavior.

Also, as discussed in Chapter 6, in our culture there is still a strong association between sexuality and power, especially the notion that men are not capable of responsibility for their sexual drive. For example, rape and its prevention were long considered women's responsibility, not men's. Results from a
large national, longitudinal survey of adolescent males representing Hispanic,
white, and African American populations, ages 15 to 19, conducted by Joe Pleck
and his colleagues, indicated that perceptions of ideal manhood, which many

males internalize, contain elements promoting unhealthy risk-taking, nonconsensual sexual relationships, and rejections of appropriate social norms (Pleck, 1995). Kahn, Mathie, and Torgler (1994) reported that many rape victims do not identify their rape as rape because they have a rape script of violent rape by a stranger that does not match their experiences of being raped in a less forceful manner by someone with whom they are acquainted.

It is important to note, however, the development of rape prevention programs aimed at men (Lonsway, 1996). These programs emphasize the importance of male responsibility and men's ability to understand women's feelings and socialized responses to men. Unfortunately, at this point, research indicates that the effects of a single 60- to 90-minute workshop has little lasting impact on undergraduate white men's rape myth beliefs (e.g., Heppner, Humphrey, Hillenbrand-Gunn, & DeBord, 1995).

The mental health consequences of nonconsensual sexual relationships and battering are very complicated and differ from individual to individual, depending on the resources available and one's own coping resources and history (Koss & Harver, 1991). For many women healing is a lifelong effort, as the moving vignette from an anonymous student makes clear (Box 7.4). Discussions of treatment modalities are beyond the scope of this chapter. Resources helpful for counselors appear at the end of this chapter.

BOX 7.4   One Young Woman's Experience

I had a very upsetting encounter as a youth. I was fifteen and off on a church campout. My sister was with me and we were the only young people there. The others were a lot older and then there was the minister who was recently widowed. I had never met him before but had no reason to doubt his sincerity when I told him I was freezing at night. My sleeping bag wasn't warm enough. Well, he told me the less clothes I wore the warmer I would be in my sleeping bag. That night while in my bag, away from the men, I took my shirt and shorts off and went to sleep. It did seem toastier in my bag, but I was petrified when a hand came into my bag and held onto my breast. I couldn't move; I was so scared. I pretended I was asleep, but remember hearing him almost quiver as he held on. It seemed like an eternity but I'm sure it was only seconds. His hand slid out of the bag and he was gone. I didn't go back to sleep that night and have never forgotten that night. Someone I trusted, who held such a meaningful position, betrayed me. That incident has left its scar on me forever. I told my sister the next day and we were like Siamese twins from then on until we ended that nightmare camp-out. That week I lost something. A part of me that was young and innocent and a man in a high position took it. A man of God whom we are all taught to trust and put our faith in. I have never been that trusting again.

—Anonymous student, 1990

Source: Unger, R., & Crawford, M. (1996). *Women and gender: A feminist psychology.* New York: McGraw-Hill. Reprinted with permission of The McGraw-Hill Companies.

Gender Issues Associated with Integrating Work and Family Life in Dual-Earner Families

Few American families today fit the traditional model of a two-parent family with children, a wage-earning husband, and a homemaker wife. For married women with children under 6 years old, more than 59 percent are in the labor force, and of these, at least 70 percent are employed full-time. For married women with children under the age of eighteen, these percentages increase to at least 67 percent employed and 73 percent employed full-time (Barnett & Rivers, 1996). The average working wife with full-time employment contributes approximately 40 percent of the family's annual income, with 55 percent of employed women bringing in half or more of their household income (Gilbert, 1993; Shellenbarger, 1995).

Both women and men combining occupational work and family life is now the norm, and it is a norm that presents different practical, psychological, and social issues for women and men (Barnett & Rivers, 1996; Gilbert, 1987b, 1993). That is why women more than men push for dual-earner marriages, despite the lack of equality at home and work, and why, when resistances emerge, women more than men accommodate. This section identifies two gender issues that can cause difficulties in dual-earner relationships. The first is role conflict and self-definition, a variation of the women and men as equals dominant discourse described in Chapter 5. The second issue, the politics of housework, was initially introduced in Chapter 2.

Role Conflict and Self-Definition

Many changes are occurring in women's and men's self-concepts and self-definitions. Turning first to women, historically in most cultures women accommodated to men's needs, regardless of their own talents and abilities. Their efforts to act autonomously and to broaden their interests beyond the sphere of the family were met with great skepticism mostly because such actions ran counter to "women's nature" and "women's place." (This is not the case for African American women, as noted earlier.) Personal ambition and self-definition were antithetical to what made a woman desirable and worthwhile. In the past, many women reconciled their achievement desires and societal views of women by choosing female-dominated occupations, not expecting to advance in their careers, or finding ways other than paid employment to use their talents and abilities.

The situation is different today but not everyone is happy with the changes. Some view women who desire careers and families as selfish. Others view them as destroying the nuclear family and displacing men at work. We have never had a man come into our offices worried about being too competent or too self-assured or not looking professional enough, but many women have. They describe struggles with the negative reactions they receive from male peers, professors, and employers for showing their knowledge, challenging the ideas of others, or not looking or playing their expected part.

Women who do not need men's approval, women who make choices separate from the needs of men, women who are at times more capable than men, may seem out of place and perhaps even scary—to women and men alike. Ellen DeGeneres, a sitcom personality, says her last name is an anagram for the as yet uncoined word, "genderees," a word that might describe people like herself. De-Generes knows she is a woman, feels she is a woman, and does not dress or act like a woman is expected to. "I don't like dresses or panty hose, or heels . . . I guess I'm just a woman trapped in a woman's body . . . She does everything that other women do, only she does it in pants and sneakers and going forward" (Leibovitz, 1996, p. 70).

Some young women come to therapy feeling that they have to choose between a career and a family or accommodate to a husband if they do marry (Lerner, 1988). If the male partner is unwilling to engage in an egalitarian relationship, the woman may view the choice as one between equality and marriage. Indeed the literature indicates that a number of women find themselves doing more than their share, and resenting it. At the same time, they may feel reluctant to challenge male partners because they fear losing the relationship or feel less competent and assured than the male partner (Gilbert, 1985).

What about men and their changing self-views? Although the traditional emblems of masculinity abound in the culture at large, many men today question the usefulness of traditional male norms and seek new definitions of self-worth and self-confidence (Levant & Pollack, 1995). Men's greater involvement in relationships, caring, and parenting is likely the hallmark of the 1990s.

Research surveys show that 33 to 41 percent of working fathers have refused a new job, a promotion, or a transfer that threatened to reduce their family time (Lewin, 1995; Malcolm, 1991). Half the men polled by the largest executive recruiting firm in the financial field reported that they would be willing to reduce their hours and salary by up to 25 percent in order to have more family time (Ball, 1989). An example is a man who came to counseling conflicted about the demands of his employer that he travel more. He reported a close relationship with his child and greatly valued and enjoyed the day-to-day tasks of parenting. When asked why he came to counseling, he said, "I do not know of a way to tell my five-year-old that I don't have time for her, that I have something more important to do."

However, similar to some women, some men seem confused about their roles, with some trying to redefine masculinity and still others trying to ignore the obvious changes in women's lives. Findings from a study (Weiss, 1991) of upper middle-class heterosexual white men who "do well at work" provide a good illustration. Although most of their spouses were employed, the 70 men in the survey showed little interest in their wives' lives or with how they managed to juggle work and family. Their concern was with their own success.

The focus on how well one is doing by traditional standards of male success can keep men from seeing the reality of women's lives and from supporting changes that would benefit their partners. Rather than pitching in to cook dinner or clean up, they may wait to be asked. Their time may be viewed as too important to devote to "women's work." One male client, who lived with a female partner, took her out to dinner whenever she complained that he was not doing his fair share of the meal preparation. He saw this as "fair"; she saw it "as his not getting it" and eventually left the relationship.

In summary, many women and men are struggling with self-definitions that allow love and work to be at the center of their lives, although more women than men are actively thinking about how to accomplish this. The reason for this difference is that women have expressed much more dissatisfaction with how tradition has defined and limited their lives than men have.

The Politics of Housework

For some time now, partners have struggled with what has come to be known as the "politics of housework." This situation causes a good deal of conflict for families and has produced a huge literature ranging from studies on coping to studies on work–family policies (e.g., Blain, 1994). Generally speaking, relationships do better when partners hold similar attitudes about women's and men's roles (e.g., Huston & Geis, 1993). When both partners hold egalitarian views, the more the couple shares the responsibilities of the household and parenting, the greater is their marital happiness (Sanchez & Kane, 1996; Thompson & Walker, 1989).

Issues of who is entitled to what remain a struggle. Many men and women who try to develop egalitarian partnerships are attempting to do so in a society that has little historical precedence for gender equality between women and men in their private lives. Jessie Bernard (1982) put her finger on this key problem when she noted that it is easier to push for men's and women's equality in the workplace than to push for equality in heterosexual relationships. It is easier for a man to want equal justice for women in the world at large than it is for him to embrace in his heart that a woman who is his partner is also his equal. For some men, doing so may require the man to hand over his image of himself as a man (Pleck, 1995).

There is ample evidence that discourses of gender equality have emerged in some families, however. Approximately one-third of dual-career families achieve a role-sharing marriage, while others remain fairly traditional in role behaviors within the home (see Gilbert, 1993). Traditional and egalitarian role-sharing marriages basically differ on two dimensions—power (the extent to which the husband is more dominant than the wife) and role specialization (the extent of role specialization between the spouses). The discourses in egalitarian marriages acknowledge that marital roles are socially constructed and gender based, that they may have had some relevance in the past, and that they are subject to change. One man commenting on his role-sharing marriage captured this very well. "Sometimes I think, my father didn't do it this way, many of my friends don't do it this way, why should I? But then I realize how those rules aren't in effect and it turns things from black and white into gray" (Gilbert, 1993, p. 92).

Communication is particularly important in negotiating egalitarian roles, particularly in asking for and receiving support. As described in earlier chapters, the language of interactions, especially language that reinforces or disrupts conventional assumptions about gender, provides important information to therapists about how partners communicate concern, support, and liking in their efforts to maintain a loving relationship. A female partner who tells her spouse that she wants to be listened to and heard, and does not want his solutions to her problems, would be disrupting traditional gender discourses as would be a male partner who tells his spouse he just needs to be held. In describing examples of how they provided mutual support, one husband in a past study provided an illustration of how spouses can disrupt dominant discourses about work and parenting. He said, "After our daughter was born I kept reassuring her about the quality of her work (they were in the same profession) and she kept reassuring me that I was a competent and loving father" (Gilbert, 1985, p. 70).

How partners combine their work and family roles depends on many factors and varies a great deal from couple to couple. There is no right way and there is no blueprint. Chapter 8 presents a case example of Rick and Darlene, a couple struggling with how to handle parenting and home roles after the birth of their first child. See also Box 8.1 for a summary of factors that influence how partners combine their occupational and family roles.

Concluding Remarks

Gender issues are complex. This chapter described common gender issues that enter counseling through clients' presenting concerns. For both women and men, they are tied to long-standing societal views of what makes women desirable and what makes men desirable as well as to views of what it means to be a man or a woman. Still today, women and men must counter and grapple with internalized societal mandates of male superiority and female nurturance and care, conflicts that result in depression, stress, relationship difficulties, and for some women and men, dysfunctional and harmful behavior.

In Part II we have argued that therapy needs to acknowledge and understand gender issues to be fully therapeutic. Each chapter focused on a somewhat different way in which gender enters into the theory and practice of counseling. In Part III we apply these various ways gender enters counseling to different aspects of the counseling setting—the client, the counselor, and their interaction in the process of counseling.

Discussion Questions

1. You are working as an intake consultant at a university counseling center. A homosexual undergraduate comes in requesting to work with a therapist on relationship issues. You have the opportunity to recommend the client to therapists of equal ability and strength. What might be some advantages and disadvantages associated with matching the client with a female counselor? With a male counselor? Would you recommend that the client work with a homosexual counselor? Discuss your rationale. Respond first for a male client, and then respond for a female client.

2. When asked if his first lover was a man or a woman, a well-known writer replied, "I was too polite to ask." Based on what is presented in this chapter, what are the implications of this question and the answer?

Suggested Readings

Banks, R. (1989). *Affliction*. New York: Harper & Row. A poignant and tragic story of one man's struggle to live within society's view of what a man should do.

Koss, M. P., & Harver, M. (1991). *The rape victim: Clinical and community approaches to treatment*. Lexington, MA: Stephen Greene Press. An informative book based on solid research.

Mintz, L. B., O'Halloran, M. S., Mulholland, A. M., & Schneider, P. A. (1997). Questionnaire for eating disorder diagnoses: Reliability and validity of operationalizing DSM-IV criteria into a self-report format. *Journal of Counseling Psychology, 44*, 63–79. This article describes in depth the problems of questionnaires and self-report measures used to diagnose eating disorders and describes a more valid and reliable assessment tool.

Applications

Part III

The four chapters in the last part of the book describe in greater detail the connection between gender and the practice of counseling and psychotherapy. In contrast to Parts I and II, in which relatively brief cases were presented at the beginning of each chapter and then discussed throughout the chapter to illustrate key points and issues, in Part III more extensive cases are placed at the end of each chapter and used to provide a more detailed analysis of material presented in the chapter. In addition, throughout these chapters we provide opportunities for the reader to consider ways to "undo gender" and illustrate this process with examples from the counseling setting.

In Chapter 8 we describe what makes up a person who comes for counseling with special reference to gender, and in Chapter 9 we look at how gender can influence various aspects of the counseling process, including what is seen and heard and what is less visible. The cases of Jonathan and Allison (Chapter 8), and Donald and Eloise (Chapter 9) not only further elaborate on material presented in the chapters but also illustrate gender case analyses using the four faces of gender described in Chapters 1 and 2.

In Chapter 10 we examine in greater detail crucial aspects of the counseling process associated with the doing and undoing of gender in therapy. We describe problematic areas in counseling, including the particularly troublesome area of sexual relations with clients, which violates the ethics of all the helping professions. A more extensive gender analysis of the case of Anthony and Rose appears as an appendix to the chapter. Finally in Chapter 11 we consider what is needed for ethical practice.

8 Gender and What Clients Contribute

Shawna, a 26-year-old African American pharmaceutical representative came to therapy because of a recurrent nightmare of losing her grip on the hand of her younger sister and subsequently losing sight of her during an urban riot. The image was very graphic, although Shawna could never see the child's face clearly. She had been having the dream for about 6 months and would wake up in a cold sweat with extreme anxiety and an inability to fall asleep again for several hours. Her therapist was an African American woman in her middle forties.

A constantly evolving and changing process, counseling is influenced by all that the client and therapist are. In this chapter we first consider what makes up a person who comes for counseling with special reference to gender. This includes gender socialization and ongoing interactions that perform or create gender, such as women acting to protect the male ego and men sexualizing women, processes that occur within most cultures and societies. We then turn to how individuals do gender, and how that becomes manifest in a client's presenting problem and interactions with the therapist. We use the cases of Jonathan and Allison, presented at the end of the chapter, to illustrate gender case analyses using the four faces of gender described in Chapters 1 and 2.

The Case of Shawna

A good deal of the effect gender has in therapy has to do with the assumptions clients and therapists make about women's and men's qualities and the manner in which we as therapists then locate those qualities, and our assumptions about them, in the client rather than in our own psyches. A woman client complains (do male clients complain or do they just report?) of her husband's infidelity. The counselor immediately offers ways of dealing with this situation through negotiation, confrontation, or accommodation. The woman says, "No! I am going to throw the bastard out and I need your help in what to do with his mother who lives with us in a house I own." The counselor believed that women are dependent and therefore assumed that this woman needed some way to work things out with her husband because she could not get along without him. That could be true in some cases, but it is best to find this out from the client rather than making so major an assumption.

People bring to counseling what and who they are and what they have experienced. What and who they are include the qualities they possess, qualities they might like to possess, and qualities they have lost through trauma or other life experiences. All of this creates a startling mosaic with tiles easily seen and tiles barely discernible but with no clear integrated pattern. Illuminating the obscured tiles, and thus the mosaic's pattern, as the process of therapeutic unfolding occurs is the task of counseling.

The case example of Shawna well illustrates this process. The therapist believed that the recurring dream which prompted Shawna to seek counseling was highly significant. She suggested they come back to the dream in their next session and use this first session for the therapist to learn more about Shawna, her family, and her current life situation. Shawna was a graduate of an historically black college and the daughter of a schoolteacher and an electrician. Her father had not attended college, having learned his trade in the army. Her mother had a master's degree and had always worked. There were three children in the family and Shawna was the youngest; she had two brothers, one older by 2 years and the other 5 years older than she. She had a large extended family who were close knit.

Shawna had held her current job since she graduated from college and was advancing in a generally satisfactory manner, although she did feel some job dissatisfaction. She expressed discomfort with the condescending manner in which she was often treated by the office staff of some of the physicians on whom she had to call. She was never clear whether it was because she was a woman, an African American, or someone who invited condescension. Her supervisor, a white man, offered little assistance or understanding, however, because he did not detect such behavior when he accompanied her on these visits, as he did several times a year.

During the second counseling session, Shawna and her therapist began to look at her dream of losing her younger sister. What emerged from Shawna's associations and thoughts led to a very rich and therapeutic experience for her and took the better part of a year. Briefly, dream analysis began with the therapist exploring the anomaly of Shawna's not having a younger sister. They came to understand the dream as a need for Shawna to protect a tender part of herself that was damaged by the manner in which our culture treats African American women, mainly the way in which she felt disenfranchised, unseen, and dismissed. The persistent experience of this combination of sexism and racism made her feel small and young and is what that aspect of the dream represented.

Shawna associated other elements of the dream with her feelings that she needed to be more sophisticated and knowledgeable to be accepted. The urban mob came to be understood as representing urbane people whom she believed were better than she and who thus contributed to her poor self-image. Shawna came to recognize the anxiety she experienced as tied to her fear of losing the status she had gained and her family had struggled for so diligently.

Examining the dream and what subsequently emerged from her associations was helpful for Shawna in seeing herself more fully and understanding better the ways she had learned to cope with various aspects of her life as an African American woman. She worked hard in her therapy and emerged with deeper knowledge of both herself and societal factors as well as with greater inner peace and strength, although she knew that she still had to face what at times was a hostile and difficult world.

What Makes Up a Person Who Comes for Counseling with Special Reference to Gender

An individual's history is a complex amalgam of all that is bequeathed to and experienced by the person as life is lived. A good deal of that history is random and outside of an individual's control. Who can control the fact that one's father is the greatest tangoer in Omaha, or that Granny was an orphan, or that Uncle Hal likes to fondle young children, but there is an effect nonetheless. Did she have chickenpox? Was he too tall or too short, fat, thin, freckled, African American, Catholic, rural, gay, smart, or gap-toothed? All of these qualities play a role in our history just as trips to the seashore, breastfeeding, older or younger sibs, bullies, chopsticks, hamburgers, and TV play a role. What we make of all that, or do not make of it, how we integrate it or do not is part of our history and that history is what we bring with us to the counseling encounter.

Thus, enumerating all the qualities that comprise a person is likely an impossible exercise. Instead we elucidate here those qualities most significant in examining gender in the counseling process.

Gender does not exist within a person. It exists in the warren of expectations and behaviors that an individual is trained to accede to, incorporate, and engage in, based on the sex with which that person is born. Existing outside the person, gender is a dark cloak, often obscuring the person who struggles to wear it comfortably. The counselor who recognizes the extrapersonal quality of gender needs to know what makes up a person and how that person is affected by gender.

Earlier chapters described the manner in which gender plays a major role in how our history develops, how and what we experience, and how we internally articulate that experience. It starts immediately. Little girls are seen as more fragile than little boys (they aren't) and so they are not treated as roughly or as encouraged to develop their physical strength. The first thing adults ask is which sex is the child. It should not matter but it does. It would be nice if people asked how loud the kid could scream or how fast it could eat, but the obsession is with the child's sex.

The child's sex is significant to the parents too, and marks the child for certain roles and expectations. Typical traits for the sex are rewarded and nontypical traits extinguished through nonreward and being ignored. Most of this shaping is nonconscious and begins at birth, maybe even before in parents' visions of what their child will be like. With this shaping the individual begins to interpret the world in such a manner as to fit with the expectations generated by gender. Boys know that the President of the United States is a man because men are entitled to lead. Girls know men are more powerful because the President is a man. In counseling, male clients often attempt to take over the counseling process through whatever force is necessary because they have a history of feeling entitled to power so as to keep them from feeling unsafe. Some women in therapy, especially with male therapists, allow the therapist to be the expert, even the expert about the client, because their history has trained them to expect men to be more knowledgeable and in charge and for women to accept and value that power. Power is a part of the culture in which our personal history is created.

The manner in which culture affects a client in counseling is, of course, as varied as the individuals coming for counseling and their cultures. However, in the United States there is a good deal more cultural similarity than we might prefer to believe. The reason for this similarity is the impact of Western culture on our personal lives. Society evolves with culture and provides the internal and external supports of culture. Culture is the collection of mores and folkways, laws, and traditions that govern people and create the manner in which people see much of their world and respond to it. The articulation of cultural imperatives occurs through societal requirements. In this culture, where power is of such importance, people are raised not to question certain forms of authority associated with gender.

Many counselors work with women trapped in marriages that are destructive at worst and nonenhancing at best. These women were encouraged in myriad ways from advertisements to movies to songs to stand by their man and always be available to him, and discouraged about education and work advancement that could have led to greater independence (Lerner, 1988). The problem in this kind of counseling interaction is both individual and societal. The counselor will do well to help such clients to see their problem (and indeed their husband's) as part of the cultural and societal structure. Men are also victims of the same system (Pleck, 1981a, b; 1995). They are trapped, frequently in being a success object, in order to maintain the domestic structures that maintain their roles.

Closely tied with the culture and society in which an individual evolves and also affecting her or him deeply is education. Learning has both a direct component and an indirect component depending on how one is taught. We mentioned in Chapter 2 the differential experiences and expectations of women and men in the classroom, the greater attention provided to male students in all educational settings, and the formal and informal "lessons" students learn. A girl or a boy learns something about her or his "place and roles in society" from observing who gets the attention and for what reasons, from who teaches kindergarten, and from which individuals are presented as role models.

Values are another important element of human behavior, and they too can be direct and indirect, both explicit and implicit, known and hidden. Values held by clients are often organizing forces that can determine their behaviors as individuals. Behaviors here include the realm of feelings. For instance, violation of a particular value might fill an individual with paralyzing guilt, leaving the person unable to sleep and without appetite. Explicit values are those an individual can verbally articulate, and implicit values are those assumed by the individual because "that is just the way people are supposed to act," for example, it is OK to kill mosquitoes but not OK to kill dogs. Known values are those that are retrievable by the individual and that have been pondered, examined, or at least recognized. Unknown values are those that are not available to an individual until they are somehow challenged or invoked because of some unusual occurrence. An example is the young man who always thought he was against adultery until a married women comes on to him and he discovers that it is hard to reconcile his socialization as a male, which says he should take advantage of sexual opportunity, with his belief system.

Values become connected with personality traits and qualities of the individual and thus can influence what the client brings to therapy. These traits and qualities are also an integral part of what makes up a person. Traits and qualities are the characteristics, both of behavior and thought, that personify an individual and make that person separate and distinct from others.

Traits and Qualities of Individuals

The previous section considered the importance of cultural mores and practices, education, and values as factors influencing a person's presentation of self as a result of what is externally offered as one progresses through life. We now look at the internal components of the person, and then at the intrapersonal and interpersonal dynamics that also are part of what comprises a person.

We originally thought we would look at the seven deadly sins: pride, avarice, lust, envy, gluttony, anger, and sloth, in an attempt to explicate aspects of gender and personality qualities. On further reflection, these were reduced to a core three—anger, narcissism, and hunger—and then augmented by dependence, power, and fear. These six qualities are discussed in most major theories of personality (see, for example, the theories of Karen Horney and Sigmund Freud).

Although it might appear rather negative to focus on these qualities, it is the consequences of these approaches to the world that often bring individuals into counselors' offices. The obverse, or at least another facet of these qualities, are the societal-endorsed positive aspects of an individual. For example, hunger could be construed as the dark side of generosity. Moreover, who and what comprises a person is simply who and what that person is. The counselor might choose not to be like that person or even not to associate with people who have some or all of those traits. However, in the counseling interaction those stances in regard to others are unproductive and can be destructive. One does best to observe and explore rather than to observe and judge. Not liking something is not the same as judging it bad or wrong. At the same time, communicating a dislike to the client can be difficult and interpreted as disapproval. To say, "I don't like artichokes but I don't think they're bad," is clever but probably unconvincing.

In considering anger, hunger, narcissism, dependence, power, and fear it is useful to recognize that these qualities not only describe an individual but also underscore important aspects of that individual's interactions with others. Intrapersonal traits have both a self and interactive quality. Our narcissism, for example, influences how others may perceive us, for example, as conceited, distant, unapproachable, and also how we interact with those others.

Anger.   How we react to being frustrated is anger. It may be expressed, it may not, but it is there. Anger is a very significant personal and societal quality. Our culture attempts to suppress anger. Anger is not easily tolerated and the suppression of it often has powerful consequences. Open expression of anger might defuse much of the hidden and very destructive discharging of unexpressed anger. There are significant assumptions about gender and anger. An angry woman is often referred to as a bitch, but an angry man is powerful, even if he is out of control.

Narcissism.   Narcissism is a quality we all have. We just express it in different ways. Demanding narcissism is what is typically labeled as narcissism because it is so annoying. However, all people appreciate themselves in some manner and although all of us want others to do so, many learn to suppress that expectation. Interestingly enough, although women are reputed to be concerned with appearance and therefore might appear to be narcissistic, it is men who are usually labeled with a narcissistic personality disorder (American Psychiatric Association, 1987). Narcissistic feelings are likely confused with the sense of entitlement many men are taught. This sense of entitlement dovetails nicely with the mission of self-abnegation with which women are imbued.

Hunger.   Hunger is with us from birth. How that hunger is satisfied has much to with how we progress and who we become. Over the course of our development our hunger gets articulated. We move from simply desiring sustenance to desiring attention, contact, reassurance, and love. Then as a product of our socialization, these wishes become further elaborated. The sexes differ stereotypically on how hunger is manifested. Female socialization encourages women to suppress their hunger, whereas male socialization encourages men to embroider theirs. For example, society sanctions men to take what they need and women to be self-sacrificing.

Dependence.   Obviously if we are hungry and incapable of satisfying ourselves, as infants are, we must depend on others to feed us. Thus begins the lifelong conflict between dependence and independence. We want to be dependent because the consequences feel good: satiety, comfort, and well-being. We do not want to be dependent because we are then in danger from the whims and wishes of others. How to negotiate this quandary is difficult. Traditional male socialization stresses acting independent and that is how some men may appear even when, underneath, they may feel terribly dependent and unable to take care of even their basic needs. Traditional female socialization stressed being dependent on men for a sense of well-being and purpose and that is how some women may appear even when, underneath, they feel perfectly capable of taking care of themselves. However, because women have been socialized to be dependent, they frequently get themselves into situations in which they are tied to the earning power of men and thus cannot lead independent lives. Chapters 2 and 7 explored this dynamic in some detail.

Power.   How we control situations and individuals and how we are controlled by them is what constitutes power. We all want power. How we gain, use, surrender, and deny our power is a product of what we learn and how others relate to us. Dynamics in most cultures allow men to be more direct in their needs for power, women more subtle. Power, which is closely tied to gender relations, also is discussed in several other parts of the book, particularly in Chapters 2, 5, 6, and 7.

Fear.   Everyone is afraid. The root of that fear may be existential anxiety or it may be the early terror and trauma of being totally dependent on the largesse of others. Whatever its cause, fear is present and it is powerful. Part of its power lies in the attempts to deny fear because of concern that it will be paralyzing. It might paralyze but it also might be enhancing as are all our qualities once they are recognized and simply acknowledged as a part of who we are. Both sexes are taught to deny their fear. That is a terrible burden and it is often only in the counseling interaction that people can confess how frightened they are, indeed frequently terrified.

These six qualities, which we have looked at only briefly, are interactive and function to create, enhance, and maintain each other. Dependence may frustrate us and so we must gain power to get what we need but also to escape the dependence. Fear may come from worry about being abandoned and thus unable to satisfy our hunger. There are many intricate interactions and pathways among our personal qualities, some involving intrapersonal and interpersonal dynamics.

Intrapersonal and Interpersonal Dynamics

Part of the makeup of people is the dynamic quality of their personalities. This includes qualities that are of an intrapersonal nature in addition to qualities of an interpersonal nature. These dynamic qualities are human qualities, and occur just as regularly in the lives of women as of men. Obsessive behaviors, for example, constitute an intrapersonal dynamic frequent among both men and women as does deference, an example of an interpersonal quality. Stereotypes can induce misperceptions of the sexes that leave the erroneous impression that certain intrapersonal and interpersonal dynamics belong to women or men exclusively, such as women are deferent, men are not; men are obsessive, women are not.

Intrapersonal Dynamics.   Intrapersonal dynamics refers to the enactment of a personality quality in which there is no direct consequence to another. This distinction is similar to that between intransitive and transitive verbs. As an example, we might look at qualities of self-love and self-hate. These qualities are tied up with narcissism, dependence, power, and fear. An individual with high levels of narcissism and low levels of dependence who also desires power and has little fear of acting on all these qualities will be high on self-love, thinking well of the self and anxious to do whatever will be self-aggrandizing or self-promoting. Individuals who are opposite on the continua of these qualities will tend to be more self-hating.

Jessica was a talented actress who was self-possessed and aggressive. She came to counseling because she could not maintain a relationship and had experienced several unhappy love affairs. What emerged was a woman who was very positive about herself but unaware that such a positive view and such strong self-love made her inaccessible to others. She and the counselor worked on her being more sensitive to those people who entered her life while at the same time maintaining her positive feelings about herself, which was a great asset. Michael, on the other hand, was an overweight and slovenly individual. He had little interest in establishing relationships and tended to be involved with domineering and deprecating people when he did enter a relationship. Very quickly in the initial session Michael confessed to powerful self-loathing. His desired accomplishment in therapy was to stop wanting to kill himself. The counseling was to focus on changing the messages he gave himself about his liabilities and shortcomings and to desist from relationships that supported the negative messages on which he consistently ruminated.

Interpersonal Dynamics.   The manner in which individuals present themselves to the world and interact with the world is a function of the interpersonal dynamics of their personality. Whether an individual does or does not desire sharing power in a relationship, for example, reflects aspects of her or his personality and values. Clearly, the way in which individuals see themselves and feel about themselves will make a difference in how they present themselves to and interact with others.

All of these dynamic qualities of individuals are intertwined. The use of language, for instance, is related to whether an individual wishes to be dominant in an interaction. Should a person wish to dominate, her or his language will often contain many more self-referents and statements rather than questions about the other person and the ideas or values she or he holds. Demonstration of affection is reduced in persons desiring control but is used if such demonstration can disempower the object of control. One way in which male employers can show dominance over their female staff is to engage in touching behaviors, such as putting their hands on women's arms or shoulders or hugging them—nonverbal behavioral patterns characteristic of individuals of unequal status (see Chapter 5 for a summary of research in this area).

In thinking about gender and interpersonal dynamics, one important element is that of dominance and submission (Foa, 1961). The manner in which individuals externalize those qualities and characteristics of which they are made influences the degree to which they need to be in charge in relationships. This continuum of domination is separate from such intrapersonal dynamics as self-love, of which we have spoken earlier; some individuals who dominate may feel self-hate and use dominance to reassure themselves that they are of worth because they control others. In most cultures, women are to be submissive in relations with men, and men are to be dominant in relations with women. Obviously, this view has been challenged, and is changing. It is still widely held though, and subtly and not so subtly, shapes the behavior of individuals partially by shaping the interpersonal dynamics of an individual's self.

The Case of Rick and Darlene.

As a way of summarizing some of the key aspects of what individuals bring to counseling, we consider the hypothetical situation of Rick and Darlene, a dual-earner couple struggling with how to handle parenting and home roles after the birth of their first child. Important characteristics that individuals and couples in dual-earner families bring to counseling appear in Box 8.1 on page 134. These will be useful in considering counseling considerations for Rick and Darlene.

Rick, a 36-year-old carpenter, comes to you for counseling. Darlene, his 31-year-old wife, is a product manager with a major food corporation. They are a mixed-race couple and they live in a small city in the South. Rick is white and Darlene is African American. They have recently found out that she is pregnant, something they both very much want. Darlene assumed she would take the maternity leave offered by her company and then return to work after that 3-month period. Rick feels that she should stay home with the child full-time and that if the mother is not the primary person in the baby's life, especially during the first year, the baby will have psychological problems. He also believes she would be missing out on an important aspect of womanhood. He is very anxious and upset over their past arguments in this regard.

Darlene has tried to accommodate his fears by suggesting that she use the flex-time options of her company and he change his work schedule for that year to do childrearing, which he can do because he works independently. He feels

BOX 8.1   Important Characteristics That Individuals and Couples in Dual-Earner Families Bring to Counseling

Each Partner's Intrapersonal and Cultural Characteristics

- World views and racial identity (e.g., stage of racial identity, degree to which partner holds a Eurocentric or Afrocentric world view, view of gender roles)
- Personality (e.g., how important is a person's need to dominate, be emotionally intimate, be highly successful in her or his field?)
- Attitudes and values (e.g., person's beliefs about rearing a child, family and work roles, gender and power issues, relationship with and responsibility for extended family)
- Interests, abilities, stages in careers (e.g., person's commitment to occupational work, family relations; partner's work satisfaction and career plans, is one partner peaking careerwise and the other thinking about retirement; is one partner unemployed and having difficulty finding employment)
- Cultural and family background of each partner
- Acceptance in one's community or in one's field (does one feel isolated at work; does neighborhood or work setting hold racist or sexist views)
- Strategies for self-care

Interpersonal Factors within the Couple

- Equity and power (e.g., how are decisions made; what seems fair; how do partners come to agreements about household work, parenting, money; how to deal with sexism and racism in their own lives and in the lives of their children)
- Partners support (e.g., can partners count on each other for support in all areas)
- Shared values and expectations (e.g., do partners share life goals, views of gender roles, philosophy regarding childrearing practices and support of extended family, importance of instilling a sense of racial pride in children)
- Extended family and community support (e.g., how important is contributing to the welfare of other members of extended family, or one's ethnic or racial community?)

Environmental/Societal Characteristics

- The work situation (e.g., are work hours flexible, any sex discrimination, race discrimination, are there health care benefits, and if so, are partners covered)
- Employer's views (e.g., kinds of family policy provided, general attitude about employees who involve themselves in family life)
- Child care availability and quality
- Support systems (family, friends, colleagues, church, community)
- Family responsibilities to parents and other relatives
- Racial and ethnic views/discrimination

that she is being unreasonable and that she is asking too much of him. Although feeling strongly about his opinions, he questions whether he is going to be sorry in the long run. He is worried about what this is going to do to their relationship.

In counseling Rick initially, and perhaps Rick and Darlene as a couple, depending on what ensues in the first session, all three kinds of characteristics identified in Box 8.1 appear relevant and in need of exploration. *Intrapersonal* attitudes and values tied to race and gender and Eurocentric and Afrocentric world views are likely a good starting point, but interests, abilities, career, and societal characteristics may be as important to explore.

Perceptions and understanding of the roles of work, family, and marriage are influenced by a person's world view, and Darlene and Rick may for the first time in their marriage realize that they do not necessarily share the same world view. (World view refers to the customs, values, and beliefs of an identified group of people.) African American women have a history of employment, sharing in the financial responsibilities of family life, and establishing a relatively egalitarian sharing of home and employment roles. Rick may hold a different world view, having been reared in a European American culture that encourages a more traditional patriarchal family situation. Darlene's racial identity would also be important to the kind of decision made (Cross, 1971). African Americans go through stages in achieving their racial identity, stages that range from a strong positive identification with whites and a concomitant negative evaluation of African Americans to a more racially transcendent view, in which the individual is very positive about African Americans and black culture, but is accepting and appreciative of whites.

Gender-related intrapersonal characteristics such as feelings of dominance in each partner, needs for and beliefs about intimacy, power, parenting, and career commitment may need to be considered. For example, Rick may feel Darlene is not being sufficiently sensitive to disruptions to his work. He is self-employed and works by word-of-mouth referrals; as a white man reared to evaluate himself through his provider role, he may feel more threatened than reassured when she reminds him that her position offers greater financial stability than his, in addition to providing their health care coverage.

An *interpersonal* relationship factor that may be particularly important to explore is partner support. Neither Rick nor Darlene may feel supported at the moment, and instead both may feel that one is trying to push the other into a decision both are reluctant to make. By focusing on how Darlene and Rick typically support each other and exploring how each would like to be supported in this area, new options are likely to emerge—options perhaps related to the environmental and societal characteristics summarized in Box 8.1. Thus, although Rick may have the more flexible work situation, Darlene may be able to arrange more flexible work hours so that parenting can be better shared between them.

The counselor's job in this situation likely centers around helping Rick, and perhaps Rick and Darlene as a couple, explore their basic beliefs and increase their awareness of the values they are currently using to make decisions. However, given the value-laden aspects of the situation regarding women's and men's traditional roles, counselors may need to first explore their own values in the areas of work and family and decide whether they can ethically work with Rick or with Rick and Darlene. Counselors act as the carriers and enforcers of values in their work with clients. They can reinforce racial and gender stereotypes, patriarchal values, and heterosexist beliefs that limit all women and men interested in nontraditional family lifestyles (Gilbert & Bingham, in press).

Identifying Gender Dynamics in Therapeutic Work — Two Case Examples

Illustrations of what individuals bring to counseling are provided in the cases of Jonathan and of Allison. Following each case we indicate (1) how *not* understanding the faces of gender could inhibit therapeutic progress, and (2) how understanding the faces of gender could inform work with the client.

The four faces described in Chapter 1 are:

- Gender operating as difference
- Gender operating as structurer or organizer
- Gender operating as interpersonal process
- Gender operating as dominant discourse

The Case of Jonathan

Referred by a local physician, Jonathan, a high school principal, was suffering from a depression brought on by the unexpected and quite sudden end of a 2-year relationship that he had wanted to continue. He described himself as sad, tired, lethargic, depressed, and inconsolable. He was 35 years old, divorced for 3 years after a 5-year marriage, and had no children.

Jonathan was the youngest child and only son of two schoolteachers; he has two sisters. He has grown up in a fairly traditional family in a mid-sized city close to where he is now employed. He had gone away to a good state university where he had gotten both a bachelor's and master's degree and was currently pursuing a doctoral degree part-time. He reported an idyllic and spoiled upbringing and generally uneventful life. His report did not match a depression as deep as the one he was experiencing.

The counselor, a female, was aware of a desire to embrace Jonathan, an unusual feeling for her with regard to a client during the first session. She also was aware of how increasingly attractive both physically and emotionally he became during the course of the session, as if his face and his psyche became recomposed. The struggle with tears and sadness that characterized him at the start of the session slowly dissipated as time wore on and he seemed to be benefiting from her attention, interest, and concern. He answered all questions fully, carefully, and insightfully.

Gender as Interpersonal Process.   Jonathan provides a good example of a client whose individual contribution to the counseling interaction is quite traditional and provides a fair number of pitfalls for a counselor unaware of how the person's way of being in the world can be tied to gender expectations and to a counselor and client "doing gender" in therapy. This could occur in a number of ways in counseling Jonathan.

First, Jonathan is an only son and youngest child, who reports being spoiled. This is a clue that he has likely gotten a good deal of attention, especially from women, because there were three of them in his family, and they spoiled him. So his view of himself was of an entitled individual, a common view in our culture for men, but magnified by growing up as the only son in a traditional home with two older sisters. He was accustomed to women being interested in him, and thus acted in ways that demanded the counselor's attention and interest, for example, the counselor experienced him as increasingly attractive physically and emotionally (Westkott, 1986). The counselor also was aware of a desire to embrace the client and to take care of him, again a not uncommon gendered dynamic in which men "take care" and women "give care" (Pogrebin, 1983). Should the counselor act out of these feelings, rather than use them to understand and address the gendered dynamics that were likely occurring, she and the client would "do gender."

Second, the woman with whom Jonathan had been most recently involved had dumped him. Although the counselor would not yet know this until she asked about his other relationships, she sensed this was an unusual occurrence. A clue to that was his use of the word *inconsolable*. Jonathan is inconsolable because he does not believe anyone should be able to treat him as he has been treated and he is not going to be pacified by anyone. His fear is presented in his behavior. Under the depression and sense of not being consolable is likely anger, a feeling which the client has not at all acknowledged or expressed in the counseling, and which may eventually transfer from the other women in his life to the female counselor. Should the counselor find herself not only taking care of Jonathan but also working to express his emotions for him, especially his unexpressed anger, they would again be doing gender. Stereotypically, and paradoxically so, women are often viewed as the cause of men's anger and rage and also as having the ability to express men's emotions for them (Brooks, 1990; Pleck, 1981b).

The Case of Allison

A dark-haired and modishly dressed woman of 29, Allison came to see this male counselor because she was unable to advance beyond lower middle-management in the large prestigious accounting firm for which she had worked since graduating from college. She reported her work performance as excellent and usually got superior ratings from her supervisor and although she got reasonable salary increases, the promotions she wanted never materialized.

Allison, an only child, had grown up in the large urban area where she still lived. Her parents had divorced when she entered college and she was close to each of them, although she did have some difficulty with her father's new wife. Both parents were very attentive to and concerned about her.

She had come for counseling because she was getting increasingly frustrated and increasingly self-critical as a result of her failure to advance. Unwilling to come initially, she eventually gave in as her work situation became more upsetting. She had been referred by her roommate, whose boyfriend had been a client of this male counselor.

The counselor did not feel particularly engaged with Allison, although he did feel that she was genuine about seeking help. The client presented herself in a distant and somewhat cool manner, there was little demonstration of affect and although attentive to what the counselor said she seemed more introspective than interested in his input. In light of how he experienced her, the key issue which emerged for him was, what might Allison be doing to sabotage her own progress?

The counselor also hypothesized that her personal characteristics, such as her relative disinterest in what he had to say, might be an important element in her not seeking out more information about her not being promoted. His thoughts along this line were confirmed when Allison reported that she was an only child and thus less likely in his mind to have developed the social skills of most other children. The fact that she was not particularly interested in dating men also suggested to him that she lacked the skills to socialize well either with friends or at work. The goals of the counseling increasingly focused on improving Allison's social skills and increasing her ability to show affect interpersonally.

Gender as Difference and Gender as Dominant Discourse.   The most obvious personal quality the male counselor identified in Allison was her relative disinterest in others, a characteristic not unusual in men, especially male accountants. However, because this characteristic is not the traditionally expected behavior in women, the counselor, using erroneous notions of gender as difference, conceptualized the client's problem as not acting the way women should act. Moreover, her apparent disinterest in men did not fit traditional discourses about how the female life plot (Ker Conway, 1995) and about how women (healthy women) should focus their priorities and their lives.

Gender as Structure.   Women have had a great deal of difficulty advancing in the kind of organization that employs Allison, making structural barriers to her achieving in this situation highly likely. These are ignored by the counselor.

Rather than examining the client's work situation and the possibility that she may be somewhat traumatized from the way she is being treated in her workplace, the counselor focuses the therapy on Allison not meeting his views of how she should present herself as a woman. In this kind of situation, the gender-aware counselor must ask some pointed questions and make some inferences from what the client says in order to determine whether she has an understanding of gender discrimination and is not blaming herself for not advancing when few if any females have advanced in this corporation. Should they come to an agreement that she is experiencing sex discrimination, strategies need to be considered for dealing with her situation effectively. This would include ways to deal with her trauma as well as steps to change the situation. Finally, it would be crucial for the gender-aware counselor to examine with a colleague or a supervisor what appears to be a negative reaction to Allison's distant style and her apparent lack of interest in his input. His perceptions of Allison, if accurate, could provide her with important feedback about how others may experience her interpersonally. If his perceptions, however, stem from personal feelings of hurt or anger by her lack of interest in his insights or proposed solutions to her difficulties or a personal difficulty in working with emotionally reserved women, then the problem resides within the counselor, not with Allison.

Concluding Remarks

The individual client brings much to the counseling situation. A good deal of what is brought is a result of the process of development, which is powerfully influenced by the gender socialization of the individual and how that process has been articulated. The impact and contribution of gender are inescapable. Our obligation as counselors and therapists is to know as much as we can about how gender affects individuals and how to work with that in our interactions with our clients.

As the ancient Chinese knew, "When the idea is learned the words are forgotten." Therefore, if we are deeply conversant with the influence of gender on individuals including ourselves and embrace the goals of gender aware therapy, then our store of knowledge will serve us when appropriate.

Discussion Questions

1. It has been argued that the traditional female gender role is oppressing while the traditional male gender role is constraining. What are your thoughts on the matter? Discuss your own experiences, observations, as well as what you have read.

2. Presented here for your consideration is the case of Luis, a Latino man who seeks counseling for issues related to male gender role strain. Using the two cases presented in the chapter as models, speculate about ways in which the four faces of gender could become manifest in working with Luis. In responding, indicate who the counselor is, the estimated length of the counseling, and how cultural aspects of the case would be considered.

   Luis, a 42-year-old married father of three sons came to counseling because of several episodes of rage at work. He works in a bank in the large southwestern city where he grew up and attended college. He received an MBA at the local university, too. His career at the bank has been one of a rapid rise and an equally rapid leveling off, although he has been given reasonable salary increases and greater responsibility but no advancement in rank or membership in the inner circle of directors.

   Luis's sons are academically inclined and have done well in their studies; two are in college and the third is in high school. They are athletic and popular, although somewhat docile and petulant at home. Lorena, Luis's wife, is a nurse who has always worked and is a devoted mother and wife. The couple has been successful financially through hard work and careful budgeting. Their life appears full and happy.

   In one incident in which Luis erupted in rage at work, Luis yelled at a male customer who challenged his honesty and implied that Luis was treating him cavalierly. The customer was a Latino several years younger than Luis who was trying to negotiate a loan to maintain his fledgling business. Another incident of anger involved an employee of the bank who refused a request for information from Luis, saying that this information was classified and could only be released by a superior. Luis again erupted in rage when a Latina female teller lightheartedly accused Luis of staring at her salaciously.

   Luis's boss suggested he take the day off after the last incident and get himself together before he returned to work. In talking with Lorena, Luis realized that something was amiss with him and that he had better get some assistance before he endangered his job. This was not an easy decision for this proud and independent man. Luis was the child of immigrants and was the first in his family not only to graduate from high school but to go on to college and then to university. He was a professional in an extended family of blue-collar workers and he took his success and status very seriously. His achievements were his own and to have to approach another for aid was a new and unwelcome experience.

Suggested Readings

Espiritu, Y. L. (1996). *Asian american women and men: Labor, laws, and love.* Beverly Hills, CA: Sage. Using a gender lens, this book explores the Asian American experience starting with historical forces and immigration and moving to contemporary experiences with racism, cultural resistance, and relationships between women and men.

Gilbert, L. A. (1993). *Two careers/one family: The promise of gender equality.* Beverly Hills, CA: Sage. A thoughtful, highly readable presentation of how gender processes influence life as a dual-earner family.

9 Gender and the Dynamics of Counseling

Gender is a major shaping force in the counseling process just as it is a major element in how we live our lives and interact with the world. As much as we might wish otherwise, it is abundantly clear that were we the other sex we would respond to people and they to us differently from the manner in which we do. This is also the case in counseling (Scher, 1994). We respond to our clients in myriad ways, most of which are nonconscious. This requires knowledge of all our stereotypes and stereotypic and nonstereotypic reactions to the other sex and also to our own self as a woman or a man (see Fiske, 1993; Steele, 1997). The male counselor comfortable with what he perceives or construes to be "seductive behavior" in female clients may be quite undone by what he experiences as "seductive behavior" in male clients. Not only does he not expect these kinds of experiences with male clients, but they also could hit him in the blind spot of homophobia. In this chapter we briefly review material presented in Parts I and II of the book and then provide detailed examples pertinent to understanding how gender can enter into the counseling process. We then consider the case of Eloise and the case of Donald.

Revisiting and Integrating Earlier Key Points about Gender

The language and dialogue of counseling is often "gendered." For example, as described in Chapter 5, boys and men are more likely to interrupt and to determine the nature of the conversation than are girls and women. Similar dynamics will certainly occur in therapy and counseling, with male counselors more likely to interrupt and move away from the client's story than female counselors. This pattern of behavior on the part of male counselors would likely affect the counseling process insofar as it may leave the client feeling unheard, and by so doing, depending on the sex of each member of the counseling dyad, mirror or create power differentials or power struggles within the dyad that reflect dynamics in the society.

Nonverbal Aspects of Gender and the Counseling Process

It is erroneous to assume that the only element of counseling that must be scrupulously studied with regard to gender bias is verbal communication. That nonverbal aspects of communication are also subject to gendering is well documented (see Chapter 5). Also well documented is the important role of nonverbal behavior in therapeutic interactions (see Hall, Harrigan, & Rosenthal, 1995, for a comprehensive review). Nonverbal behaviors appear particularly important in the establishment of rapport and trust between client and therapist and in the client's feeling heard and understood. In addition, nonverbal behaviors such as nodding, eye contact, leaning forward, and facial expression are important to the client in perceived counselor empathy and competence. Inconsistencies between verbal and nonverbal behaviors also influence counseling interactions: Therapists who give off inconsistent messages are perceived as less genuine by their clients and cause clients to distance themselves emotionally from their therapists (Gelso & Fassinger, 1990).

A number of nonverbal aspects of behavior may have a gendered quality (e.g., Abbey & Melby, 1986). Female counselors' offices might be more welcoming and homey than those of male counselors; male counselors are expected to shake hands with all new clients, especially new male clients; male counselors may feel a greater freedom to dress casually than female counselors, because their perceived competence is perhaps less tied to their appearance, and so forth. Areas of nonverbal behavior particularly important in considerations of gender dynamics are personal space and touch, time, facial positivity, and emotional expression (see Box 9.1).

Touch and personal space can become interconnected in therapeutic settings, with counselors more likely to violate, ignore, or consider as unnecessary female clients' personal space and to engage in touching behavior more with female clients than with male clients (Pope, 1994). These differences are moderated by dynamics of power and status. Our basic belief about touching clients is that it should be restricted to a handshake at the start of therapy and a handshake or perhaps hug at the termination of therapy. Touch is a potent and frequently misunderstood communication between people. Therefore, in an attempt to reduce miscommunication, it should be avoided at least until client and counselor are comfortable with each other and it fits naturally into the ongoing therapeutic process.

BOX 9.1   Nonverbal Ways That Gender Enters Counseling and Therapy

- Personal Space and Touch

   Are female clients touched more? Are they given less personal space?

   Is touching done without seeking clarification about what is communicated?

- Time

   Any patterns among clients with whom you "go over" session limits, or with whom you watch the clock, hoping time would move more quickly?

- Emotional Expression and Facial Positivity

   Any patterns in how you respond to emotional expression in clients?

   Do you use your own facial positivity to control or manipulate clients' feelings and behavior?

Is the use of touch ever justified? Yes, but only under certain circumstances. The counselor should be experienced enough to know when touch is self-enhancing, and *not* helpful to the client; when it is not consistent with what is transpiring in counseling; and when it is discordant with the client's persona. Holding the hands of a sobbing client whom you have been seeing regularly for 2 years who suddenly lost an adult child in a hiking accident would be such an example of justifiable use of touch. Holding the hands of a new client, regardless of the concern presented, would not be appropriate. As a powerful modality, touch must be handled carefully and sparingly; a little goes a long way. The ethical dilemmas and dangers of touch are further explored in Chapters 10 and 11.

Time represents another important aspect of nonverbal behavior. How often one looks at one's watch during a session and how one monitors time as a boundary in the practice of therapy are obvious and pertinent examples. Time defines the limits of a session and provides structure and even containment for some clients (Gutheil & Gabbard, 1993). Important questions for us to ask ourselves as counselors include: Do I tend to go "over" the time scheduled with clients I like more, find more difficult to end a session with, or feel physically attracted to? There is evidence that therapists involved in sexual misconduct cases scheduled clients with whom they had sexual relations for the last hour of the day.

Emotional expression of feelings is another strong nonverbal form of communication. Tears and laughter are of tremendous import, as are the facial expressions and body language of both the client and the counselor. Because emotional expressions are often accorded stereotypic gendered meaning, their actual meaning for a client or therapist may be lost or misconstrued. Therapists need to be careful about making stereotypic internal interpretations in this area. The shedding of tears by a male client during a session, for example, may routinely be accorded greater importance than similar behavior in a female client because it is assumed to be harder for a male to cry. A female client who expresses powerful and contained anger may be labeled as histrionic and her feelings dismissed or not honored by the therapist through misattribution.

Finally, one is in danger of reproducing gender dynamics by looking at women's bodies or into space rather than at their faces, returning their nervous smile with a stony stare, or listening to their recounting of their experiences with obvious disapproval or disinterest.

Language and the Counseling Process

How we use language reflects our thoughts and our construction of the world. Counselors need to be aware of how they use language and whether their use of language lacks gender awareness. Referring to women as girls or using the pronoun "he" generically are obvious examples. More subtle examples include the use of terms that judge male or female clients' experience, such as referring to a female client's sexual behavior as promiscuous, when a similar level of sexual activity on the part of a male client would receive no comment, being viewed as normal. Another common example is referring to the sensitive, caring aspects of a male client as feminine, or their female part. Women do not "own" caring behaviors; they are human characteristics. This way of using language perpetuates notions of gender as difference.

How clients describe what brings them to counseling, and how they subsequently respond to our probing and our words, can help us to enter into their worlds and to know them and those worlds. We must listen for what is said, and what is not said, and how what is not said may relate to gendered lives. The male client who avidly describes his occupational work but rarely mentions his marital relationship or his three children is telling us a good deal about how he construes his life. The female client who uses the most stereotypic female terms for describing her behavior and the most stereotypic male terms for describing a former male counselor whom she found very helpful is telling us something about how she views female–male relationships. Lesbian and gay clients unsure that they feel sufficiently safe to reveal their sexual orientation may avoid using a partner's name and the pronouns *he* or *she* in therapy, and instead use the plural pronoun *we*.

It is always intriguing how people reveal themselves. What is even more intriguing is how often most of us miss what we are being told. We do this by denying what we have heard or by making excuses for anything discordant to the flow of communication. In counseling we have a responsibility not to let such misspeaking pass by. We do not have to mention these discordances to the client but we do have to note them to ourselves. For example, the misuse of pronouns, which is not unusual in common parlance, in counseling must be attended to. One client continually used *I* when talking about himself and his wife, when the correct grammatical construction would have been *me*. Suddenly he shifted to using the pronoun *me*. The counselor mentioned this and then went on to suggest that perhaps the client was now feeling like an object rather than a subject. The client indicated that he had been feeling much less in control in the marriage and in the rest of his life. Another client frequently told stories involving himself without saying *I*. With the counselor's assistance he realized he did not have much of a positive self-image and was more interested in the behavior and attitudes of others.

Word choice is another example of how individuals reveal the gendered way in which they see themselves, their world, and the people in that world. One client, a physician, constantly referred to his female patients as "girls." What this revealed was that he saw himself as big and therefore in charge of these patients whom he viewed as childlike and less capable of taking care of themselves. This made him feel both powerful and competent, but it also made him feel overly responsible and burdened by what he perceived as their dependence on him.

Counseling is not conversation. Therefore, the counselor must be aware when discourse has become too chatty or informal with a client and if this occurrence is related to unconscious motivations or dynamics such as a personal interest in clients or an inability to connect with their issues for reasons of disinterest, bias, or fear. We mentioned, in Chapter 3, a male therapist's difficulty in listening to a gay male couple discuss aspects of their sex life. Other examples related to possible gender bias include listening less closely to women than to men, fear of engaging with angry female clients or tender male clients, or lack of interest in experiences associated with usual aspects of the male or female experience in our society.

Internalized Views of Women and Men and the Counseling Process

It is usually a shock to realize that we have very highly articulated views of men and women that are not easily retrievable to consciousness but which nonetheless greatly influence how we interact with people. Counseling, a subset or microcosm of relationships, is similarly influenced by the views of women and men brought to it by its participants—clients and counselors.

Earlier chapters described how women's traditional socialization focuses on relationships and men's on making a mark on the world. This is an almost schematic way of describing an intricately articulated dance of individual, dyadic, group, and societal behavior. Although some aspects of gender socialization appear obvious, many aspects remain unseen and unknown. For example, many people today no longer believe that women are the best caregivers for children or that women have no place in the workforce if they have a man to support them. However, women still earn 68 to 74 percent of what men earn on average, and women experience a good deal of resistance to their entering the professional paid work world still dominated by men (O'Donohue, 1997; U.S. Dept. of Labor, 1991). Counselors need to be sensitive to the generally exploitive and condescending manner in which women are viewed and treated in our culture.

How our internalized views of men and women play out can be surprisingly subtle and varied. Some of these subtleties were made apparent in the exploration of nonverbal and verbal aspects of counseling. There are, of course, others. A classic example is channeling women into less prestigious professions or less prestigious positions within a profession (U.S. Dept. of Labor, 1995). There is concern today, in fact, that professions, such as counseling and psychology, will become less prestigious because too many women are entering these fields (Pion et al., 1996). A current example is viewing women, but not men, as having the choice of working or staying at home with children.

The obverse side of the situation for women is the overloading of men with occupational obligations. Although many men rebel against this, the general ethos still holds and can cause much struggle and suffering, as we discussed in some detail in Chapter 7. Counselors may find themselves encouraging men to shoulder their responsibilities and get on with their lives and obligations.

In many ways our society trains women to be interested in men, and trains men to be interested in themselves. This works out nicely if we believe that women ought to be subservient caretakers of men. Should we think otherwise we have to function quite differently from the ways we have, especially in counseling. For example, male therapists need to be aware of how they reproduce this dominant discourse when they allow their female clients to attend to them through interest, support, and flattery while not challenging and confronting those same clients for fear of wounding them. Similarly, female therapists may reproduce dominant discourses about male-female roles when they try to take care of male clients and feel hurt when that care is taken for granted (a possible dynamic in the case of Jonathan, described in the previous chapter), but expect female clients to respond more appreciatively to much less care.

The manner in which gender affects our work is wide-ranging. From the simple fact that men interrupt discourse more often than women and actually have greater verbal production (e.g., Tannen, 1994), to the subtle and complex manner in which sexuality is expressed and suppressed (e.g., Kitzinger, 1985; Zilbergeld, 1978), we are constantly exercising the elements of our closely held views of how men and women supposedly are and ought to be. The intricate behaviors involved in this, as we have pointed out, influence the process of counseling. We now turn to the counseling process and its interactions with gender.

Gender and the Process of Counseling

Another way to understand gender's contribution to the counseling interaction is by using the paradigm of Foa (1961). Foa postulated that the structure of interpersonal interactions could be understood by placing them on the two perpendicular axes of power and affect. The power dimension refers to who is in control and the affect dimension refers to how that control is manifested in the interpersonal interaction. His paradigm also includes the dimension of ongoing expression of positive or negative affect from each participant toward the other.

Foa's Model

We have chosen this paradigm because the qualities of interpersonal power and affect are central to gender roles in our culture and perhaps in most cultures. How males and females use and abuse power and how they feel about each other and themselves are central to their conceptions of self and how those conceptions require tending through counseling.

Power.   Use of the word *power* is deliberate. Many of the interactions from a gender role perspective involve the attempt by one party to direct or control the other. Much of adult behavior involves trying to feel in control of one's life and destiny. This is important for dealing with existential anxiety as well as for sensing the autonomy that is so valued in Western culture. To feel this power one learns to compare oneself to others and to measure one's degree of control in a situation. All clients bring the struggle for control of their lives into the counseling interaction, although a client's needs in this area are a product of the history of ethnic, cultural, historical, and gender influences. The counselor, too, is also a product of these determinants.

Foa's model can be useful in assessing the process of counseling and providing a way to recognize nonconscious gender-related dynamics. For some clients, initially low on the power axis, for example, because they are feeling so bad about themselves and so defeated that they think they neither merit nor can achieve control with others or in the counseling situation, movement toward being in control or just struggling actively to gain control over their lives is a sign of improvement and empowerment. For other clients who immediately try to control the interaction because they feel intimidated by perceptions of the counselor's power, movement away from that struggle and the attendant willingness to trust the counselor is a sign of positive movement.

Affect.   The axis crossing power is that of affect. Affect here does not mean emotionality, although that could be a representation or expression of it. Rather what we are referring to here is the continuum of positive and negative feelings that underlie and affect the development of connection in the therapeutic process. There are other coexistent continua, such as acceptance and rejection. In any interaction, the participants will be in a dynamic process of feeling positive or negative affect toward each other and to what is transpiring in the encounter.

Knowing the affect level helps in framing useful questions and in gauging the mood of the client and making some conjectures as to what may be fueling that mood. Gender schema differ in how clients are supposed to behave, and women more than men are expected to pay attention to others. Some women often find themselves at a disadvantage interpersonally, having been taught to be concerned with what others think of them and whether or not they are liked by others.

The influence of ethnic and cultural factors on the affect dimension of counseling must be considered, with various ethnic groups not being deeply concerned about a positive quality in the interaction and in fact actively hostile toward counselors who might be perceived as members of an oppressive group, for example, bureaucrats. Again, determining the place on the affect continuum will aid the counselor in judging how things are going and what kind of progress is being made. In some cases, it may be essential to hold the interaction toward the negative end of the continuum in order to aid the client in expressing anger and rage or in learning to be confronting and challenging. Positive affect is not necessarily of greater value, although it may make the counselor feel better. In fact, it may be counterproductive, depending on the situation.

Working Effectively

We all know horror stories of counselors supporting stereotypic views of women and men. These horrors span the gamut from blaming women for being sexually abused to discouraging men's involvement with their children. Avoiding these kinds of outcomes in one's own work involves not only our own understanding of gender dynamics, but also our clients' understanding, so that they, too, can grasp more deeply the contributions of gender socialization and ongoing gendered dynamics in society to the paths they have taken. This might also involve understanding the differing life trajectories determined by gendered scripts.

In that process, counselors also need to be aware of how they influence clients and shape their behavior and world view. All of counseling is an ongoing, mutually influencing interaction. A female client once told a male counselor that she was feeling inferior to him. When quizzed as to why, she thought for a minute and blurted out, "You're a man!" That was a very powerful realization for both of them and helped bring into the counselor's awareness, and into the counseling, ways he and the client were "doing gender."

To a great extent Carl Rogers (1961) explicated the essential qualities for a therapeutic effect when he talked about unconditional positive regard, nonpossessive warmth, and accurate empathy. These are the building blocks for effective therapy. However, we must go beyond these in promoting successful process. Listening carefully, screening out our own issues, knowing the effects of contemporary pressures, trusting the client, not being afraid of the client or the problems presented, and being willing to enter fully into the encounter largely determine the success of the enterprise. Being able to do all of this is determined by our training, life experience, self-analysis, our own experience of therapy, and our willingness to trust ourselves and to take risks. This is not a profession for the faint of heart.

Identifying Gender Dynamics in Therapeutic Work — Case Examples

The Case of Eloise

A somewhat overweight woman Eloise, the wife of a physician, had a caustic and bitingly sarcastic wit. Her verbal production was in contrast, almost a contradiction to, her overtly nurturing demeanor. She came to counseling because she was having recurring dreams of killing her father who had Parkinson's disease and was living in a nearby nursing home. The counselor, Vanessa, a 30-

year-old slender and attractive Latina woman was eager to listen to Eloise's story and did so enthusiastically. A therapeutic alliance, both emotional and contractual, was established and counseling undertaken. After eight sessions the counseling was going well insofar as the two participants indicated satisfaction, but Eloise was not progressing in her feelings toward her father and the feelings of anger directed at her husband, which had surfaced.

Examining the process of this counseling interaction presents some clues as to the lack of progress resulting from the dynamics of the individuals and that of their interactions. Both women had been treated poorly by men who were neglectful of them early on in their relationships but became increasingly dependent on and demanding of them as they aged. This engendered a good deal of anger in both client and counselor. It surfaced in not acceding to the conventional female striving for physical attractiveness and deference in Eloise and a hard-boiled independence in Vanessa, her counselor. Therefore although the outward appearances differed, much of the motivation was the same, that is, to tell the male-dominated society that these women were not buying into the expected behaviors. This created an alliance of anger which did not allow Eloise to focus on how to get beyond it.

There was also a desire to be nurtured and dependent on the part of the client, because she had needed to be self-reliant from an early age. The counselor desired to be nurturing but was reluctant to allow clients to depend on her because of her own life experiences. However, she wished to overcome that by choosing a helping profession. This struggle, although not obvious to most of Vanessa's clients, was sensed by Eloise. In addition they were mutually put off by the other's appearance, with Eloise resenting how attractive Vanessa was and Vanessa wanting Eloise to shape up. Vanessa, on the other hand, sensed the subtle condescension of a white economically secure nonworking woman to her, a woman professional of color.

There was a good deal of struggle for a sense of control in the counseling. Eloise generally felt disenfranchised in her life by a powerful father and subsequently a powerful husband as well as by sons who loved her but saw her as an endlessly flowing breast. This caused Eloise to try to gain control in situations that did not involve men. Vanessa, who had labored to overcome the Hispanic culture's lack of support for her as a professional was consistently in need of control in most interpersonal situations. This mutual struggle kept the encounter moving along on the dimension of power. The affect dimension was slightly harder to delineate because each of the women wanted to like and be liked by the other. This kept the interaction friendly, although Eloise's vitriol leaked out and was quickly followed by apologies when Vanessa reproached her for it.

Eloise and Vanessa each tried to maintain power. This concentrated too much energy in the counseling without suitable exploration of what was transpiring between them. Had they been able to explore and understand their interactions, a good deal of light would have been shed on Eloise's psychological problems and likely some more progress would have resulted.

This case also helps illustrate how a client may feel rejected or abandoned if therapists' own issues prevent them from being able to provide nurturing or do not allow a client to be dependent on them as part of the client's working through an important developmental dynamic. This is especially the case with individuals who are phobic about being dependent either because of gendered messages and societal practices or because of other formative life experiences. Therapists need to be sensitive to such reactions and assure clients that feelings of dependence in counseling do not represent a permanent state of affairs, but rather part of a process of developing a self-view that allows feelings of dependence and independence to ebb and flow within the context of the mutuality that characterizes interpersonal relationships.

The Case of Donald

Donald, a 32-year-old single white man came for counseling because he was unable to keep a job and was urged by his lover to look at some possible reasons for that. Donald had no special vocational training, although he had graduated from college with a degree in English. He had a series of jobs including receptionist, waiter, executive assistant, and salesperson. At best, he kept the job for a year or two and at worst, for several months. He did not understand why he could not retain the jobs and was generally mystified as to why he was usually let go or made to feel sufficiently uncomfortable that he would quit.

He was affable and friendly, reasonably bright and well-spoken, nice-looking, attentive, and almost charming. He presented himself as interested in understanding what caused him to have so checkered a work history. He had no insight into what was happening and hoped the counselor could provide the solution. His counselor, Maya was a woman with a good deal of experience in vocational counseling.

Maya's initial inclination was to do some testing with Donald, but some intuitive sense urged restraint and she decided to hold off on the testing until she had more time to interact with Donald. The more she talked with him, the more she became aware of her changing reactions to him, and the more she began to look at the process of their interactions in therapy.

The first thing that intrigued her was her awareness of having flashes of anger toward Donald, which seemed inappropriate as he was invariably pleasant and responsive. She also found herself having a hard time listening and paying attention. All of this was disconcerting to her. Donald went blissfully on answering her questions and appearing to gain insight into his behavior as they explored his job history. Yet the counselor had the feeling that nothing was really changing, and that it was unlikely that he would improve in his work.

She asked Donald during their third session what he felt the dynamics were between them. He answered brightly, "Just like with my mother, you only want to take care of me and make everything better for me." "Do you like that?"

she inquired. "You bet, it makes me feel good to be cared about." "Do you care about me?" she asked. He replied, "Not really, but I haven't known you very long. Maybe I could after some time." All this was said with complete sincerity. The counselor felt a twinge of sadness and a strange aching feeling, which she suddenly realized was her reaction to abandonment.

At that moment she got it. Donald made himself extremely likable, especially to women, and easy to be with, in the hope that they would take care of him. They usually did. He, however, had no idea as to how to care for another person and really did not want to as he was far too needy himself. This caused him to refuse to reciprocate the caring and concern and, in fact, to emotionally retreat. This left others feeling "drawn or pulled in" and then discarded or abandoned. What usually happened at work, the counselor surmised, is that when supervisors or peers then retreated from Donald, his work performance suffered and they wound up firing him or he would quit.

The counselor's task she realized was somehow conveying to Donald what the dynamics of his behavior were and how he might do some things differently. Being sophisticated to the process dimension of counseling, the counselor pointed out to Donald when he exhibited the bits of behavior which led her to construct her analysis. He was able to grasp what she was talking about and could then look at ways in which he could be gratified outside of the work environment and thus not make the demands he usually did.

This counseling could have been turned into long-term psychotherapy but the client had not come with that intention and the counselor felt that the client could learn to handle his problem with some alternative behaviors even though the deeper roots of the behavior were not dealt with. She pointed out to him that he could enter into therapy if he so chose, but for now she was helping him to improve his chances of keeping his job and finding satisfaction in it. Perceiving, understanding, and using the process of the counseling interaction made this solution possible.

In this case, the counselor used her self-awareness and her understanding of the emerging gendered interpersonal process to gain insights into what might be motivating behaviors of difficulty to Donald. Moreover, her knowledge that white middle-class male socialization practices can leave some men unempathic to others and divorced from their own strong feelings of inadequacy assisted her in sensing what might be underneath the engaging chatter and superficiality she experienced in sessions with Donald.

The case also illustrates ways to use the transferential and countertransferential elements of counseling in promoting client awareness. Essentially, transference is the sum total of the client's reception of the counselor as some other person in the client's life, past or present. Countertransference is the reaction of the counselor to the transference as well as the counselor's own transference to the client. In this case the counselor used Donald's transference, and her immediate awareness of possible countertransferential reactions to it, in the "here and now" to help Donald recognize a dysfunctional interpersonal pattern that was also occurring in the counseling relationship. Thus, in saying to Donald, "What did you feel when your last supervisor said she could no longer help you?" she used her understanding of her momentary feelings to assist Donald in entering into explorations of his own pain.

Concluding Remarks

The counseling process incorporates the behavior of the participants as well as the history and culture each brings to their encounter. Behaviors considered in the chapter included those that are more and less visible and obvious. Nonverbal and verbal behaviors and dynamics can convey gendered meanings and perpetuate nonconscious views of how one should be as an acceptable and desirable woman or man. Counseling can move in ways more determined by therapists' internalized views of how a person should be, or how the counselor wants to be, rather than by wishes and desires congruent with what the client wants for herself or himself.

The counselor must pay attention to gender-related clues and to gender itself to maximize the success of counseling. This necessitates knowing much about gender role socialization and ongoing gendered discourses and interactions that influence clients, therapists, and their interactions in the process of counseling.

Discussion Questions

1. As mentioned in the chapter, lesbian and gay clients may avoid using a partner's name and the pronouns he or she in therapy, and instead use the plural pronoun we, when they do not feel safe to reveal their sexual orientation. As a personal exercise, have a 3-minute conversation with a person in the class in which you describe something you did this weekend with a friend, lover, or partner of the other sex. However, do not mention that person's name and do not reveal the person's sex. What did you observe about yourself? The other person?

2. This three-part question concerns how notions of power and privilege affect client-therapist dynamics and therapeutic outcomes. In responding, address how in your experience power and gender can play out in a counseling relationship. To the extent possible, use examples from your own counseling and therapeutic work (as counselor or client) to illustrate your points.

a. What themes of power and gender may play out when the dyad is same sex versus when the dyad is not the same sex?
b. What themes of power and gender may play out when the counselor is male and the client is female? When the counselor is female and the client is male?
c. How do you as a therapist work with a client who tries to have power over you? Would the therapy differ depending on the sex of the client? In responding make clear what you mean by a client having power over a counselor.

Suggested Readings

Comas-Diaz, L. & Greene, B. (Eds.). (1994). *Women of color: Integrating ethnic and gender identities in psychotherapy.* New York: Guilford. A comprehensive and in-depth discussion of cultural imperatives relevant to the mental health treatment of African American, Asian, Asian American, Latina/Hispanic, American Indian, and East and West Indian women.

Morrison, T. (1970). *The bluest eye.* New York: Pocket Books. The story of a young girl who believes her life would be different if she had blue eyes.

10 Strategies for Disrupting Gender Processes

A theme of the book is that gender is an active process that emerges between counselors and clients. In the complex process of development across the life cycle each of us internalizes societal-based constructions of women and men and each of us to varying degrees is encouraged and rewarded for playing them out in our interpersonal interactions. As made clear in earlier chapters, as counselors we do gender when we make certain assumptions about women's and men's differing capacities and act on these assumptions as if they are "truth" in counseling clients. We do gender when we behave differently with male and female clients and attribute the difference to their dynamics and not to our own. Finally, we do gender when we hold certain views of how women and men should be and use these views to implicitly or explicitly guide our counseling.

The focus of this chapter is the doing and undoing of gender in therapy. We start with a model for understanding these "alive" aspects of gender in therapy and then describe problematic areas in counseling, including the particularly troublesome area of sexual relations with clients, which violates the ethics of all the helping professions. Throughout we provide opportunities for the reader to consider ways to "undo gender" and also illustrate this process with examples from the counseling setting. Finally in an appendix to the chapter we provide an illustrative gender analysis of the case of Anthony and Rose.

A Model for Understanding the Interactive Aspects of Gender

In 1987, Deaux and Major published an interactive model of gender-related behavior. We have adapted their model to help explain the role of gender within social interactions such as counseling. The model conceptualizes gender as a component of the interactions between a perceiver and a target within a situational context. According to the model, the perceiver (in this case a counselor or therapist) enters the interaction with expectancies based on a set of gender beliefs which, in turn, may interact with and/or activate the target's (in this case the client's) own gender self-schemas and goals. A male counselor, for example, may assume when a married female client with children seeks his assistance that women want to put the needs of their husband and children before their own needs. This assumption may activate gender-related beliefs that color how a female client's present circumstances and concerns are considered. These interrelated events are depicted in Figure 10.1.

Moreover, because interactions occur within a context such as the office of a knowledgeable therapist, the context itself may influence whether an individual acts in accordance with the perceiver's expectations. In general, individuals are more likely to act in accordance with a perceiver's expectations, including

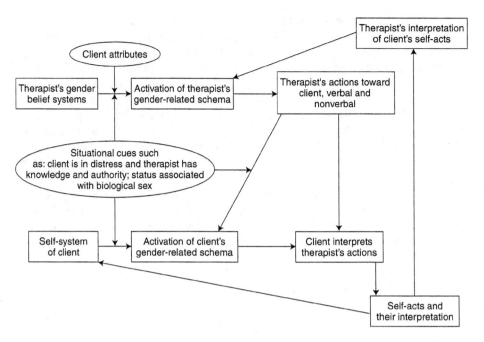

FIGURE 10.1 **Pictorial Representation of Therapist and Client Doing Gender**

sex-role expectations, when perceivers have more status and power. The rather complex set of events depicted in Figure 10.1 helps make this clear. In the model, situational cues are depicted as influencing the activation of both the therapist's and the client's gender-related schemas as well as how the therapist acts toward the client.

Let us return to the counseling example of the female client seeking help and to its context. This situation involves a woman in distress, who in seeking assistance from an esteemed helping professional may find herself acting in ways that preserve his views of women and his esteem for her as a wife and mother. The socially desirable, stereotypic behavior that emerges in the interaction, which may remain out of the awareness of both the perceiver and the target, would further serve to reinforce the gender expectancy of the perceiver as well as the target. That is, in responding in ways that are consistent with the counselor's expectations of women, the female client acts to preserve these expectations for herself. The model in Figure 10.1 depicts this possible sequence in the set of boxes starting with the self-system of client, to activation of client's schemas, to client interprets therapist's actions, to client's self-acts and interpretation of self-acts, and then back to the client's self-system and on to the therapist's interpretation of the client's self-acts.

Themes of Gender as Interpersonal Process in the Counseling Setting

Counseling and psychotherapy is an optimal place for gender as interpersonal process to emerge. As we noted in Chapter 4, the notion of therapists establishing egalitarian relationships with clients became a fundamental principle of feminist therapy for this very reason. Many women had entered into therapeutic relationships with well-meaning male therapists only to find themselves engaged in a paradigmatic contract between unequals, which operated to accentuate and deepen the initial inequality between the female client and the male therapist—the very doing of gender we are talking about here. In this situation, interpersonal processes based on assumed or nonconsciously held views of male superiority implicitly or explicitly maintained interpersonal dynamics that kept male counselors in a dominant position with their female clients. Let us now turn to common themes that could emerge as the doing of gender.

Using the Power and Influence Inherent in the Role of the Counselor, with Case Examples

Individuals seek assistance from counselors and therapists because of their supposed expertise. This situation sets up a power differential between those seeking help and those providing help, with one needing what the other can provide. Such a situation can put clients in a vulnerable position vis-à-vis counselors and place counselors in a position of unique power and influence.

Counselors need to be aware and respectful of this power differential and not use this difference in power to limit the counseling or harm the client. One way to minimize the potential for harm is by clarifying one's professional roles and obligations to clients (American Psychological Association, 1992). Counselors have the responsibility to determine where and when counseling takes place and to make clear to clients the rules applying to the counseling (e.g., when payment is due, how long sessions are, and how missed appointments and telephone calls in between sessions will be handled). Thus, the procedures and the boundaries of counseling are set, monitored, and enforced by the counselors. Clients, on the other hand, need the counselor's assistance in learning what the rules are so they can decide whether they want to abide by them.

Case Example 1.   A client at a community service agency has missed two appointments, calling after the second missed appointment to reschedule with the secretary but not explaining the reason for missing the first time. A third appointment is scheduled and the client shows up after having explained to the secretary that both missed sessions were because of child care difficulties. How does the counselor respond?

Does one attend to the difficulties of child care and how those can be dealt with or does one conceptualize the missed appointments as elements of a power struggle with the counselor that may need to be addressed? How does the counselor deal with possible feelings of anger, self-doubt, and concern caused by the missed appointments complicated by the client's calling afterward and rescheduling and then finally showing up. Can all these elements be dealt with simultaneously and briefly?

The answer to this last question is yes and no. The counselor may not know very much about the client's child care situation and this needs to be clarified. Also needing clarification is the agency's policy concerning missed appointments. It is also possible to make clear that the counselor and the agency cannot continue to serve clients who make a practice of missing appointments. This must be done carefully so as not to alienate the client while demonstrating that both the counselor and client have choices and responsibilities in this situation.

Clients struggling to master the counseling situation may elicit different reactions from male and female counselors. Should the client and therapist in this situation both be women, we might view the situation quite differently than if they were both men or if they were each of a different sex. A female counselor, for example, might be less likely to view the situation as having to do with power and more to do with the realities of the woman's life, and counseling not having the priority of other important priorities in a stressful life; a male counselor might be more likely to view the situation as having to do with challenges to his power and authority. Should the client be male, a resistance to seeking help hypothesis might emerge for both male and female counselors, which perhaps could result in greater accommodation of the missed appointments and less willingness to be firm in laying out the agency's policies.

Case Example 2.   Pope (1994) describes the case of a very prominent and highly respected psychiatrist who was charged with sexual involvement with seven female and male patients. The psychiatrist persuaded patients that sexual activity with their psychiatrist was part of their therapy and that he trusted that if they reported the incidents, their stories would not be believed. (In reality, legal actions in the case resulted in a revocation of his license and a prison term.)

This case illustrates how someone who is well aware of professional responsibilities and standards can use authority and position to exploit clients. It also illustrates some therapists' attempts to portray sexual involvement as a legitimate part of treatment. Many clients are unaware that ethics codes of all major mental health associations explicitly prohibit sexual intimacies with clients and thus clients without this knowledge are not in a position to challenge what the therapist says. Also wanting or needing to feel special with a therapist or trusting a therapist's intentions may result in clients believing the therapist's declaration that this situation is special and falls outside the domain of professional ethical standards.

Needing Female Clients to Please and Emulate the Counselor, with Case Examples

Counselors must examine their own affectional responses toward clients in an attempt to determine what is happening and to gauge what may be going on with the client. Counselors are in the business usually because they are positively disposed toward people. This can be a confounding element and must be considered whenever assessing the progress and status of a particular client, as there may be distortion in a positive direction.

It is fair to say that most counselors prefer feeling that their clients like them. The question of the doing of gender enters in when a counselor, male or female, needs clients to like them, and engages in gendered behaviors to bring about this liking. What motivates the behavior is the counselors' needs, not the clients', but the need itself may be situated in gender socialization. For example, as a result of their socialization, men as a group are more likely than women to assume that their clients want to please them, especially female clients, and that engaging in this kind of behavior reflects positively on clients' psychological health. In addition, they may unwittingly encourage or reinforce this kind of behavior but project the motivations for the pleasing on the needs of female clients to be liked and esteemed by powerful men rather than on their own need to be viewed in this way by women.

A client seeking approval may hang on every word of the counselor and attempt to implement what is suggested or perceived to be suggested. At the same time, the counselor may be trying to be helpful or brilliant so as to gain the approval of the client. The greater the need for approval in either participant the more the counseling will be about approval seeking and the more likely the interaction will be characterized by helpfulness and congratulation.

Case Example 1.   Beverly came to see a female counselor because of a miscarriage and the depression which followed it (see Sprock & Yoder, 1997, for an update on women and depression). She was feeling depressed, suicidal, and abandoned. She wanted a divorce. The counselor became aware that Beverly was a person who tended to avoid people and to abandon what few relationships she had enjoyed in an attempt to avoid being abandoned herself. She was defensive and presented herself as fragile.

The counselor, who had a great deal of experience and self-knowledge and understanding, worked quite well with Beverly helping her to feel valued and secure in their counseling relationship. Her ability to do this was a product of her experience and skill but also of her desire to nurture and protect people. The counselor's desire to nuture was a product of her own abandonment by her parents and the subsequent rescue by her maternal grandparents. She had an ongoing desire to be valued by people and the client was quite willing to do that while her own needs for safety and security were being met by the counselor. The counselor could be effective because she was aware of many of her internal dynamics and how they often got played out because she had sought therapy, supervision, and consultation to grasp what she was about as a person and as a therapist.

Case Example 2.   A very attractive woman in her middle thirties, Lorraine came for counseling because she was feeling quite sad and unmotivated. She had always been very dynamic with a passionate interest in the interior design business that she had developed with her sister and mother but had left it early in her marriage when her children were born. She had "everything" and yet she was not able to appreciate or enjoy her life as much as she thought she ought to. Her husband was somewhat older than she, a successful physician with a passion for golf who treated her like the trophy she appeared to be: a useful and functional adornment. She loved her children but often found herself in a rage with them just as she did occasionally with both her mother and sister. She was anxious and frightened because she was beginning to feel out of control.

Her counseling was short-term. She felt better after the first three sessions and came back for a fourth session in which the gains Lorraine made were examined and consolidated. The counselor, a man in his late forties, was very attracted to the client, although he was unsure why he felt a decided pull toward her, and liked her as a person. He found himself a bit annoyed with her at first because she was not realizing her potential. He also felt himself making some judgments about her choices in life, a part of him feeling that she had only herself to blame for her predicament of having bought into the traditional gender system of our culture. He was, however, aware of his thoughts and feelings toward her and thus could keep his interventions cleaner and more therapeutic than would have been the case were he unaware of his reactions.

The counselor allowed his genuine liking for the client to emerge in a positive manner in order to make her feel welcomed and admired, accomplishing this through both his verbal and nonverbal behavior. This caused her to warm to the counselor and to the task despite her anxiety. It became quickly apparent that Lorraine had an investment in making people (especially men) think she was not overly bright. The counselor made several comments about her adeptness at grasping his meaning and that he wondered why she was hiding her true competence. This gave her some permission to be more honest and proud of who she was and aided in the improvement she was to accomplish.

Understanding the danger of his putting Lorraine in a stereotypic pigeon-hole, the counselor asked appropriate questions to understand better why she had made the choices she did and what her life was like. She was quite happy with those choices and even with insight into the stereotypic quality of her gen-der role decisions, she would not have chosen otherwise. What did emerge, however, was a lack of understanding that with both children in school she was not getting enough emotional sustenance at home. The counselor had to be care-ful not to be smug and self-satisfied about his insight into her behavior but rather help her work with her choices. He did this by supporting her choices but also urging her to consider other options that would be in contradiction to the roles expected of her. She warmed to the support and began to look at options that would take her out of the house.

The relationship with her husband, which was not sufficient for her now that she was no longer so nurtured by her children's need for her, was also ex-amined. Together Lorraine and the counselor developed some strategies for her to increase her interactions and commonality with her husband. In working these tasks out together, the counselor was helping her to discover a way of working with her husband. He pointed this out and helped her to see how she could easily adopt and, if necessary, adapt the problem-solving and cooperative skills she had just used in counseling. Although the counseling centered around traditional choices for a woman, it was gender-aware insofar as the process of exploring Lorraine's choices and experience of herself enabled Lorraine to take more control of her participation in the marital relationship and in constructing a life that better met her needs.

The case of Lorraine is particularly instructive in that it illustrates clearly how counselors can effectively work with clients to disrupt gendered dis-courses. For example, the counselor gently confronted Lorraine on the possibil-ity that she hid her true competence and he genuinely encouraged, supported, and modeled her not needing to "do gender" with him in this way. The coun-selor was also mindful of the danger of his putting Lorraine in a stereotypic pi-geonhole and assuming he knew all there was to know about her. Instead, he viewed Lorraine as the expert on her own life and sought to understand better why she had made the choices she did and what her thoughts and feelings were now about those choices.

There is also the possibility that some doing of gender occurred in the counseling, despite the therapist's keen gender awareness and the counseling's positive outcome. In the process of the counselor's showing his liking for the client, probably a common experience for Lorraine who was very attractive and socially poised, he may also have engaged her in a nonconscious dynamic to get her to please and emulate him as an esteemed man who wants to help. More-over, his own gendered need to be esteemed and valued by a beautiful woman may have been activated. Some evidence for this hypothesis comes from the counselor's self-congratulatory feelings about how well the counseling with Lorraine progressed.

Conceptualizing Clients' Concerns within Gender Role Constraints and Dominant Discourse Themes, with Case Examples

Working against gender stereotypes is hard, particularly when those seeking our help may not be aware of the influence and power of those stereotypes in the counseling interaction with individuals representing the status quo (Fiske, 1993). Especially detrimental to women and men personally and interpersonally are internalized myths and conventional discourses about what it means to be a desirable woman or man. Common discourses descriptive of female clients' concerns include accepting husbands' authority, accepting belittling attitudes of women, and accepting physical and sexual abuse. Common discourses for men include believing "real men" need no one, depending on women to express for men, and assuming men are entitled to nurturance from women and entitled to their bodies. It is crucial for counselors to personally reflect on their work with clients and consider how they work "either to reproduce or disrupt conventional assumptions about gender" (Hare-Mustin & Marecek, 1990a, p. 4).

Case Example 1.   A good illustration of disrupting discourse about gender comes from a therapy demonstration in a training group in which a male student in the group volunteered to work with the female trainer. The theme of their work together that day was his wanting to feel empowered. At one point she asked him if there was any way in the moment that he could perhaps feel more empowered. "Yes" he said, "if I could somehow be superior to you." The counselor moved from her chair and sat on the floor and asked him to stand on his chair so that he could be far above her. This change in positions had an immediate and obvious impact on the male trainee and led into a very moving and spontaneous dialogue about his not knowing how to relate to powerful women as equals. The female trainer felt very secure as a woman, and did not feel at any risk of doing gender by giving up power so that he could feel empowered. She was able to let him struggle to come to a new meaning for himself of how he could feel powerful with a woman, not needing to disempower her in order to feel powerful himself.

Case Example 2.   Victor, a 20-year-old college sophomore at a prestigious college, was experiencing feelings of longing for his roommate. He had recurrent images of caressing and fondling the other young man. When he masturbated, images of his roommate kept intruding even though he tried to focus on women. He was becoming increasingly panic stricken, especially as he had inadvertently brushed against the naked roommate and had immediately become very aroused. He sought counseling at the college counseling center where he was assigned to Stan, a 35-year-old male counselor.

Victor missed several appointments when he was given Stan's name, and not that of a female therapist as he requested. Stan called and left him messages urging him to come in to the center, informing him that he could not be assigned another therapist until he spoke with him. When he finally did come for counseling he was very embarrassed and shy with Stan. Stan was active, asking lots of questions and volunteering information in a kind and interested manner. Victor slowly relaxed and began to talk about himself and his fantasies. He experienced a great deal of shame and fear about his interest in his roommate, worrying that he was gay, unmanly, and his future was empty. He was getting increasingly hopeless and depressed.

Stan was very patient and supportive and gently helped him to understand that his experience was not unusual and was in fact fairly normal. He was careful not to make him feel like a statistic and to explore with him the possibility that his was not a typical late adolescent homosexual panic but rather might be an indication of his being homosexual. This turned out not to be the case and Victor emerged from counseling with a deeper appreciation of some of the issues surrounding the gay world as well as a greater sensitivity to his own psychological makeup.

In exploring the dynamics of this counseling interaction we are aware of the power of the male role in frightening those who are to maintain and promote it while at the same time falling victim to it. Victor felt unmanly because of his homosexual yearnings. Stan, a man who was comfortable with homosexuality, could be nonjudgmental and supportive of Victor no matter what the outcome. This was aided by his generally nurturing and supportive approach in counseling (Scher, 1980). Victor responded well to his sense of comfort and care and let himself be open to Stan's support of him through his fear and anxiety. By allowing himself to depend on another man in this process he was able to listen to what he had to say and thus move beyond what was causing him extreme anxiety and panic and to feel empowered by his increased self-knowledge.

Constraining Oneself as the Counselor in Gendered Ways, with Case Examples

The dynamic of conceptualizing within gender role constraints and dominant discourse themes is double-edged in that it applies to how counselors conceptualize clients and how they conceptualize themselves in their work as counselors. The previous section concerned work with clients; in this section we turn to ourselves as counselors and therapists. Generally speaking, female counselors need to be mindful not to restrict themselves to support and nurturance and to find ways to feel comfortable using their power to influence, change, repair, or create that which is called for in the counseling setting. Men need to be mindful to be more nurturing and to let things emerge rather than control them.

Case Example 1.   Amy, a 26-year-old computer consultant, came to see Stephen, a 44-year-old psychologist because of severe headaches, that had no discernible physiological basis. Amy worked 80-hour weeks in the interest of getting ahead and earning a lot of money. In fact, she made more money than Stephen, who had a modest practice because he had little drive to work harder than he had to. He preferred a life of contemplation and leisure with opportunity to garden and go antiquing. They entered into a therapeutic relationship that went on for a year. At the end of the year Amy was still working as hard, had gotten engaged, and still had the headaches although their frequency and intensity had diminished. She terminated therapy against Stephen's advice.

There was a very subtle and interesting gender role dynamic in this particular case. Stephen was aware of how his occupational drive was counter to the competitive and ambitious mode most men followed and that he had to be careful not to try to influence other men to be as he was. Interestingly enough, he was seeing a young woman behaving as a man ought to. He was careful not to discourage her from being ambitious because women ought not to be and because he thought he should be more ambitious. He was successful in not discouraging her ambition, especially considering the likelihood that Amy's headaches were stress related as a result of her drive and hard work. It was all right with this male counselor for his female client to be ambitious.

However, Stephen was not aware of his gender programming when he advised Amy to remain in counseling. He wanted to take care of her and was convinced that through his ministrations she could eventually be headache free. Amy intuitively knew that she was on her way to curing herself of her headaches not entirely because of Stephen's assistance, but mainly through her own efforts and she was quite capable of continuing the process herself. She resisted his efforts to keep her dependent by being resolutely independent, something Stephen did not like.

Case Example 2.   Ernestine had been a counselor in a rural mental health center for 12 years when Cristina came to see her for counseling. Cristina was 17 years old and very depressed. She was an intelligent young woman who had come because of obsessive thoughts of suicide after her boyfriend of four years had dumped her. Ernestine, a single mother of three, had educated herself and her children without help or involvement from her former husband. She remained in this rural area because her aged parents needed assistance. She was an only child and therefore the burden fell on her. Cristina's parents were prominent members of the community who did not want her to go for counseling so she had come on her own without their knowledge.

Cristina stayed in counseling for 6 months and left feeling good about herself, determined to go to college to become a social worker, resolved to put off dating, tenuously reconciled with her parents, and was deeply grateful to Ernestine. On the surface one would think that this is an excellent outcome for such a counseling interaction and indeed it was. At the same time, on closer inspection we can discern that some dynamics were elicited in Ernestine as a result of her socialization and experiences as a woman. For example, she obviously supported and encouraged Cristina's independence and autonomy in contradiction to traditional gender role traits. She did not encourage her to involve herself with her parents or solicit their support. She not only helped her to get over the feelings of rejection by and need for male companionship but supported a kind of renunciation of that need, obviously a partial reflection of her own adjustment to abandonment by her ex-husband. She did, however, support Cristina in pursuing a career as a social worker without examining the transference.

Cristina aroused in Ernestine a vicarious wish to do her own life differently and she supported and encouraged that in her. This is not necessarily bad or wrong but it is obvious that gender role dynamics and dominant discourse themes played a part here and Ernestine could have been more empowering of Cristina's self-definition were she more aware of her own values and expectations with regard to women's roles and desires.

Engaging in Sexual Relations with Clients

Sexual intimacy between therapists and clients continues to be a serious problem (Pope, Sonne, & Holroyd, 1993; Stake & Oliver, 1991; Thoreson, Shaughnessy, Heppner, & Cook, 1993). In 1988 cases based on violation of the Ethical Principles of Psychologists accounted for 25 percent of the cases reported to the American Psychological Association Ethics Committee—more than twice the number reported for any other category of the ethical principles for that year (American Psychological Association, 1990, 1991). Complaints in this area have increased each year since 1979, when sexual intimacies with clients were specifically defined as unethical in the Ethical Principles of Psychologists.

Recent reports indicate that the problem is no better. Sexual misconduct was the underlying behavior in 47 percent of the cases opened by the Ethics Committee in 1994 and 48 percent of the cases opened in 1995 (American Psychological Association, 1995, 1996). The only other categories involved in more than 5 percent of the complaints were insurance and fee problems (14 percent), test misuse (9 percent), termination and supervisory matters (8 percent), child custody evaluations (7 percent), practicing outside one's competence (5 percent), and confidentiality violations (5 percent).

As has been the pattern all along, the major area of sexual misconduct violations continues to be male psychologist with adult female client. For cases in 1994, 91 percent of the violations were for a male therapist with a female client. For 1995, it was 90 percent. These figures are consistent with earlier figures of approximately 1 in 10 men, but only 1 in 50 women, self-reporting erotic contact with clients, nearly all of whom were female (Pope, 1990; Pope & Bouhoutsos, 1986). These figures are also consistent with reports from the Ethics Committee each year from 1988 to the present time.

Female therapists appear to have little interest in being sexually intimate with male clients; the motivations and needs of male therapists appear stronger. This situation, which is extremely harmful to clients, appears tied to the misuse of power and the doing of gender in the counseling setting.

Gilbert and Scher (1992) analyzed men's socialized entitlement and needs for power over, and dependence on, women in elucidating this pattern of unethical and harmful behavior. Their review of the literature indicated that the reasons typically given for why this happens fall under the category of male entitlement, an entitlement that results in some male therapists reproducing conventional assumptions about gender and the male sexual drive discourse (see Chapter 5 for a discussion of this topic). Illustrative themes include the needs and wants of the therapist becoming the focus of the therapy; the therapist creates and exploits an exaggerated dependence on the part of the client; and the therapist uses rationalizations to discount harm to the client.

Male counselors and therapists who do not feel dominant or special in their own lives outside of counseling and therapy may be particularly prone to look to sexual expression with a female client to feel empowered. In addition, a sense of entitlement to female nurturance and to women's bodies may lead male counselors to overlook any of the improprieties involved. Moreover, because female clients may respond in ways that meet the male counselor's needs—a situation made likely by female socialization—the counselor may have little incentive to question his motives. The particular sexual behaviors reported to occur, for example, are usually characterized by submissive behavior on the part of the client such as performing fellatio on the counselor (Gutheil & Gabbard, 1993; Pope, 1994).

Pope and Bouhoutsos (1986, p. 4) described the most common themes describing male therapists' motivations. Many of these themes are consistent with Gilbert and Scher's (1992) analysis, particularly the themes of Role trading, Svengali, True love, It just got out of hand, Time out, and Hold me.

- *Role trading:* The therapist and client trade roles and the needs of the therapist become the focus.
- *Sex therapy:* Sex with the client is presented as the preferred mode of treatment.
- *As if . . . :* Positive transference is interpreted as if there were no therapy relationship involved.
- *Svengali:* Client's dependence on therapist is exaggerated and exploited.
- *Drugs/rape:* Therapist uses drugs or physical force and intimidation to force sex on the client.
- *True love:* Therapist rationalizes that he is in love.
- *It just got out of hand:* Therapist fails to handle the emotional boundaries of therapy.
- *Time out:* Therapist rationalizes that time between sessions is not part of therapy or terminates therapy to have sex with a client.
- *Hold me:* Client's needs for closeness and attachment are exploited by the therapist.

Counselors do not wish to harm their clients. Often counselors have not worked through their own gender socialization in the area of sexuality and eroticism, do not recognize their own doing of gender with clients, and are not prepared to deal constructively with sexual feelings in counseling. Box 10.1 presents some "dangers" to pay attention to in counseling. If you find yourself engaging in any of these dynamics or behaviors with a client, seek supervision from a colleague. Supervision will allow you to step back from the situation, honestly consider what is going on with you, and work out ways to get counseling back on course. In some cases, referral may be in the best interest of the client.

In preventing the sexual abuse of clients, it is important for counselors to develop a comfort with their sexuality and their sexual feelings, hold a deep commitment to the importance of boundaries in counseling and therapy, and should clients feel attracted to their counselor, know how to validate the client's experience while using the experience to explore ways they as counselors may be hiding sexual attraction and erotic feelings.

Also likely is that a female client you are seeing will report in the process of counseling that she has been in a sexual relationship with a previous therapist. Studies indicate that 44 to 65 percent of therapists surveyed reported that at least one client they treated had been sexually involved with a previous therapist (Pope, 1994). Working with such a client presents a number of complex challenges, for the counselor has no automatic way of knowing how the client experienced the relationship and what she is feeling now. Every client is unique in this respect. A client may be unaware of the ethics violations involved. Clients may expect, want, or fear sexual involvement with a subsequent therapist. They may

---

BOX 10.1   Signals That a Male Counselor May Be Denying Erotic Feelings and Headed for Trouble in Counseling a Female Client

- Sexual voyeurism—Sessions begin to focus around the sex life of the client.
- Self-protection—In supervision or in case notes, sexual material/feelings of counselor's attraction are not reported.
- Pathologizes the client—The client is viewed as obsessed with sex, overly dependent on men, needy, having poor boundaries.
- Hard to say no—The client is reluctant to challenge the counselor and believes he has her best interests at heart.
- Patronizes the client—The counselor feels overly self-protective of the client and/or views women as needing to take care of men's emotions.
- Fears allowing sexual feelings—The counselor denies ever having sexual feelings about a client.
- Sexualizes intimacy—The client seeks an emotional intimacy which the therapist experiences as sexual and erotic.
- Has difficulty in saying no—The counselor experiences the client as so arousing it is difficult to say no to his own needs.

feel powerless to prevent this from occurring and may seek a female therapist for this reason. On the other hand, they may feel protective of the previous therapist and reluctant to hear that he was not behaving ethically. In this situation it is crucial to validate the client's experience and at some point to inform her that this kind of behavior is prohibited, that it was not her fault, and that she has a right to file a complaint with the appropriate state board or licensing agency. (The client reporting this kind of incident may also be a male, but if so, it is much more likely that the counselor also was a male rather than a female.)

Also complicating therapy with a client who has been in a sexual relationship with a previous therapist is the counselor's own feelings and reactions, and the extent to which these are consistent with stereotypic views of women' sexuality and nature. Common responses of therapists reported by Pope (1994) include disbelieving that it happened, assuming little harm occurred, believing the client is sick or dangerous, or believing the client brought it on herself and should be held responsible, and fearing sexual attraction to the client.

As a gender-aware counselor you may feel angry that this happened, and that the client was abused and harmed by someone whom she trusted to help her. Here again, supervision or discussion with a colleague is called for. It is important to keep the counseling focused on what the client is feeling and not to let your own feelings of outrage determine its process and goals.

Concluding Remarks

This chapter centered around the active processes of gender that emerge between counselors and clients. We discussed four areas particularly vulnerable to the doing of gender: using the authority inherent in the counselor role, needing clients to please and emulate, being constrained by conventional gender roles and discourses, and engaging in sex with clients. By focusing on examples of the doing, and the undoing of gender, we hope we have provided readers with clear ways to detect these "alive" aspects of gender in their counseling and by so doing ways to engage in more effective practice. Finally, in an appendix to this chapter we use the case of Anthony and Rose to provide an example of how one can do a gender analysis of one's work as a therapist or counselor. We suggest you also use this kind of analysis in considering client cases that appear in various case books and textbooks.

Discussion Questions

1. In addition to learning a lot of objective material from this book, we hope it also increased your awareness of personal biases and belief systems in

the areas of gender and sexuality. In responding, please give at least two examples for each part of the question.

   a. In what ways do you see your beliefs, expectations, and understanding of human development and behavior influenced by this book?
   b. Are there ways that you see and think about yourself differently from how you did when you started the book?

2. Throughout the book we have emphasized the importance of recognizing the multiple cultural, historical, and social relational influences that structure any particular discourse. In this chapter we have examined a few ways gender as a cultural construct might implicitly structure assumptions guiding the therapeutic process without participants' full awareness. Discuss three examples from your own life experiences that illustrate this affect.

Suggested Readings

Pope, K. S. (1994). *Sexual involvement with therapists: Patient assessment, subsequent therapy, forensics*. Washington, DC: American Psychological Association. An information-packed volume for counselors and therapists working with clients who have been sexually involved with a previous therapist.

Pope, K. S., Sonne, J. L., & Holroyd, J. (1993). *Sexual feelings in psychotherapy*. Washington, DC: American Psychological Association. A highly readable and useful resource for therapists and counselors.

Appendix A: An Illustrative Gender Analysis of a Client Case

The Case of Anthony and Rose

Anthony was a 59-year-old recently retired man. Both he and his wife of 36 years, Rose, were adjusting to his new status. Rose was a few years younger than Anthony. They married when she was 20 and he was 23. They had no children and Rose had cared for their home over the years and occasionally did part-time work or volunteer activities. They had relocated three or four times within the same state and had lived in their current city for nearly 10 years. They were each in good health and were physically and socially attractive people. He sought therapy with a man, also white, about his age who had been recommended by a recently retired former colleague.

Anthony wanted therapy because he was having overwhelming fears of impotence, and subsequently had begun to lose interest in sex. He had only experienced the loss of an erection recently, in fact. However, it had become such an obsession that he was not enjoying sex and was not able to be a very satisfying lover to Rose. These fears were very new to him, as he had never had any sexual dysfunction before and had always viewed himself with a stronger than average male sexual appetite. He had not told Rose what was happening psychologically and thought she was unaware of his worries, as she had been very reassuring that everything was basically fine and would go back to normal any day now.

These thoughts of impotence had begun to occur more frequently during the day rather than just when the couple was having sex, as was originally the case. Anthony was getting more frantic as each day passed and began immediately to pressure the therapist to solve his problem.

The therapist found it easy to establish rapport with Anthony and quite enjoyed his practical manner and obvious intelligence. He also appreciated his getting to the basic issue quickly and his willingness to do what was needed to resolve the problem. He commented positively on Anthony's ability to quickly pick up on the drift of his queries and his ability to think and express himself so clearly.

As the therapist questioned and listened to Anthony, some additional significant information began to emerge. It bothered Anthony that he was pressured to retire because he had always assumed he would be the one to decide when to retire. It also bothered him, although he did not know why, that he had worked so hard and been so successful but had no children to pass things on to. It was also unclear to him why he and Rose had no children. Neither of them had used birth control to his knowledge but pregnancy just had never happened. In addition, Anthony revealed the secret of a relatively long-term affair with a married woman. This woman had moved abroad, forcing the affair to end approximately 6 months ago.

Rose was a caring and trusting woman who had willingly created a comfortable home in the several locations necessary for Anthony's work. He thought not having a child had been hard for her, because he had noticed that on more than one occasion when individuals asked Rose what she did, her response was, "I am nothing." If she knew he was having an affair she never let on and continued to be the nearly perfect wife for him—always available sexually and emotionally and very eager to please him. He affectionately referred to her as his soft side. Anthony thought she did not know of his infidelity and he had done everything he could to keep it from her as he did not want to upset Rose or cause her to leave. He was very devoted to her and would never want to hurt her.

The counseling initially focused on what it meant for Anthony to have both his career and his love affair end at about the same time. Anthony had never thought about that coincidence and how this set of events might be related to his current anxiety about impotence. It emerged that Anthony's work as an engineer was clearly at the center of his life and that he felt "at sea" and "unanchored" having to retire. He had never given a good deal of thought to why he was involved in the affair and had more or less attributed it to his strong sex drive. However, he did agree with his counselor's thought that these events contributed to his feelings of having less power and his questioning his virility and status. Although he enjoyed sex with Rose, he liked the idea of also having sex with other women. In fact, it made him feel more alive and vital and he is quite sure he would not have ended the relationship if the woman had not moved so far away.

After the third session, the counselor recommended that it might be useful for Rose to come to a session with Anthony. Anthony's anxiety was decreasing, since he had been able to maintain an erection two times in the previous week. However, the counselor was concerned that there might be some other issues in the relationship affecting Anthony's anxiety that were not immediately obvious to him. Rose was at first reluctant to come with Anthony but agreed because she wanted to do all she could to have Anthony "feel better and be himself again."

The three sessions with Anthony and Rose together were useful for the counselor and the couple. It emerged that Rose was having a difficult time adapting to Anthony's being at home. She felt she had to be accountable to him for how she spent her time and she was also feeling increasingly defensive and self-conscious about how she spent her time. Anthony would read professional books and journals, spend hours on the Internet, and watch CNN, activities that she found foreign and uninteresting. She admitted always having felt intellectually inferior to Anthony, a feeling magnified by her not having come close to completing her undergraduate degree, while Anthony had completed two master's degrees in both engineering and management. Anthony always reassured her, as he did in the session, that he loved her as she is and had no need for her to get a degree. She also admitted that she thought his sexual problems must be somehow related to his being at home, to the pressure she felt at having to be sexually available at any time, and to his seeing her not at her best. "We never had any problems until Anthony retired, and now he may not respect me as much." In the next two sessions of counseling Anthony came to see the importance of work in his life and decided to take on a three-quarter time consulting position. This decision eased the situation considerably with Rose as well as Anthony's preoccupation with not getting an erection.

A Gender Analysis of the Case

One way to approach a gender analysis is to ask oneself how might gender issues associated with the four faces of gender have entered into and informed the therapy. We identify several issues here, knowing that many others are possible. It is important to note that the four faces are interactive (see Figure 1.1) and thus may appear in a different form under more than one face or category.

Gender as Difference

- The counselor challenges neither Anthony's use of sex as a way to define and enhance his sense of masculinity nor Rose's sense that she may be the cause of his difficulties because she is not a desirable enough sex object.

- Anthony's sexual functioning and satisfaction are an index of whether counseling is successful; Rose's satisfaction in this area is never addressed.
- Anthony sees no reason for Rose to feel a need for an education although he himself earned two advanced degrees.
- What Rose does in the relationship is considered the "soft side."

Gender as Structurer and Organizer

- By being asked to retire, Anthony gives up power, which is what he also does when he is forced to give up the affair. This kind of analysis by the counselor is consistent with traditional views of men's power at work becoming associated with their sexual power and entitlement as, for example, in dynamics associated with sexual harassment.
- Anthony and Rose have developed a marriage around traditional notions of male and female roles. The counselor appears to accept this arrangement as a given, a structure not to be challenged or questioned.

Gender as Language and Discourse

- Anthony attributes his affair to the male sexual drive discourse and his entitlement as a man; this dominant discourse goes unchallenged by the counselor.
- Rose sees herself "as nothing," a perception seemingly tied to her not being a mother and thus not fulfilling her destiny as a woman; this represents another dominant discourse not addressed in the counseling.

Gender as Interpersonal Process

- The counselor never questions the central importance of Anthony's career. Its importance is emphasized throughout the counseling with much less emphasis given to other aspects of his life or to his emotional life.
- The counselor validates Anthony's intelligence and ability and uses these to establish rapport.
- The counselor accepts at face value that Rose is satisfied with "being nothing" and seeks a solution that leaves her in the same situation she was in before Anthony sought counseling.

◈ Discussion Questions

1. Would the case have played out differently with a white female therapist of about the same age as the male therapist? For example, would Anthony have been as open about the affair and his motivations for engaging in it?

2. The counselor did not challenge Anthony's defining himself in terms of his performance at work or in sex. Anthony is getting older. Has the counselor done him a disservice by putting him back on track, so to speak, and not exploring Anthony's performance-based self-evaluations?

3. The issues of sex and children were not explored, although the loss of not having a child emerged in discussions with Rose and Anthony. Both partners may carry feelings of inadequacy about why they never had children. Is it too late to raise these kinds of issues with the couple? Would it be important?

4. What do you think is going on with Rose?

11 Ethical Practice

Ethical codes are guides to effective therapy, and effective therapy is a guide to ethical behavior. We cannot be effective therapists without behaving ethically. The ethical counselor knows what appropriate behavior is, even if that behavior seems inconsistent with professional standards. That counselor also knows that consultation with colleagues and professional boards is essential should such inconsistency arise. Ethical principles and codes of conduct are arrived at by mental health professionals attempting to protect the profession from regulation by external agencies. Implicit in the ethical codes, however, is a model for the client-counselor relationship that fosters the goals of mental health. Just as ethical codes have been given specific content in standards for providers of mental health services, ethical codes can be given specific content in the counseling relationship. It is the responsibility of therapists and counselors to incorporate ethical standards into their practices so that clients' rights will be an integral part of the therapy (Hare-Mustin, Marecek, Kaplan, & Liss-Levinson, 1979; Lerman & Porter, 1990).

As the public seeking therapy and the means of providing such assistance have multiplied, the potential for harm has also increased, making counselors' and therapists' responsibilities to clients all the more important. Clients need to be provided with information that allows them to make informed decisions about their counseling and with a statement that outlines the counselor's expectations (e.g., fees, length of sessions, relationship boundaries). In addition, clients need to be informed of their rights and responsibilities, which includes challenging counselors who practice outside their areas of competence and knowing where they can file ethical complaints (Hare-Mustin et. al, 1979). The difficulty in conceptualizing standards for practice to cover every possible situation has also increased and that is why it is important to be conversant with the ethical principles and codes of conduct governing one's profession and to be willing to question those principles and codes with the assistance of consultation and deep thought should that be necessary.

The impact of gender issues on the ethical practice of counseling has been of inordinate significance. This impact has been largely the result of the work of writers on feminism and feminist therapy (Lerman & Porter, 1990). The manner in which women had been treated in therapy was cause for great concern and led to a major rethinking of ethical principles governing fairness and oppression. New codes of behavior are to some extent a result of the courageous challenging of patriarchal and hierarchical concepts of therapy and the professions that delivered it. A new broom does sweep clean and so all people benefited from the changes.

What Is Ethical Behavior?

Obviously we cannot definitively answer a question that has plagued humankind since communities emerged. However, we can think about it in terms of gender and the ethical implications involved in how gender affects counseling and how counseling affects gender role behavior. This leads us to the following opinion about ethical behavior in counseling: Ethical behavior is that which promotes the fullest expression of all people while honoring the rights of individuals to safety from subjugation and oppression.

We understand that there are shortcomings in this statement but we hope that the spirit will be honored. That spirit is a proclamation that a new wind of freedom from artificially created historical restraints to the full functioning of women and men must blow through the musty offices of counselors in order to freshen and sweeten the atmosphere of a profession dedicated to assisting people in living their lives amply.

What Is Effective Counseling?

This is another question that is difficult to answer definitively. So again we look at the answer from the perspective of gender roles and we attempt a response. To us effective counseling is the professional interaction that

1. Challenges modes of gender enactments in counseling and in clients' lives
2. Promotes a deeper understanding of and encouragement toward the appropriate divesting of those artifacts of gender roles and gender enactments that oppress and constrain individuals, keeping them from realizing the potential possible from their skills, education, talents, and personal history
3. Provides a safe place for alternate discourses about self to emerge

If we counsel ethically then we aid clients in understanding the constraints imposed on them by the historical accumulation of behaviors, traditions, beliefs, and standards associated with gender constructions. The counselor aids the client in exploring alternatives to these constraints, never demanding nor expecting that the client will shed these constraints if that is not the desire of the client. In the explication and examples to follow the link between ethical practice and effective therapy will be made clearer.

Ethical Difficulties Counselors Confront

Each of the disciplines that trains counselors has a code of ethical principles and codes of conduct. These include the American Counseling Association *Code of*

Ethics and Standards of Practice (1995), the American Psychological Association (APA) *Ethical Principles of Psychologists and Code of Conduct* (1992), National Board for Certified Counselors' *Counseling Services: Consumer Rights and Responsibilities* (1987), and codes established for marriage and family therapists, licensed professional counselors, and licensed clinical social workers.

These codes bear great similarity. We are most familiar with the APA principles and code and use it as the prototype in discussing ethics in counseling. We believe that ethical behavior is a function of good education and meaningful introspection by professionals who have confronted their own psychological issues in therapy. The latter helps ensure ethical and effective professional behavior.

The major stumbling block to working ethically is a narcissistic belief in the rightness of our own opinions and the necessity of gratifying our desires and impulses. Obviously, we can all deny caving in to either of these beliefs as they are transparently counterproductive. However, when we are under pressure and are somehow not being nourished in our own lives it is far easier to give in to impulses that we would normally hold in check. For this reason it is essential to maintain therapeutic and consultative relationships with peers to help in avoiding unethical and indeed harmful behavior to our clients and ultimately to ourselves.

Ethical standards should be carefully studied, digested, and applied through reading casebooks about ethical issues and dilemmas. Because practicing ethically involves a whole host of decisions, it is important to know what one's profession deems appropriate. This extends from advertising one's services to carefully informing clients of what to expect in counseling and what it will cost, to being judicious in the keeping of records, to conducting research, to avoiding dual relationships, to shunning sexual contact, to terminating counseling appropriately.

It is clear that most of these issues are amenable to learning, for example, what is appropriate in advertising one's services. What is appropriate, incidentally, has changed over the years as a result of cultural and legal pressures. Ethical principles and codes of conduct are a product of the general culture and therefore are living documents that evolve and change, as professions and cultural expectations evolve and change. Some ethical issues are not straightforward and need careful study and consideration. It is to some examples of these issues that we now turn.

Challenges to Ethical Behavior

The major challenges to ethical behavior from the perspective of sex and gender are issues and dynamics that prevent equality between the sexes, socially, politically, and economically. A key example is dual relationships. A dual relationship occurs when the therapist and client have contact or involvement in a context other than therapy, such as the client is a student, employee, supervisee, or friend of the therapist. Dual relationships pose problems in counseling for a variety of reasons, not the least of which is the power differential that exists and is magnified in such relationships, particularly between female clients and male counselors and therapists.

Avoiding dual relationships with clients involves not knowing or interacting with them outside of the counseling situation. This sanction extends to not being involved with others who are involved with these clients directly. Counseling works best when it presents a clean and clear interaction between two parties who did not know each other before therapy and will not know each other after therapy. If there is any kind of dual relationship, those optimum conditions are compromised. Certainly, it is possible that a dual relationship will abet counseling but the risks usually outweigh that potential.

In the real world, however, that is not always possible (Brown, 1991). There are times when clients unexpectedly enter a counselor's social or occupational sphere. For example, your client may be an elementary school teacher who happens to work in the same school as the spouse of your brother, or your daughter or son may transfer to a school and be in the same class as the son or daughter of one of your clients. Berman (1985) used the term "overlapping relationships" to refer to situations in which therapists' and clients' lives overlap despite all efforts to avoid dual roles. These kinds of situations require therapists to clearly think through the steps for boundary management. An important first step is to acknowledge and validate that an overlapping relationship exists (rather than, for example, hoping you will never see the person, knowing full well that you will). Doing so facilitates anticipating possible problems and thinking through ways to handle these situations when they arise (Brown, 1991).

It is important to exercise common sense when considering the issues of dual relationships. For example, it is not necessary to ignore clients when they are encountered in the supermarket or at a movie. However, it is wise to allow the client to extend a greeting first as that preserves the confidentiality of the relationship, which incidentally belongs to the client and not the counselor. Discussing such chance meetings early in the counseling is helpful in aiding the client to understand how this is not conversation with an interested friend but rather a professional relationship that has standards, limits, and rules.

The confidential nature of the therapeutic interaction is also considered in raising the issues inherent in the structure of counseling. Counseling is a privileged relationship, which means that without the client's permission what is divulged cannot be reported. Of course, there are variations to this rule by state depending on characteristics of the client and the situation, and the counselor must be conversant with these differences. Confidentiality, which underscores the anonymity of the counselor for the client, is an essential element in the effectiveness of this therapeutic interaction. Inroads into this privileged relationship must be guarded against and fought when they occur. Without it, therapy becomes just two people having an intense chat.

As discussed in Chapter 10, sexual improprieties in counseling are to be avoided because they are uniformly destructive and unethical in nature. As we have explored it elsewhere, it is not necessary to explain but simply to restate that counseling is a relationship of unequal power. Therefore, any sexual behavior in the context of therapy is exploitative. The counselor is the professional whose role has associated with it certain responsibilities and privileges. If the power and authority associated with that role are used for sex or seduction, regardless of how it comes about, it is an exploitation of the client.

There are so many ways of being sexual and it is important to understand therefore that counselors must be aware of their own erotic needs and behaviors as well as the potential in the counseling encounter. The introspective and self-aware counselor will know, for example, when touch is likely to be sexual as opposed to comforting or affectionate. In the latter cases it may still be inappropriate.

Working Effectively

Working ethically is tantamount to working effectively, that is, one cannot be unethical and effective. Once again, we reiterate the importance of knowing one's profession's code of ethical behavior and consulting with colleagues and boards of professional practice whenever there is a question about a particular action the counselor wishes to make.

In order to be effective we must understand that situations will always arise that test the limits of ethical behavior. There is no way to avoid this because human behavior is complex and often messy. We have been counseling long enough to know that sometimes we need to weigh several factors in coming to a decision that we believe is in the client's best interest and congruent with our understanding of the ethics of our profession.

We want to look at a few areas where such messiness is bound to occur and think about ways of dealing with it, or at least understanding that the ethical dilemma may have to be lived with. Common examples include counselors finding themselves on community committees with current and former clients or the partner of a client, or having a client meet and befriend a close friend or former partner of the counselor. These kinds of dilemmas are particularly likely to occur in small communities or in lesbian and gay communities where lesbian or gay therapists are also very active in their community (Brown, 1991).

Lydia, a therapist in private practice in a small town in Nebraska, received a phone call from her accountant. He was in a personal crisis and wanted to see her immediately for counseling. Lydia carefully explained that she would not see him because it was a violation of ethical standards to establish a dual relationship that might be inimical to effective counseling. She told him she would refer him to another therapist in town. He refused saying that he knew she was a superior therapist and that he would not go to see anyone else because he trusted her skills and her confidentiality as a result of their long association. Lydia did not think he was suicidal but he was desperate. She realized her choice was to see him and get supervision or consultation for the case so as to minimize the effects of the dual relationship or not to see him and run the risk of his not getting any counseling, which he very much needed. She also would have lost an excellent accountant as well as had her reputation damaged in a small town where dual relationships had to be a way of life. After all, the stockbroker's doctor was also his customer and had to assume that he would be treated professionally even if he recommended an investment that failed. The counselor decided to take on the therapy of her accountant for several months until the crisis passed and then she referred him to another counselor in a nearby town.

Did this therapist violate the letter of the ethical code? The case is instructive because it shows us that knowing ethical principles and incorporating them into one's work and being enables the counselor to serve the public well. She was wise enough to share and explain her dilemma to the client when the time was appropriate so that he would not feel rejected or abandoned but would be willing to move to another therapist when he felt the crisis was past and he was on his way to being more centered and coping better.

When counselors behave unethically there are a variety of consequences, not the least of which is that they run the risk of losing their license and putting their livelihood in danger. Counseling is a humane profession and so we must apply ourselves and our skills humanely. This may mean making decisions and taking actions that are in the spirit of the codes but not abiding by the letter. For example, a client in real crisis may not be able to listen to a recitation of what can be expected in counseling on entering the counselor's office because the pressure of divulging the trauma that was the impetus for coming is too great. The counselor risks alienating the client by rigidly adhering to the principles. The counselor must decide. Experience helps in knowing what is likely the best course of action. It is, however, no guarantee.

Behaving unethically, in a manner that damages the client or the therapy also damages the counselor ultimately and of course casts the whole profession in a poor light. It is incumbent on all of us as practitioners to be cognizant of our ethical principles and code of conduct and to act in accordance with them.

Aside from circumstances of geography or practice that may cause us to make carefully thought out departures from ethics, there are circumstances which encourage departures that are not well thought out or are the product of denial and self-delusion. These must be carefully guarded against. Practicing outside one's area of competence is not helpful to anyone.

Counselors who are under personal strain are vulnerable to acting in an inappropriate manner. It is essential that they have resources for exploring their personal difficulties and traumas as well as to have been in therapy and to use it as a regular resource to maintain their own equilibrium. Failure to do so results in potential damage to their work and to their clients. It is hard to encourage introspection and change in others when one has avoided it for oneself. All of us are subject to the whims and difficulties of life and at times need assistance in coping. That assistance does not have to come from a professional but it often has to come from someone outside the self.

An example follows that demonstrates how not being aware of the stresses in one's life or ignoring them can do damage to a client. A 35-year-old male counselor whose wife was in her sixth month of pregnancy and had been cautioned to refrain from sexual intercourse was feeling depressed. He was unaware that his sexual frustration was not just physiological but was fed by his depression as a result of unresolved fears of abandonment. His wife's inability to have sex with him made him feel deserted. He had a very attractive young man in his practice who was sexually active and had come to counseling as a result of a seeming inability to maintain relationships. The counseling was going well and the client and counselor were forming a good therapeutic relationship. As the counselor became increasingly depressed, he began to ask for more and more detailed accounts of the client's sexual exploits. This was all carefully couched in appropriate sounding questions relating to the young man's interpersonal dynamics. After three or four sessions of this, the client abruptly terminated the counseling. The client had been damaged without having sex with the counselor but their interaction had been voyeuristically sexual. Had the counselor been more aware of his own needs and sought assistance for them this sad eventuality would have been avoided.

Case Examples to Consider

In an attempt to make explicit some ethical dilemmas and how one might deal with them we will examine a few illustrative cases.

1. Simon, a colleague in the counseling division of the community agency where you work, is a charismatic and well-respected member of the staff. One of your clients mentions that her 8-year-old niece is getting excellent help from Simon; the girl has no male figure in her life since the death of her father. Your client says that Simon frequently holds the young girl in his lap and gives her small presents when she comes for her sessions. The little girl is thriving and has become very attached to Simon. You subsequently find out that Simon and the little girl attend the same church. You feel uncomfortable when this information is revealed to you and you wonder what to do.

Your concerns as Simon's colleague are related to ethical issues of dual relationships. At a deeper level, it is the blurring of boundaries and possible inappropriateness of therapeutic technique that are at issue. Additional questions are prompted by gender-related issues. Is Simon abusing the power of his position? Is he being sexual with this client? What kind of messages is he giving the client about how males behave toward females? Interestingly enough, these questions would be equally relevant were Simon a female because it is the power dimension of the counseling interaction that is most significant in these concerns.

What should be done? First, as Simon's colleague you should approach him to explore with him those concerns. This is a very hard thing to do in most cases. We are often reluctant to challenge our colleagues, especially if they are senior to us in age, experience, or reputation. Most of us will become defensive if our judgment, technique, or ethics are challenged or even questioned. Therefore, one must be careful when questioning behaviors to stay professional and not get into personalities. In the best of scenarios Simon will carefully explain why he does what he does, what the effect has been, and how he plans to work with the client in weaning and terminating her from his methods so that she can use the counseling and his interventions in the most positive manner.

Should Simon become irate, defensive and dismissing, you should then consult with another colleague, preferably in the same agency to determine whether the concerns held have substance. Should it be determined they do, then consultation with the appropriate ethics committee must be made. The chair of the committee will then decide how the case is to proceed.

2. After seeing a client for several months it occurred to Marvalene, a counselor in a city clinic, that there might be some physical abuse being inflicted on the children of her client by the client's boyfriend who frequently lived with her for extended periods of time. Marvalene was unsure because the client never explicitly said it was happening and, in fact, denied it when confronted. However, reading between the lines Marvalene kept wondering whether such behavior was going on. As much as she wanted to believe the client, there was still doubt. A very disturbing dream that Marvalene explored in a therapy session with the client led to the conclusion that this situation had to be explored further. Her supervisor concurred. Consultation was sought with a colleague who specialized in child and domestic abuse cases. The consultant was quite sure that abuse was taking place but cautioned that there were issues of confidentiality and the potential for damage to the therapeutic relationship with the client if action were taken. Marvalene immediately called the appropriate state agency to report the suspected abuse. The client was apprised of the report and reacted with fury and threats canceling all subsequent sessions.

Several weeks later the client called and scheduled an appointment. She thanked Marvalene for forcing her to confront a situation she wanted to deny and even though she faced protracted involvement with the state and could even lose her children she knew that what had happened was the best thing possible for her and for them.

In most states there is a law that suspicions of child abuse must be reported. The confidentiality in the relationship is not binding on the counselor and the counselor is not liable if there is sufficient reason to justify investigating the alleged abuse. Therefore, this is an example of how important it is to be acquainted with the statutes that pertain to our work and what our rights and obligations under the law are as well as what the rights and obligations of our clients are.

3. Marco, a newly credentialed therapist, was assigned a young, handsome male client who was experiencing a great deal of anxiety and depression but was not sure of the cause of his feelings. In the course of the first session he revealed that at a party another young man had made a pass at him and he found it quite arousing. He was obsessed with having a sexual encounter with this man even though he had always been heterosexual in his behavior and thoughts. He was tormented by the obsession and had even thought about suicide. Marco found himself very interested in the young man's plight and scheduled an extra session that week. To his surprise, he found himself thinking about the young man a great deal more than he usually thought about his clients. He snapped out of a daydream realizing that he had fantasized about the client naked and in a sexual position.

Marco was most disturbed by his thoughts because they did not fit with his usual patterns and he was even more concerned for their potential to interfere with his ability to aid the client. Marco initially thought he would seek consultation with a colleague at his agency but decided he was risking the client's privilege and might put himself in a bad light. Marco requested an emergency appointment with a therapist he had once seen to explore the personal issue of the case for him as well as to get some guidance from a more experienced counselor about the potential ethical issues.

As a result of this consultation, this therapist determined to enter counseling to work out some of the issues raised for him. He also determined that as a young counselor with little experience he needed supervision for this particular case. Such supervision was not offered at his agency but he worked out time release and some assistance with the supervisory fee with the agency director, who did not require specific information about the case and was very supportive about the counselor's concerns.

Being cognizant of ethical issues in the effectiveness of our work often arouses anxiety. However, it also saves us pain and usually instructs us in powerful and helpful ways.

Concluding Remarks

Effective counseling is ethical counseling, and ethical counseling is effective counseling. A knowledge of professional ethics and the active integration of ethical standards into the being and doing of the counselor is essential. The effective counselor is not hampered by ethical standards and practices; rather the counselor's ability to assist clients is enhanced and magnified.

Willingness to look at ethical issues and struggle with them are also required for good work. We must be willing to use the expertise of others for assistance in understanding and applying ethical standards in situations in which we are unsure about such issues. Consultation with colleagues, state ethics boards, and the boards of ethics of professional organizations is a resource, although not essential in every case generating ethical concerns.

Finally, working ethically requires an understanding of the complexities of gender. Gender is far more than a role assigned to women and men. Gender becomes involved in the defining of women's and men's desired characteristics and behaviors and is enacted and reenacted millions of times a day verbally and nonverbally, in everyday and legal language, in institutional policies and practices, and in societal norms and standards. Ethical practice asks that we who practice counseling and therapy work as allies with our clients "in the process of transforming patriarchal oppression" (Brown, 1994, p. 207). Ethical practice requires that we examine ourselves as possible contributors to our clients' oppression and dominance. Finally ethical practice demands that we remain ever mindful of the political context and power relationships of our work with clients.

Discussion Questions

1. You find yourself thinking about a client you terminated with a year ago. You remember and reexperience the attraction you had for her or him. You think about calling her or him to go out for coffee. What should you do?

2. You suspect that a woman in your class/program is having a romantic relationship with her therapy/clinical supervisor. She answers vaguely when you ask about this possibility. What do you do?

Suggested Readings

Lerman, H. & Porter, N. (Eds.). (1990). *Feminist ethics in psychotherapy*. New York: Springer. A thoughtful and informative collection of essays covering many aspects of counseling and detailing the Feminist Therapy Institute Ethical Code.

Pope, K. S., & Vasquez, M. J. T. (1991). *Ethics in psychotherapy and counseling*. San Francisco, CA: Jossey-Bass. A good book for mental health professionals in the early years of their practice.

 References

Abbey, A., & Melby, C. (1986). The effects of nonverbal cues on gender differences in perceptions of sexual intent. *Sex Roles, 15,* 283–298.

Ad Hoc Committee on Women (Division 17). (1979). Principles concerning the counseling and psychotherapy of women. *The Counseling Psychologist, 8,* 21.

Aldous, J. (1990). Specification and speculation concerning the politics of workplace family policies. *Journal of Family Issues, II,* 355–367.

Amaro, H. (1995). Love, sex, and power. Considering women's realities in HIV prevention. *American Psychologist, 50,* 437–447.

American Association of University Women (AAUW). (1991). *Short-changing girls, short-changing America.* (Available from AAUW, 1111 16th NW, Washington, DC 20036–4873.)

American Counseling Association (ACA). (1995). *Code of ethics and standards of practice.* Alexandria, VA: Author.

American Psychiatric Association. (1987). *Diagnostic and statistical manual of mental disorders* (3rd ed., rev.). Washington, DC: Author.

American Psychological Association. (1975). Report of the Task Force on Sex Bias and Sex-Role Stereotyping in Psychotherapeutic Practice. *American Psychologist, 30,* 1169–1175.

American Psychological Association. (1990). Report of the Ethics Committee. *American Psychologist, 45,* 873–874.

American Psychological Association. (1991). Report of the Ethics Committee. *American Psychologist, 46,* 750–757.

American Psychological Association. (1992). Ethical Principles of Psychologists and Code of Conduct. *American Psychologist, 47* (12), 1597–1611.

American Psychological Association. (1995). Report of the Ethics Committee. *American Psychologist, 50,* 706–713.

American Psychological Association. (1996). Report of the Ethics Committee. *American Psychologist, 51,* 1279–1286.

Aries, E. (1987). Gender and communication. In P. Shaver & C. Hendrick (Eds.), *Review of personality and social psychology* (pp. 149–176). Newbury Park, CA: Sage.

Attie, I., & Brooks-Gunn, J. (1989). Development of eating problems in adolescent girls: A longitudinal study. *Developmental Psychology, 25,* 70–79.

Backman, E. L., & Backman, L. R. (1997). Sexual harassment and rape: A view from higher education. In R. F. Levant & G. R. Brooks (Eds.), *Men and sex: New psychological perspectives* (pp. 133–155). New York: John Wiley.

Ball, A. L. (1989, October 23). The daddy track. *New York Times,* pp. A52–A53.

Banks, R. (1989). *Affliction.* New York: HarperCollins.

Barnett, R. C., & Rivers, C. (1996). *She works/He works: How two-income families are happier, healthier, and better off.* New York: HarperCollins.

Beal, C. R. (1994). *Boys and girls: The development of gender roles.* New York: McGraw Hill.

Belensky, M. F., Clinchy, B. M., Goldberger, N. R., & Tarule, J. M. (1986). *Women's way of knowing: The development of self, voice, and mind.* New York: Basic Books.

Belkin, L. (1989, August 20). Bars to equality of sexes seen as eroding slowly. *New York Times,* pp. A1, A26.

Bem, S. L. (1993) *The lenses of gender: Transforming the debate on sexual inequality.* New Haven: Yale University Press.

Berman, J. S. (1985). Ethical feminist perspectives on dual relationships with clients. In L. B. Rosewater & L. E. A. Walker (Eds.), *Handbook of feminist therapy: Women's issues in psychotherapy.* New York: Springer.

Bernard, J. (1975). *Women, wives, and mothers.* Chicago, IL: Aldine.

Bernard, J. (1982). *The future of marriage.* New Haven, CT: Yale University Press.

Betz, N. E. & Fitzgerald, L. F. (1993). Individuality and diversity: Theory and research in counseling and psychotherapy. *Annual Review of Psychology, 44,* 343–381.

Biernat, M. (1993). Gender and height: Developmental patterns in knowledge and use of an accurate stereotype. *Sex Roles, 29,* 691–713.

Bigler, R. S. (1995). The role of classification skill in moderating environmental influences on children's gender stereotyping: A study of the functional use of gender in the classroom. *Child Development, 66,* 1072–1087.

Blain, J. (1994). Discourses of agency and domestic labor: Family discourse and gendered practice in dual-career families. *Journal of Family Issues, 15,* 515–549.

Block, J. H. (1984). *Sex role identity and ego development.* San Francisco: Jossey-Bass.

Boston Women's Health Collective. (1996). *The new our bodies, ourselves.* Boston, MA: Scribner.

Bradshaw, C. K. (1994). Asian and Asian-American women: Historical and political considerations in psychotherapy. In L. Comas-Diaz & B. Greene (Eds.), *Women of color: Integrating ethnic and gender identities in psychotherapy* (pp. 72–113). New York: Guilford.

Brannon, R. (1985). A scale for measuring attitudes about masculinity. In A. Sargent (Ed.), *Beyond sex roles* (pp. 110–116). St. Paul, MN: West Publishing.

Brod, H. (Ed.). (1987). *The making of masculinities—The new men's studies.* Boston: Allen & Unwin.

Brooks, G. R. (1990) Psychotherapeutic approaches with traditional men. In P. A. Keller & L. G. Ritt (Eds.), *Innovations in Clinical Practice: A Source Book* (pp. 61–74). Sarasota, FL: Professional Resource Exchange.

Brooks, G. R. (1997). The centerfold syndrome. In R. F. Levant & G. R. Brooks (Eds.), *Men and sex: New psychological perspectives* (pp. 28-60). New York: John Wiley.

Broverman, I. K., Broverman, D. M., Clarkson, F. E., Rosenkrantz, P. S., & Vogel, S. R. (1970). Sex-role stereotypes and clinical judgments of mental health. *Journal of Consulting and Clinical Psychology, 34,* 1–7.

Brown, L. M., & Gilligan, C. (1992). *Meeting at the crossroads: Women's psychology and girls' development.* Cambridge, MA: Harvard University Press.

Brown, L. S. (1991). Ethical issues in feminist therapy: Selected topics. *Psychology of Women Quarterly, 15,* 323–349.

Brown, L. S. (1994). *Subversive dialogues: Theory in feminist therapy.* New York: Basic Books.

Butler, J. (1990). *Gender trouble: Feminism and the subversion of identity.* New York: Routledge.

Cancian, F. M. (1987). *Love in America: Gender and self-development.* London: Cambridge University Press.

Castaneda, D. (1996). Gender issues among Latinas. In J. Chrisler, C. Golden, & P. D. Rozee (Eds.), *Lectures on the psychology of women* (pp. 166–181). New York: McGraw-Hill.

Chesler, P. (1972). *Women and madness.* Garden City, NY: Doubleday.

Cisneros, S. (1989). *The house on Mango Street.* New York: Vintage Books.

Clatterbaugh, K. (1990). *Contemporary perspectives on masculinity: Men, women, and politics in modern society.* Boulder, CO: Westview Press.

Comas-Diaz, L. & Greene, B. (Eds.). (1994). *Women of color: Integrating ethnic and gender identities in psychotherapy.* New York: Guilford.

Courtois, C. A. (1988). *Healing the incest wound: Adult survivors in therapy.* New York: W.W. Norton.

Crawford, J., Kippax, S., & Waldby, C. (1994). Women's sex talk and men's sex talk: Different worlds. *Feminism & Psychology, 4,* 571–587.

Crawford, M. (1995). *Talking difference: On gender and language.* Thousand Hills, CA: Sage.

Crawford, M., & Marecek, J. (1989). Psychology constructs the female. *Psychology of Women Quarterly, 13,* 147–166.

Cross, W. E. (1971). Negro-to-Black conversion experience: Toward a psychology of Black liberation. *Black World, 20,* 13–27.

Davis, B. M., & Gilbert, L. A. (1989). Effect of dispositional and situational influences on women's dominance expression in mixed-sex dyads. *Journal of Personality and Social Psychology, 57,* 294–300.

Deaux, K. (1985). Sex and gender. In L. Porter & M. Rosenzeig (Eds.), *Annual review of psychology, 1985* (Vol. 36, pp. 49–81). Palo Alto, CA: Annual Reviews.

Deaux, K., & LaFrance, M. (1998). Gender. In D. Gilbert, S. Fiske, & G. Lindzey (Eds.), *Handbook of Social Psychology.* New York: McGraw Hill.

Deaux, K., & Major, B. (1987). Putting gender into context: An interactive model of gender-related behavior. *Psychological Review, 94,* 369–389.

deBeauvoir, S. (1970). *The second sex.* New York: Bantam.

Deveny, K. (1994, December 5). Chart of kindergarten awards. *Wall Street Journal,* p. B1.

Doyle, J. A. (1984). *The male experience.* Dubuque, IA: William C. Brown.

Driggs, J. H., & Finn, S. E. (1990). *Intimacy between men: How to find and keep gay love relationships.* New York: Dutton.

Duke, L. (1995, August). *From Seventeen to Sassy: Teen magazines and the construction of the model girl.* Paper presented at the annual meeting of the Association of Education in Journalism and Mass Communication, Washington, DC.

Eagly, A. H., & Johnson, B. T. (1990). Gender and leadership style: A meta-analysis. *Psychological Bulletin, 108,* 233–256.

Eldridge, N. S. (1987). Gender issues in counseling same-sex couples. *Professional Psychology: Research and Practice, 18,* 567–572.

Enns, C. Z. (1993). Twenty years of feminist counseling and therapy: From naming biases to implementing multifaceted practice. *The Counseling Psychologist, 21,* 3–87.

Espin, O. (1994). Feminist approaches. In L. Comas-Diaz, & B. Greene (Eds.), *Women of color: Integrating ethnic and gender identities in psychotherapy* (pp. 265–286). New York: Guilford.

Espiritu, Y. L. (1997). *Asian american women and men: Labor, laws, and love.* Thousand Oaks, CA: Sage.

Estrada, E. (1989). *Gender influences and the diagnosis of antisocial and borderline personality disorders.* Unpublished doctoral dissertation. University of Texas at Austin.

Fassinger, R. E. (1991). The hidden minority: Issues and challenges in working with lesbian women and gay men. *Counseling Psychologist, 19* (2), 157–176.

Fine, M., & Macpherson, P. (1994). Over dinner: Feminism and adolescent female bodies. In H. L. Radtake, & H. J. Stam (Eds.), *Power/gender: Social relations in theory and practice* (pp. 219–246). London: Sage.

Fiske, S. T. (1993). Controlling other people: The impact of power on stereotyping. *American Psychologist, 48*, 621–628.

Fitzgerald, L. F., & Nutt, R. (1986). The Division 17 principles concerning the counseling/psychotherapy of women: Rationale and implementation. *Counseling Psychologist, 14*, 180–216.

Foa, U. G. (1961). Convergences in the analysis of the structure of interpersonal behavior. *Psychological Review, 68*, 341–353.

Fouad, N. A., & Bingham, R. P. (1995). Career counseling with racial and ethnic minorities. In W. B. Walsh & S. H. Osipow (Eds.), *Handbook of vocational psychology: Theory, research and practice* (2nd ed., pp. 331–366). Mahwah, NJ: Lawrence Erlbaum Associates.

Freedman, R. (1986). *Beauty bound.* Lexington, MA: Heath.

Friedman, W. J., Robinson, A. B., & Friedman, B. L. (1987). Sex differences in moral judgments? A test of Gilligan's theory. *Psychology of Women Quarterly, 11*, 37–46.

Gandara, R. (1995, November 9). Teens and rape: Forced sex OK in certain cases, young people say. *Austin American-Statesman,* pp. E1, E7.

Gelso, C. J., & Fassinger, R. E. (1990) Counseling psychology: Theory and research on interventions. *Annual Review of Psychology, 41*, 355–386.

Gilbert, L. A. (1980). Feminist therapy. In A. M. Brodsky & R. T. Hare-Mustin (Eds.), *Women and psychotherapy: An assessment of research and practice* (pp. 245–265). New York: Guilford Press.

Gilbert, L. A. (1985). *Men in dual-career families: Current realities and future prospects.* Hillsdale, NJ: Lawrence Erlbaum.

Gilbert, L. A. (1987a). Female and male emotional dependency and its implications for the therapist-client relationship. *Professional Psychology: Research and Practice, 18*, 555–561.

Gilbert, L. A. (Ed.). (1987b). Dual-career families in perspective. (Special Issue) *The Counseling Psychologist, 15* (1).

Gilbert, L. A. (1988). *Sharing it all: The rewards and struggles of two-career families.* New York: Plenum.

Gilbert, L. A. (1992). Gender and counseling psychology: Current knowledge and directions for research and social action. In S. D. Brown & R. W. Lent (Eds.), *Handbook of counseling psychology* (pp. 383–416). New York: Wiley.

Gilbert, L. A. (1993). *Two careers/One family: The promise of gender equality.* Beverly Hills, CA: Sage.

Gilbert, L. A. (1994). Reclaiming and returning gender to context: Examples from studies of heterosexual dual-career families. *Psychology of Women Quarterly, 18*, 539–558.

Gilbert, L. A., & Bingham, R. P. (In press). Career counseling with dual-career heterosexual African American couples. In W. B. Walsh, S. Osipow, R. Bingham, M. Brown, & C. Ward (Eds.), *Career counseling for African Americans.* Mahwah, NJ: Lawrence Erlbaum Associates.

Gilbert, L. A., & Osipow, S. H. (1991). Feminist contributions to counseling psychology. *Psychology of Women Quarterly, 15*, 537–547.

Gilbert, L. A., & Scher, M. (1992). The power of an unconscious belief: Male entitlement and sexual intimacy with clients. *Professional Practice of Psychology, 8*, 94–108.

Gilbert, L. A., & Walker, S. J. (1998). Dominant discourse in heterosexual relationships: Inhibitors or facilitators of interpersonal commitment and relationship stability? In J. M. Adams (Ed.), *Handbook of Interpersonal Commitment.* New York: Plenum.

Gilbert, L. A., Walker, S. J., Goss, S., & Snell, J. L. (1997, August). *Negotiating sex in heterosexual dating: Can dominant discourses be challenged?* Paper presented at the Annual Meeting of the American Psychological Association, Chicago, IL.

Gilligan, C. (1982). *In a different voice.* Cambridge, MA: Harvard University Press.

Good, G. E., Gilbert, L. A., & Scher, M. (1990). Gender aware therapy: A synthesis of feminist therapy and knowledge about gender. *Journal of Counseling and Development, 68,* 376–380.

Good, G. E., Heppner, M. J., Hillenbrand-Gunn, T., & Wang, L. (1995). Sexual and psychological violence: An exploratory study of predictors in college men. *Journal of Men's Studies, 4,* 59–71.

Good, G. E., & Mintz, L. B. (1993). Toward healthy conceptions of masculinity: Clarifying the issues. *Journal of Mental Health Counseling, 15,* 403–413.

Good, G. E., Wallace, D. L., & Borst, T. S. (1994). Masculinity research: A review and critique. *Applied & Preventive Psychology, 3* (1), 3–14.

Goodchilds, J. D., Zellman, G. L., Johnson, P. B., & Giarrusso, R. (1988). Adolescents and their perceptions of sexual interactions. In A. W. Burgess (Ed.), *Rape and sexual assault II* (pp. 18–43). Newbury Park, CA: Sage.

Goode, W. J. (1982). Why men resist. In B. Thorne (Ed.), *Rethinking the family: Some feminist questions* (pp. 131–150). White Plains, NY: Longman.

Goodman, L. A., Koss, M. P., & Russo, N. F. (1993). Violence against women: Physical and mental health effects. Part I: Research findings. *Applied & Preventive Psychology, 2,* 79–89.

Greene, B. (1994). African-American women. In L. Comas-Diaz & B. Greene (Eds.), *Women of color: Integrating ethnic and gender identities in psychotherapy* (pp. 10–29). New York: Guilford.

Gregory, B. A., & Gilbert, L. A. (1992). The relationship between dependency behavior in female clients and psychologists' perceptions of seductiveness. *Professional Psychology: Research and Practice, 23,* 390–396.

Gutek, B. A. (1986). *Sex and the workplace.* San Francisco: Jossey-Bass.

Gutek, B. A. (1993). Responses to sexual harassment. In S. Oskamp & M. Costanzo (Eds.), *Gender issues in contemporary society* (pp. 197–216). Newbury Park, CA: Sage.

Gutheil, T. G., & Gabbard, G. O. (1993). The concept of boundaries in clinical practice: Theoretical and risk-managament dimensions. *American Journal of Psychiatry, 150* (2), 188–196.

Hall, J. A., Harrigan, J. A., & Rosenthal, R. (1995). Nonverbal behavior in clinical-patient interaction. *Applied & Preventive Psychology, 4* (1), 21–38.

Hare-Mustin, R. T. (1983). An appraisal of the relationship between women and psychotherapy: 80 years after the case of Dora. *American Psychologist, 38,* 593–601.

Hare-Mustin, R. T. (1994). Discourses in the mirrored room: A postmodern analysis of therapy. *Family Process, 33,* 19–35.

Hare-Mustin, R. T., & Marecek, J. (1990a). Gender and the meaning of difference: Postmodernism and psychology. In R. T. Hare-Mustin & J. Marecek (Eds.), *Making a difference: Psychology and the construction of gender.* (pp. 22–64). New Haven, CT: Yale University Press.

Hare-Mustin, R. T., & Marecek, J. (Eds.). (1990b). *Making a difference: Psychology and the construction of gender.* New Haven, CT: Yale University Press.

Hare-Mustin, R. T., Marecek, J, Kaplan, A. G., & Liss-Levinson, N. (1979). Rights of clients, responsibilities of therapists. *American Psychologist, 34*(1), 3–16.

Harrison, J. (1987). Counseling gay men. In M. Scher, M. Stevens, G. E. Good, & G. Eichenfield (Eds.), *Handbook of counseling and psychotherapy with men.* Newbury Park, CA: Sage.

Heilbrun, C. G. (1988). *Writing a woman's life.* New York: Ballantine Books.

Henley, N. M. (1977). *Body politics: Power, sex, and nonverbal communication*. New York: Prentice-Hall.

Henley, N. M. (1995). Body politics revisited: What do we know today? In P. J. Kalbfleisch & M. J. Cody (Eds.), *Gender, power, and communication in human relationships* (pp. 27–62). Hillsdale, NJ: Erlbaum.

Henley, N. M., & LaFrance, M. (1984). Gender as culture: Difference and dominance in nonverbal behavior. In A. Wolfgang (Ed.), *Nonverbal behavior: Perspectives, applications, intercultural insights* (pp. 351–371). Lewiston, NY: C. J. Hogrefe.

Heppner, M. J., Humphrey, C. F., Hillenbrand-Gunn, T. L., & Debord, K. A. (1995). The differential effects of rape prevention programming on attitudes, behavior, and knowledge. *Journal of Counseling Psychology, 42*, 508–518.

Holland, D. C., & Eisenhart, M. A. (1990). *Educated in romance: Women, achievement, and college culture*. Chicago: University of Chicago Press.

hooks, b. (1981). *Ain't I a woman: black women and feminism*. Boston: South End Press.

hooks, b. (1995). *Killing rage: Ending racism*. New York: Henry Holt.

Horney, K. (1934). The overevaluation of love. In H. Kelman (Ed.), *Feminine psychology* (pp. 182–213). New York: W.W. Norton.

Huston, T. L., & Geis, G. (1993). In what ways do gender-related attitudes and beliefs affect marriage? *Journal of Social Issues, 49*(3), 87–106.

Hyde, J. S. (1990). *Understanding human sexuality* (4th ed.). New York: McGraw-Hill.

Hyde, J. S. (1994). Can meta-analysis make feminist transformations in psychology? *Psychology of Women Quarterly, 18*, 451–462.

Hyde, J. S. (1996). *Half the human experience: The psychology of women*. Lexington, MA: D. C. Heath.

Hyde, J. S., Fennema, E., & Lamon, S. J. (1990). Gender differences in mathematics performance: A meta-analysis. *Psychological Bulletin, 107*, 139–155.

Hyde, J. S., & Plant, E. A. (1995). Magnitude of psychological gender differences: Another side of the story. *American Psychologist, 50*, 159–161.

Ibsen, H. (1959). The doll's house. In R. F. Sharp (Trans.), *Four Great Plays by Henrik Ibsen* (pp. 1–68). New York: Bantam Books. (Original work published in 1879)

Jacklin, C. N. (1989). Female and male: Issues of gender. *American Psychologist, 44*, 127–133.

Johnston, J. E. (1997). Appearance obsession: Women's reactions to men's objectification of their bodies. In R. F. Levant & G. R. Brooks (Eds.), *Men and sex: New psychological perspectives* (pp. 61–83). New York: John Wiley.

Jones, J. (1987). Black women, work, and the family under slavery. In N. Gerstel & H. G. Gross (Eds.), *Families and work* (pp. 84–110). Philadelphia: Temple University Press.

Jordan, J. V. (Ed.). (1997). *Women's growth in diversity: More writings from the Stone Center*. New York: Guilford.

Jordan, J. V., Kaplan, A. G., Miller, J. B., Stiver, I. P., & Surrey, J. L. (Eds.). (1991). *Women's growth in connection: Writings from the Stone Center*. New York: Guilford.

Kahn, A. S. (1984). The power war: Male responses to power loss under equality. *Psychology of Women Quarterly, 8*, 234–247.

Kahn, A. S., Mathie, V. A., Torgler, C. (1994). Rape scripts and rape acknowledgment. *Psychology of Women Quarterly, 18*, 53–66.

Karney, B. R., & Bradbury, T. N. (1995). The longitudinal course of marital quality and stability: A review of theory, method, and research. *Psychological Bulletin, 118*, 3–34.

Keller, E. F. (1992). *Secrets of life, secrets of death: Essays on language, gender, and science*. New York: Routledge.

Ker Conway, J. (1994). *True north: A memoir.* New York: Random House.

Ker Conway, J. (1995). Stages of a woman's life. *Bulletin, The American Academy of Arts and Sciences,* XLVIII (8), 30–42.

Kitzinger, S. (1985). *Woman's experience of sex.* New York: Penguin.

Koss, M. P. (1990). The women's mental health research agency: Violence against women. *American Psychologist, 45,* 374–380.

Koss, M. P., & Harver, M. (1991). *The rape victim: Clinical and community approaches to treatment.* Lexington, MA: Stephen Greene Press.

Krugman, S. (1995). Male development and the transformation of shame. In R. F. Levant & W. S. Pollack (Eds.), *A new psychology of men* (pp. 91–126). New York: Basic Books.

Langlois, J. H., Roggman, L. R., & Musselman, L. (1994). What's average and not average about attractive faces? *Psychological Science, 5,* 214–220.

Leibovitz, A. (1996, March 18). Under the skin. *New Yorker,* p. 70.

Leong, F. T. L. (1996). Toward an integrative model for cross-cultural counseling and psychotherapy. *Applied and Preventive Psychology, 5,* 189–209.

Lerman, H. (1976). What happens in feminist therapy. In S. Cox (Ed.), *Female psychology: The emerging self.* Chicago: Science Research Associates.

Lerman, H., & Porter, N. (Eds.). (1990). *Feminist ethics in psychotherapy.* New York: Springer.

Lerner, H. G. (1983). Female dependency in context: Some theoretical and technical considerations. *American Journal of Orthopsychiatry, 53,* 697–705.

Lerner, H. G. (1988). *Women in therapy.* Northvale, NJ: Aronson.

Levant, R. F., & Brooks, G. R. (Eds.). (1997). *Men and sex: New psychological perspectives.* New York: John Wiley.

Levant, R. F., & Pollack, W. S. (Eds.). (1995). *A new psychology of men.* New York: Basic Books.

Lewin, T. (1995, October 29). Workers of both sexes make trade-offs for family, study shows. *New Tork Times,* p. A14.

Lipsey, M. W., & Wilson, D. B. (1993). The efficacy of psychological, educational, and behavioral treatment: Confirmation from meta-analysis. *American Psychologist, 48,* 1181–1209.

Lonsway, K. A. (1996). Preventing acquaintance rape through education: What do we know? *Psychology of Women Quarterly, 20,* 229–266.

Lorde, A. (1982). *Zami: A new spelling of my name.* Freedom, CA: The Crossing Press.

Lorde, A. (1984). Sexism: An American disease in Blackface. In *Sister outsider.* Freedom, CA: The Crossing Press.

Loulan, J. (1984). *Lesbian sex.* San Francisco, CA: Spinsters/Aunt lute.

Maccoby, E. E., & Jacklin, C. (1974). *The psychology of sex differences.* Stanford, CA: Stanford University Press.

MacCorquodale, P. (1989). Gender and sexual behavior. In K. McKinney & S. Sprecher (Eds.), *Human sexuality: the societal and interpersonal context* (pp. 91–113). Norwood, NJ: Ablex.

MacKinnon, C. (1979). *Sexual harrassment of working women.* New Haven, CT: Yale University Press.

MacKinnon, C. (1995). Vindication and resistance: A response to the Carnegie Mellon study of pornography in cyberspace. *Georgetown Law Review, 83* (5), 1959–1968.

Malcolm, A. H. (1991, June 16). A day of celebration for a more active kind of Dad. *New York Times,* p. A14.

Marecek, J., & Hare-Mustin, R. T. (1987, March). *Feminism and therapy: Can this relationship be saved?* Paper presented at the meeting of the American Orthopsychiatric Association, Washington, DC.

Marecek, J., & Hare-Mustin, R. T. (1990, August). *Toward a feminist poststructural psychology: The modern self and the postmodern subject.* Paper presented at the Annual Meeting of the American Psychological Association, Boston, MA.

Markowitz, L. M. (1993, March/April). Understanding the differences: Demystifying gay and lesbian sex. *Networker,* 51–59.

Martinez, D. (1994). *Mother tongue.* Tempe, AZ: Bilingual Press.

McCarn, S. R., & Fassinger, R. E. (1995). Revisioning sexual minority identity formation. *The Counseling Psychologist, 24* (13), 508–534.

Mednick, M. T. (1989). On the politics of psychological constructs: Stop the bandwagon, I want to get off. *American Psychologist, 44,* 1118–1123.

Mill, J. S. (1970). *The subjection of women.* Cambridge, MA: MIT Press (Original work published in 1869)

Miller, J. B. (1976). *Toward a new psychology of women.* Boston: Beacon Press.

Miller, J. B., & Stiver, I. P. (1997). *The healing connection. How women form relationships in therapy and in life.* Boston: Beacon Press.

Minton, L. (1995, July 2). "They think they're joking." *Parade,* p. 20.

Mintz, L. B., & Betz, N. E. (1988). Prevalence and correlates of eating disordered behaviors among undergraduate women. *Journal of Counseling Psychology, 35,* 463–471.

Mintz, L. B., O'Halloran, M. S., Mulholland, A. M., & Schneider, P. A. (1997). Questionnaire for eating disorder diagnoses: Reliability and validity of operationalizing DSM-IV criteria into a self-report format. *Journal of Counseling Psychology, 44,* 63–79.

Morin, S. F. (1977). Heterosexual bias in psychological research on lesbianism and male homosexuality. *American Psychologist, 32,* 629–637.

Morrison, A. M., White, R. P., Velsor, E. V., & The Center for Creative Leadership. (1987). *Breaking the glass ceiling: Can women reach the top of America's largest corporations?* New York: Addison-Wesley.

Morrison, T. (1970). *The bluest eye.* New York: Pocket Books.

National Board for Certified Counselors (NBCC). (1987). *Counseling services: Consumer rights and responsibilities.* Alexandria, VA: Author.

National Women's Health Network. (1989). Taking hormones and women's health. (Available from NWHN, 1325 G St., NW, Washington, DC 20005).

Nomani, A. Q. (1995, July 7). A fourth-grader's hard lesson: Boys earn more money than girls. *Wall Street Journal,* p. B1.

O'Donohue, W. (Ed.). (1997). *Sexual harassment: Theory, research, and treatment.* Boston: Allyn & Bacon.

O'Neil, J. M. (1981). Patterns of gender role conflict and strain: Sexism and fear of femininity in men's lives. *Personnel and Guidance Journal, 60,* 203–210.

O'Neil, J. M., Egan, J., Owen, S. V., & Murray, V. M. (1993). The Gender Role Journey Measure: Scale development and psychometric evaluation. *Sex Roles, 28* (3/4), 167–185.

O'Neil, J. M., Good, G. F., & Holmes, S. (1995). Fifteen years of research on men's gender role conflict: New paradigms for empirical research. In R. Levant & W. S. Pollack (Eds.), *A new psychology of men* (pp. 164–206). New York: Basic Books.

Okin, S. M. (1989). *Gender, justice and the family.* New York: Basic Books.

Oliver, M. B., & Hyde, J. S. (1993). Gender differences in sexuality: A meta-analysis. *Psychological Bulletin, 114,* 29–51.

Paludi, M. A., & Barickman, R. B. (1991). *Academic and workplace sexual harassment: A resource manual.* Albany, NY: State University of New York Press.

Pearson, G. A. (1996, October 21). Of sex and gender. *Science, 274,* 328–329.

Pharr, S. (1988). *Homophobia: A weapon of sexism.* Little Rock, AR: Chardon.

Piercy, M. (1982). Rape poem. In *Circles on the water* (pp. 164–165). New York: Knopf.

Pion, G. M., Mednick, M. T., Astin, H. S., Hall, C. C. I., Kenkel, M. B., Keita, G. P., Kohout, J. L., & Kelleher, J. C. (1996). The shifting gender composition of psychology: Trends and implications for the discipline. *American Psychologist, 51,* 509–528.

Pipher, M. (1994). *Reviving Ophelia: Saving the selves of adolescent girls.* New York: Ballantine.

Pleck, J. H. (1981a). *The myth of masculinity.* Cambridge, MA: MIT Press.

Pleck, J. H. (1981b). Men's power with women, other men, and society: A men's movement analysis. In R. A. Lewis (Ed.), *Men in difficult times: Masculinity today and tomorrow* (pp. 234–244). New York: Prentice-Hall.

Pleck, J. H. (1995). The gender role strain paradigm: An update. In R. F. Levant & W. S. Pollack (Eds.), *A new psychology of men.* New York: Basic Books.

Pleck, J. H., Sonnenstein, F., & Ku, L. C. (1993). Masculinity ideology: Its impact on adolescent males' heterosexual relationships. *Journal of Social Issues, 49* (3), 11–29.

Pogrebin, L. C. (1983). *Family politics: Love and power on an intimate frontier.* New York: McGraw-Hill.

Pope, K. S. (1990). Therapist-patient sexual involvement: A review of the research. *Clinical Psychology Review, 10,* 477–490.

Pope, K. S. (1994). *Sexual involvement with therapists: Patient assessment, subsequent therapy, forensics.* Washington, DC: American Psychological Association.

Pope, K. S., & Bouhoutsos, J. C. (1986). *Sexual intimacy between therapists and patients.* New York: Praeger.

Pope, K. S., & Vasquez, M. J. T. (1991). *Ethics in psychotherapy and counseling.* San Francisco: Jossey-Bass.

Pope, K. S., Sonne, J. L., & Holroyd, J. (1993). *Sexual feelings in psychotherapy.* Washington, DC: American Psychological Association.

Prose, F. (1990, January 7). Confident at 11, confused at 16. *New York Times Magazine,* pp. 22–25, 37–40, 45–46.

Rencher, L. L., Schillaci, J., & Goss, S. (1995, August). *Gender as interpersonally created in the therapeutic relationship: Client considerations.* Paper presented at the meeting of the American Psychological Association, Washington, DC.

Rich, A. (1979). Taking women students seriously. In *On lies, secrets, and silence* (pp. 237–245). New York: W.W. Norton.

Rich, F. (1994, February 20). The girl next door. *New York Times,* p. E13.

Robertson, J. M., & Fitzgerald, L. F. (1990). The (mis)treatment of men: Effects of client gender role and lifestyle on diagnosis and attribution of pathology. *Journal of Counseling Psychology, 37,* 3–9.

Robertson, J. M., & Fitzgerald, L. F. (1992). Overcoming the masculine mystique: Preferences for alternative forms of assistance among men who avoid counseling. *Journal of Counseling Psychology, 39,* 240–246.

Rodin, J., Silberstein, L., & Striegel-Moore, R. (1985). Women and weight: A normative discontent. In T. B. Sonderegger (Ed.), *Nebraska symposium on motivation* (pp. 267–307). Lincoln, NE: University of Nebraska Press.

Rogers, C. R. (1961). *On becoming a person.* Boston: Houghton Mifflin.

Rose, S., & Larwood, L. (1988). *Women's careers: Pathways and pitfalls.* New York: Praeger.

Rossman, K. M. (1994). *Gender-awareness and the psycho-social process of counseling.* Unpublished doctoral dissertation. University of Texas at Austin.

Russett, C. E. (1989). *Sexual science: The Victorian construction of womanhood.* Cambridge, MA: Harvard University Press.

Sadker, M., & Sadker, D. (1994). *Failing at fairness: How our schools cheat girls*. New York: Touchstone Press.

Sanchez, L., & Kane, E. W. (1996). Women's and men's constructions of perceptions of housework fairness. *Journal of Family Issues, 17*, 385–387.

Savin-Williams, R. C., & Cohen, K. M. (Eds.). (1996). *The lives of lesbians, gays, and bisexuals: Children to adults*. Fort Worth, TX: Harcourt Brace.

Scarr, S., & Eisenberg, M. (1993). Child care research: Issues, perspectives, and results. *Annual Review of Psychology, 44*, 613–644.

Scher, M. (1980). The art of gentle persistence: A therapeutic necessity. *Voices, 15*, 67–73.

Scher, M. (1981). Men in hiding: A challenge for the counselor. *Personnel and Guidance Journal, 60*, 199–202.

Scher, M. (1990). Effect of gender role incongruities on men's experience as clients in psychotherapy. *Psychotherapy, 27*, 322–326.

Scher, M. (1992). Eros in my consulting room. *Voices, 28*, 29–33.

Scher, M. (Ed.). (1994). Reflections on therapist gender. (Special Issue) *Voices, 30* (3).

Scher, M., Stevens, M., Good, G., & Eichenfield, G. A. (1987). *Handbook of counseling and psychotherapy with men*. Beverly Hills, CA: Sage.

Seymour, E., & Hewitt, N. M. (1997). *Talking about leaving: Why undergraduates leave the sciences*. Boulder, CO: Westview Press.

Shellenbarger, S. (1995, May 11). Women indicate satisfaction with role of big breadwinner. *Wall Street Journal*, p. B1, B8.

Sherif, C. (1982). Needed concepts in the study of gender identity. *Psychology of Women Quarterly, 6*, 375–398.

Sherif, C. (1979). Bias in psychology. In J. A. Sherman & E. T. Beck (Eds.), *The prism of sex: Essays in the sociology of knowledge* (pp. 93–133). Madison, WI: University of Wisconsin Press.

Shotland, R. L., & Hunter, B. A. (1995). Women's "token resistant" and compliant sexual behaviors are related to uncertain sexual intentions and rape. *Personality and Social Psychology Bulletin, 21*, 226–236.

Smith, D. (1997, May 1). Study looks at portrayal of women in media. *New York Times*, p. A12.

Sonnert, G. (1995–96, Winter). Gender equity in science: Still an elusive goal. *Issues in Science and Technology*, 53–58.

Spence, J. T. (1991). Do the BSRI and PAQ measure the same or different concepts? *Psychology of Women Quarterly, 15*, 141–166.

Spence, J. T. (1993). Gender-related traits and gender ideology: Evidence for a multifactorial theory. *Journal of Personality and Social Psychology, 64*, 624–635.

Spence, J. T., Helmreich, R., & Stapp, J. (1974). The Personal Attributes Questionnaire: A measure of sex-role stereotypes and masculinity-femininity. *JSAS Catalog of Selected Documents in Psychology, 4*, 43–44, MS 617.

Sprecher, S., & McKinney, K. (1993). *Sexuality*. Newbury Park, CA: Sage.

Sprock, J., & Yoder, C. Y. (1997). Women and depression: An update on the Report of the APA Task Force. *Sex Roles, 36*, 269–304.

Stake, J. E., & Oliver, J. (1991). Sexual contact and touching between therapist and client: A survey of psychologists' attitudes and behaviors. *Professional Psychology, 22*, 297–307.

Staples, R. (1982). *Black masculinity: The Black male's role in American society*. San Francisco: Black Scholar Press.

Steele, C. M. (1997). A threat in the air: How stereotypes shape intellectual identity and performance. *American Psychologist, 52*, 613–629.

Stock, W. E. (1997). Sex as commodity: Men and the sex industry. In R. F. Levant & G. R. Brooks (Eds.), *Men and sex: New psychological perspectives* (pp. 100–132). New York: John Wiley.

Sturdivant, S. (1980). *Therapy with women: A feminist philosophy of treatment.* New York: Springer.

Tan, A. (1989). *The joy luck club.* New York: Ivy Books.

Tannen, D. (1990). *You just don't understand: Women and men in conversation.* New York: William Morrow.

Tannen, D. (1994). *Gender and discourse.* New York: Oxford University Press.

Thompson, E. H., & Pleck, J. H. (1995). Masculinity ideologies: A review of research instrumentation on men and masculinities. In R. F. Levant & W. S. Pollack (Eds.), *A new psychology of men.* New York: Basic Books.

Thompson, L., & Walker, A. J. (1989). Women and men in marriage, work, and parenthood. *Journal of Marriage and the Family, 51,* 845–872.

Thoreson, R. W., Shaughnessy, P., Heppner, P. P., & Cook, S. (1993). Sexual contact during and after the professional relationship: Attitudes and practices of male counselors. *Journal of Counseling and Development, 71,* 429–434.

Thorne, B. (1993). *Gender play: Girls and boys in school.* New Brunswick, NJ: Rutgers University Press.

Tiefer, L. (1995). *Sex is not a natural act and other essays.* Boulder, CO: Westview Press.

Truman, D. M., Tokar, M. M., & Fischer, A. R. (1996). Dimensions of masculinity: Relations to date rape supportive attitudes and sexual aggression in dating situations. *Journal of Counseling and Development, 74,* 555–562.

US Department of Labor. (1995). *A report on the glass ceiling initiative.* Washington, DC: US Government Printing Office.

US Department of Labor, Women's Bureau. (1991). *Facts on working women.* Washington, DC: US Government Printing Office.

Unger, R. K. (1979). Toward a redefinition of sex and gender. *American Psychologist, 34,* 1085–1094.

Unger, R. K. (1990). Imperfect reflections of reality. In R. T. Hare-Mustin & J. Marecek (Eds.), *Making a difference: Psychology and the construction of gender.* New Haven, CT: Yale University Press.

Unger, R. K. (1992). Will the real sex differences please stand up? *Feminism & Psychology, 2,* 231–238.

Unger, R., & Crawford, M. (1996). *Women and gender: A feminist psychology.* New York: McGraw-Hill.

Vasquez, M. J. T. (1994). Latinas. In L. Comas-Diaz, & B. Greene (Eds.), *Women of color: Integrating ethnic and gender identities in psychotherapy* (pp. 72–113). New York: Guilford.

Verba, S. (1983). *Unwanted attention: Report on a sexual harrassment survey.* Report to the Faculty of Arts and Sciences, Harvard University. (Available from Office of the Dean, Cambridge, MA 02138).

Voyer, D., Voyer, S., & Bryden, M. P. (1995). Magnitude of sex differences in spatial abilities: A meta-analysis and consideration of critical variables. *Psychological Bulletin, 1995,* 250–270.

Walker, S. J. (1997). When "no" becomes "yes:" Why girls and women consent to unwanted sex. *Applied & Preventive Psychology, 6* (3), 157–166.

Webster's New World Dictionary. (1978). New York: Collins.

Weiss, R. S. (1991). *Staying the course: The emotional and social lives of men who do well at work.* New York: Free Press.

Weisstein, N. (1968). *Kinder, kirche, kuche as scientific law: Psychology constructs the female.* Boston: New England Free Press.

Weisz, J. R., Weiss, B., Han, S. S., Granger, D. A., & Morton, T. (1995). Effects of psychotherapy with children and adolescents revisited: A meta-analysis of treatment outcome studies. *Psychological Bulletin, 117,* 450–468.

West, C., & Zimmerman, D. H. (1987). Doing gender. *Gender & Society, 1,* 125–151.

Westkott, M. (1986). *The feminist legacy of Karen Horney.* New Haven, CT: Yale University Press.

Wolf, N. (1992). *The beauty myth.* New York: Doubleday.

Wollstonecraft, M. (1989). *A vindication of the rights of women.* Buffalo, NY: Prometheus Books. (Original work published in 1792)

Worell, J., & Johnson, N. (Eds.). (1997). *Feminist visions: New directions for feminist education and training in feminist practice.* Washington, DC: American Psychological Association.

Worell, J., & Remer, P. (1992). *Feminist perspectives in therapy: An empowerment model for women.* New York: Wiley.

Wyatt, G. E., & Riederle, M. H. (1994). Reconceptualizing issues that affect women's sexual decision-making and sexual functioning. *Psychology of Women Quarterly, 18* (4), 611–626.

Zilbergeld, B. (1978). *Male sexuality.* New York: Bantam Books.

Author Index

Subject Index